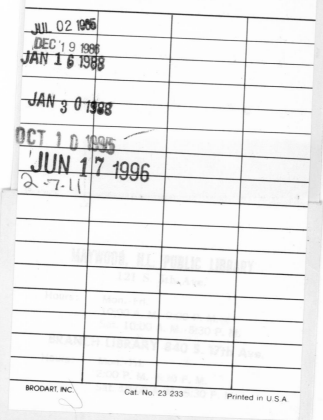

Date Due

JUL 02 1985		
DEC 19 1986		
JAN 16 1988		
JAN 30 1988		
OCT 10 1995		
JUN 17 1996		
2-7-11		

BRODART, INC.   Cat. No. 23 233   Printed in U.S.A.

COMPANIONS OF THE UNSEEN

PAUL TABORI'S NON-FICTION BOOKS

The Real Hungary
The Nazi Myth
Epitaph for Europe
Restless Summer
Peace Correspondent
Taken in Adultery
Harry Price: The Biography of a Ghost-Hunter
'48 — The Year of Revolutions (with James Eastwood)
My Occult Diary (with Cornelius Tabori)
Alexander Korda: A Biography
Twenty Tremendous Years
The Natural Science of Stupidity
The Art of Folly
The Book of the Hand
Secret and Forbidden
The Pictorial History of Love

(*in preparation:*)
A Century of Assassins
Intimate and Most Intimate
The Exiles

PAUL TABORI

COMPANIONS OF
THE UNSEEN

UNIVERSITY BOOKS • NEW HYDE PARK, NEW YORK

Library of Congress Catalog Card Number: 68-18756
University Books, Inc.©1968
Printed in Israel

Contents

Publisher's Note

MR. PAUL Tabori is particularly well qualified to present this objective study of eight mediums who during their lives evoked widely different views and opinions of their mediumistic qualities.

During his introduction Paul Tabori reminds the reader that, despite obvious...and often self-confessed...fraud on the part of the mediums themselves, there remains even today some evidence of actual psychic occurences which cannot be explained by accepted scientific methods.

Paul Tabori was a close personal friend of the late Harry Price, one of the world's most dedicated, if controversial, psychic investigators. Harry Price collected during his life-time one of the largest and most important libraries of books and documents dealing with spritualism and other psychic or parapsychological areas. Paul Tabori is the literary executor of the late Harry Price and a trustee of the HARRY PRICE LIBRARY, now housed in the Senate House of London University.

COMPANIONS OF THE UNSEEN is the first book to be published in a new series of original and reprinted books dealing with every aspect of psychical research. The editor of the series is Mr. Tabori.

Author's Introduction

ONE OF my favourite cartoons appeared in *Punch* during the nine-teen-thirties. It shows a small, gently inane looking man, sitting with his eyes closed, a broad grin on his face while another man, with a somewhat diabolic expression, is about to hit him over the head. The caption reads: "STRIKING THE HAPPY MEDIUM."

The modest pun could very well serve as an epigraph to this book—in both senses. While mediums can be happy or unhappy, honest or dishonest, stupid or intelligent—in fact, an average cross-section of humanity—practically every one of them has figured at one time or another as the subject of fierce and partisan controversy. Striking at them has been a favourite pastime of sceptics, agnostics, and materialists; they have been defended with equal fervour and tenacity. Sometimes, indeed, so confused and wild was the melée that they disappeared, figuratively speaking, in a maze of flailing arms and legs and the original cause of the dispute was all but forgotten.

This book is concerned with a representative selection of the hundreds who have offered themselves for, or participated in, psychical investigation. A motley collection of varied ages, backgrounds, nationalitites, connected only by the fact that they possessed (or were believed to possess) psychological and physical qualities which do not exist, or exist only in a rudimentary form, in the vast majority of people. And here I have tried to achieve the second meaning of the *Punch* cartoon—to steer clear of both credulity and extreme dis-belief, of denial of the possibility of the supernatural and of an uncritical acceptance of its alleged manifestations. I have never had a psychic experience but I consider it unwise to maintain that they never oc-curred or cannot happen. It is a basic principle of human progress that it consists to a considerable extent of the re-discovery of truths and facts that have become lost in the detritus of centuries. This applies particularly to psychology and the natural sciences. And it is these two great branches of learning that must be combined in effective and honest psychical research, in the investigation of mediums and their phenomena. A great deal of what has been considered rank super-stition and appalling ignorance in past ages has been found, at the least, to be prophetic insight in the light of modern scientific research. To trace this continuity is particularly difficult in anything concerning the extrasensory, intangible and so often elusive processes of the human mind. I have tried to take this into account in telling the stories of the mediums I have chosen—and in this respect at least it matters com-paratively little whether they were 'fraudulent' or 'genuine'.

★   ★   ★

In primitive civilizations things have no existence until they have been named. Those that are nameless have remained so because their existence was feared. But in our own age, with the development of the all-important science of semantics, we find that many of the names given to things and ideas, to organizations and actions have several different meanings.

This deliberate or involuntary confusion of semantics is especially dangerous and destructive in the field of what is called "the occult sciences." Though hundreds of books are published on the subject every year, though such a collection as the Harry Price Library at London University proves the scope, quantity and variety of the thousands of works devoted to it, even the simplest basic terms are again and again confused; the most general technical usages provoke completely wrong associations. "Occult" has become a synonym for "mystic"; the word "medium" is immediately connected with faked séances, ghosts made out of gauze or cheesecloth, phoney spirit photo-graphs and palpably false "spirit voices" and "rappings". Psychical research may either be treated with contempt or turned into newspaper sensations—if it is not identified with downright trickery and the criminal exploitation of bereaved families and gullible old ladies. Even though the work of such pioneers as Professor Rhine and Dr. Soal has shown the value of investigating extra-sensory perception, official science, the universities or learned bodies of natural scientists, still have considerable reserve about intensive research. Of course, the fake mediums, the commercial activity of astrologers and fortune-tellers provide good reasons for such reservations.

Occult originally meant nothing more than hidden, not understood, not experienced. Modern dictionaries define it as supernatural, magical, secret, esoteric—but at the dawn of civilization almost every process of nature belonged to this category. Ignorance was almost boundless. Today—to use a rough-and-ready classification—we can speak of three categories: that of the scientifically explored; that which is still to be discovered and understood; and finally that which cannot easily be scientifically explored—called, for want of a better word, the metaphysical. In this last category belong all the efforts to establish the "final causes of life", to draw the "supernatural" into the realm of human cognition. (If I put these words in quotation marks, it is because, semantically speaking, the very words must be vague, imprecise and open to innumerable, individual interpretations.) Yet even these categories are arbitrary. There is a difference between the extrasensory and the supernatural which has been clearly shown by the scientific and psychological results of patient research within the last few decades. Nor must scientific occultism which calls itself metapsychics be confused with the religious philosophy of the metaphysicians. Metapsychical or psychical investigators at least try to find firm ground while metaphysicians remain purely speculative. As William James said: "As in the night all cats are grey, so in the darkness of metaphysical criticism all causes are obscure."

Our first concern is with the two great fields of science—the explored and the unexplored. Even the most materialistic scientist would hesitate to forecast how many of the great riddles and secrets of Nature, still unsolved, will become clarified or understandable. Unless one writes science fiction—a by no means contemptible branch of imaginative literature—it is impossible to forecast whether we shall ever reach beyond the final verities. It is a commonplace truism that innumerable phenomena which are quite ordinary and accepted today belonged to the realm of the supernatural only a century ago—or, as in the case of atomic physics or rocket propulsion, within the life-span of a single generation. Radioactivity, hypnosis, the hover-craft, infra-red and ultra-violet rays, wireless telegraphy, television, anti-biotics—these are only a few examples of recent achievements which in past centuries would have been called witchcraft. It was not so long ago that serious scientists declared that the problem of human flight was insoluble and that travel at speeds greater than 30 miles per hour would shatter the human body.

It is better to use caution and not connect with the expression "metaphysics" anything but philosophical conceptions. There are, of course, differences between mystics and rationalists, empiricists and existentialists. But by these labels we certainly do not mean people who use a telescope to gaze into unexplored space; while the empiricists base their efforts to establish the connection between the various phenomena on scientific experience and experiment, the metaphysicians aim to discover the essentials which are not tangible, do not appear in facts and object—yet are behind all phenomena. They seek to advance beyond experience to the transcendental causes of existence, from the conditional to the absolute.

This is quite different from the usual interpretation of metaphysics—something that has become almost as discredited as the word "occultism." Metaphysics are acceptable even to the most elementary, primitive mind, side by side with metapsychics. Soon after the First World War Dr. Rudolf Schmidt, an Austrian scientist even spoke of "metachemistry"—an early label for atomic chemistry, the science which upset the ancient systems of Aristotle and Ptolemy in the beginning of our century and opened up the breath-taking world of atoms and electrons, neutrons and anti-matter which is still only just revealing its secrets and potentialities. Progress has been amazingly fast in this field; Dr. Schmidt had already spoken of every atom being not only a world in itself but a whole planetary system; of nuclei and electrons, of alpha and beta particles—and he added: "What is the aim of such metaphysics, already beyond its successful initial achievements? Nothing less than the realisation of the ancient dream of the alchemists in scientifically exact form. . ."

It took less than thirty years before atomic physics *did* realize the dream. The transmutation of metals, the splitting of the atom—these were only some of the concrete results. Early in the nineteenth century professors still spoke of the four Aristotelian elements; today we list more than a hundred—and the original four are not among them. Our concepts of the structure of the world are changing daily. The fairly recent idea that science has defined and explained everything; that there are no more fields to explore, no more discoveries to be made, has gone overboard. The comfortable and solid world of the nineteenth century has disintegrated and with it the conceit that there can be nothing beyond the physical, the tangible, the measurable.

Occultism, in its purest and most objective form, has nothing to do with mysticism. Some achievements of psychical research—for instance, experiments in telepathy—have as little mysticism about them as, say, electricity. We know just as little about some of the most important natural phenomena as about clairvoyance or thought-transference. We still do not know what life, procreation, photosynthesis or electricity are—though we can observe the manifestations, measure the effects and even reproduce them without having established the ultimate, fundamental causes. Occultism is simply whatever cannot be fitted into "official" science—science as taught in schools and universities. Some eighty years ago hypnotism was something "occult", today it is a subject of official medical science.

About forty years ago Dr. Rudolf Tischner, a German psychical researcher wrote: "Essentially we do not understand anything—we do not really understand the process of a billiard ball striking another and transferring its movements to it; we do not understand how our bodies actually grow; and least of all do we understand how the 'spirit' affects the body and how we can move an arm or a hand when we 'will' it. But this lack of understanding is tempered to a certain extent because we have been able to classify the majority of facts in the world surrounding us—classify them under certain points of view and bring them into a systematic relationship to each other. The so-called occult facts are contrary to our systematic knowledge—in any case, they cannot be coordinated easily with the generally accepted, orthodox facts. . ."

This is a cautious enough statement and can be accepted even by the most extreme materialist—though he might quarrel with Dr. Tischner's use of the expression "occult *facts*." Yet the scientifically established and whatever is still "unknown" cannot be separated by a sharp and definite limit. There is a borderland, a transitional territory, a vast domain where they meet. This is the domain of scientific occultism or psychical research. It has been also called "xenology" and it aims at the synthesis of all the unexplored or partially explored regions of science. There is no science today without such a region where knowledge tapers off into the unknown, the unexplored. Scientists might well assert that xenology is unnecessary—after all, every branch of science strives to extend its limits. Yet xenologists can be called specialists in all the fields where body and soul, spirit and mind, psychology and metaphysics meet and mingle.

It would be quite wrong to mistake scientific occultism or psychical research for a philosophy or *Weltanschauung*. This would be confusing it with spiritualism which has developed into an organized religion and a specific concept of the world. The achievements of psychical research are no more extraordinary than the discovery of X-rays or the development of cybernetics. The objection that they are "contrary to the laws of Nature" can easily be countered by remembering that these laws are abstractions from the existing, individual facts. Science is striving to classify the various processes, to unite the similar facts under a single idea and subordinate them to some rule. "The laws of Nature" are nothing but the most general rules, established according to our views and knowledge. And how many "laws of Nature" have been completely changed in the course of human progress—because the facts or their interpretations demanded these changes!

It is true that the phenomena claimed by psychical research have a bewildering and confusing effect because they are alleged to be produced by "extrasensory" or "supernatural" methods. But "supersensory" or "extrasensory" means only that there must be other senses apart from the five we generally accept. Indeed, physiology and psychology have inclined more and more to the view that these senses do exist. In any case, our "orthodox" senses have proved often enough inadequate if not totally misleading. Psychical research does not aim at upsetting the ancient structure of the natural sciences. It aims at broadening experience; to obtain a recognition of extrasensory perceptions *in addition* to those of the senses. Until the contrary has been proved, it must be assumed that these occult or supersensory events still remain within what we loosely term as Nature.

In modern psychical literature a clear distinction is made between "occult" or "supranormal" and "paranormal" phenomena. The first two terms are applied to phenomena which may be opposed to existing laws of Nature; the last to those which can still be classified within our generally accepted knowledge. For instance, clairvoyance is "occult", while a "split personality" or "automatic writing" are paranormal.

It was Professor Charles Richet, member of the French Academy of Sciences, a distinguished Nobel Prize laureate, who suggested that "metapsychics" should be used to replace the suspect and tarnished expression of "occultism"; while Max Dessoir, the Berlin university professor championed "parapsychology". Others chose "psychology in depth" or, to use the German term, "*Tiefenpsychologie*."

Occultism is said to be discredited by the "miracles" it produces. But as Dr. Karl Ludwig Schleich wrote in his brilliant *"Bewusstsein und Unsterblichkeit"* (Consciousness and Immortality, Berlin and Stuttgart, 1920): "Natural science unfortunately lost the capacity of being conscious of the miracles within its own domain—which are far greater than anything a thousand spiritualist mediums can produce. I am far less interested in table-rapping, in poltergeists or ectoplasm than in the miracle of a newborn baby, the fact that I can touch the forehead of a conscious, newly-created human being. . ."

The history of occultism could be called the history of human errors; the history of the evolution of natural science. Faith turns again and again into superstition; or superstition becomes cleansed into faith. The evaluation of superstition and faith is something completely relative. Superstitions are assumptions contrary to accepted religious or scientific tenets. Whenever such an assumption is borne out by facts it is called "magic" or "wizardry"—but here again much depends on our point of view (as it does in the case of "miracles"). Miracles were supposed to be worked by the gods or God; whenever the effect was ascribed to demons or devils, this was called "magic." Miracle-working was also named "white magic" in contrast to "black magic" —for in the East the colour black was invariably "evil" and white "good." Among the Slav people the *belibog* (white, good) and *chernobog* (black, evil) beings are also contrasted. Thus for the Jews the actions of Moses were miracles; for the Egyptians they were magical tricks.

Any successes of ancient magic remained usually mysterious to the magicians themselves as they were based exclusively on their own or on traditional experience: such "secrets" were strictly guarded within the families of the "physicians" or the caste of priests. This was, of course, simply a matter of prestige and good business—creating a monopoly of knowledge and skill.

It was only later that the innumerable scattered stones of human knowledge were combined into more or less crude structures. Gradually "magic" became the "secret lore of the East" from which the "secret sciences" of the West developed—until, finally, modern natural sciences emerged. Primitive man assumed that whatever was impersonal could not hurt him and saw behind all natural phenomena a spirit—good or bad. The task of the priest was to protect him from the evil spirits by invoking the aid of the good ones. The primitive weapons were not sufficient to combat the "elements." But the priest or the physician, through their knowledge of the forces of Nature (especially of herbs) were supposed to possess the means of protection. It was only in a much later cultural period that man's psychological activity began; he was led to the concept of the soul by the mysteries of dreams. That was to him the only possible explanation of the fact that a human body lay "unconscious," inert while the sleeper's thoughts roamed in some entirely different setting. The spirits of the dead, the good spirits, evolved into heroes who, in turn, were enthroned as gods—and finally were combined in a single, all-powerful Divinity.

Our earliest records in this respect date from Egypt and Akkad; yet much of the beliefs and ideas of pre-historic times can be reconstructed from those of the primitive tribes surviving into our age— the Stone Age civilizations of Eskimos, Australian aborigines, some North American Indian, African, Siberian and Greenland tribes. The magicians might be called shamans (in Siberia) or medicine-men, Isi-Nyanga (Zulus) or Obeah-Men and Papaloi, Ngakas (Bechuanaland) or any of a hundred different names. They were rain-makers, healers, prophets; they promised successful hunting, good harvests, victories over enemies, the satisfaction of revenge, harm to one's opponents. Usually they induced for themselves a state of ecstasy or intoxication—as the priestesses of the Delphic oracle did. And again and again we encounter the two polarities of "black" and "white" magic. The secretiveness of the privileged castes led almost without exception to the same development—whenever a new religion replaced an old one, the old faith survived in the form of superstition, part of which was often incorporated in the new religion (much of our Christmas festivities still carry echoes of the Roman Saturnalia; there are similar, ancient elements in practically all rites and rituals.). This forced the monotheistic religions—Judaism, Christianity, Islam —to make certain concessions to the converted pagans. The old always merged with the new.

Chaldean magic or "wisdom" provided some basic elements for our contemporary science. The Chaldeans were a Semitic people whose rulers founded a Babylonian dynasty in the seventh century B.C. Their original home was in the southeastern part of Babylonia, bordering on the Persian Gulf; they invaded Babylonia proper, founded a new empire and became admixed with the Babylonians. The languages spoken by the two peoples, both variations of Assyrian, also lost their distinguishing characteristics and the term "Chaldean" was used as a synonym for "Babylonian" and even for Aramaic. "Chaldean" was also synonymous with "magician" or "wise man" as Chaldea was identified with a centre of ancient, esoteric learning. In Latin and Greek, in Assyrian and Hebrew the same words are used with local variants (*Chaldaei, Chaldaioi, kaldu, kasdim*) whenever reference is intended to famous magicians. Chaldean "wizards" travelled all over the ancient civilized world. They had already found an immense accumulation of knowledge in Babylonia itself. The Babylonians, long before the dynasty of Chaldean kings, were excellent astronomers, astrologers, physicians and mathematicians. But as the Hebrews, Persians, Greeks and Romans came into contact with Babylonia only after Nabopolassar (Nabuapalazur), a former governor of the Assyrian province of Chaldea, had established his Empire, they identified all Babylonian learning with the Chaldeans. The Book of Daniel, Curtius Rufus, Strabo, Diodorus Siculus and numerous other authors all speak of the "wisdom" or the "mysteries" of the Chaldeans. It was Claudius J. Rich, Sir Henry Layard, H. Russam, G. Smith and their many successors who re-discovered and explored Nineveh and found the huge library with innumerable works in cuneiform writing.

Assur-Bani-Pal, the Assyrian King who reigned from 669 to 626 B.C. (both dates are approximate) commanded the compilation of an immense work devoted to omens and astrology; this was done largely by copying the older tablets of Babylonia, thus preserving a work of great antiquity. This gives us a fairly clear picture of the religion and demonology (that is, the ancient, suppressed faith) of the Chaldeans. Their "spirit-lore" was highly logical. They taught that the whole human life depended on spirits. But as there were so many spirits, they each had to be approached in the correct way—which only the priests (magicians) were able to do. The priests were divided into three main classes: the true conjurers of spirits, the physicians and the magicians. (Zoroaster also differentiated three groups—the '*herbeds*' apprentices, the *mobeds*, masters and the *destûrmôbeds*, the accomplished masters.) The Chaldeans had two other categories: the astrologers and the fortune-tellers, both for "events of the future."

The Chaldean or Babylonian lore found its way to the Medes, the Jews (through the Babylonian captivity), the Persians and Egyptians. Perhaps it would have spread throughout Europe if the decline and fall first of the Greek and then of the Roman civilization had not buried the whole, highly-developed cultural heritage under the debris of centuries. The Chaldean achievements were developed impressively through regular contact with the Greek philosophers and by the absorption of the large body of Egyptian knowledge. The Romans, imitators and pupils of the Greeks, also profited from them.

The first philosophers who dared to breach the none-too-solid edifice of Olympus were Pythagoras and Empedocles. They rejected the idea of Hades, the sojourn of spirits in the underworld and sought the origin of the universe in a single creator, a master-builder. Though Plato sought to strengthen scientifically the ancient belief in demons, he also coined the sentence which has become most important for modern occultism: "Nothing can be created in the world before its idea has existed." He was unconsciously echoing the views of the ancient Indian sages whose intuitive wisdom remains startling and admirable. For the earliest Indian works of religion speak of God "willing" and the world being created by His Will alone. The Hindu godhead, unlike Jehovah, did not need seven days for the literal creation. (Perhaps it is no exaggeration to say that all Roman, Greek, Etruscan, Phoenician and Persian myths can be traced back to Indian models. It is in the Vedas that the passage occurs: "He (the Great Being) thought: 'I want to create worlds!'—and they were present!")

The Jewish Philo of Alexandria, a contemporary of Christ, combined the teaching of Jehova with Greek philosophy. He wrote: "We cannot say what God is, only that He exists!" The neo-platonists—Porphyrius, Plotinus and Iamblichus—developed this idea further. They established a hierarchy of gods and demons and set above all of them a Supreme Being who was essentially Jewish. They differentiated between a "higher magic" (asceticism, religious ceremonies) to gain the favour of the "good" gods and goety (black magic) for the demons.

This was a laboriously erected house of cards which collapsed as soon as the Greeks clashed with the Persians and became familiar with Oriental learning. Greek thought was more strongly influenced and fructified when Egypt came under Greek rule. The Ptolemies were patrons of art and science and soon Alexandria became the intellectual centre of the ancient civilized world. In the Museum of Alexandria the most famous oriental mystics competed with the most outstanding Greek philosophers for the laurels. The young Christian church drank deep from this almost inexhaustible spring of wisdom. Here the first and most important dogmas were created.

This golden age of learning ended in 641 A.D. with the Arab conquest. The quintessence of this ancient body of knowledge consisted at that time of Chaldean astrology (modified through Greek and Egyptian influences) and the specifically Egyptian alchemy which was to develop into modern chemistry. The Arabs did not destroy this treasure, they guarded and increased it—and brought it much later to Europe. The Greek and Roman civilization was drowned in the confusion of the great migrations and in the bloody wars. Europe possessed nothing but her own deep-rooted magic; in this the Finns stood high above the rest. In the Far North the people of that small country had a considerable, even if much-disguised and often symbol-ridden natural science, so similar to the Chaldean (though without reaching its level) that there is justification for assuming some contact between the Finnish magicians and those of the Orient.

While in Alexandria a "magic science" developed, in Europe the early Christian era had to contend with a primitive belief in magic. The idea of occultism was unknown. Knowledge was occult only to the extent that it was kept hidden from the masses—mainly because of the commercial interests of various social classes.

In the beginning the Christian Church was extremely tolerant towards pagan customs and accepted many a compromise. But when the Crusades and contact with the Moors or Saracens (as all Arabs were called) introduced Oriental learning, the Church began to sense a danger to her dogmas and took forcible measures—of which the most terrible was the persecution of "witches" and heretics. Gradually the "darkest Middle Ages" began to lighten; the sober, unbiased scientists of Europe disentangled the chaos created by the mixture of Egyptian learning, imported by the Moors, and of native magic beliefs. Finally this purified learning was elevated to the status of "secret sciences".

There was one element which slowed down this process—the teachings of the Kabbala.

It was natural that the Jews should also practice the secret sciences—the more so as the educated or wise men of Jewry were given to the examination of metaphysical problems. But while all other people who imitated the learned magic of the Chaldeans and Egyptians, threw their own religious views overboard, the Jews retained a deep respect for their Holy Writ. This was in no way altered by the fact that the prophets of the Kabbala wrapped its origin, age and significance in the most impenetrable mysteries. They declared that according to the Old Testament (the apocryphal Book of Enoch) all secret sciences originated with the Fallen Angels. These "supermen" were supposed to know a great deal which remained unknown to ordinary mortals. According to another legend the Lord revealed on Mount Sinai not only the Ten Commandments to Moses but also various other precepts, destined exclusively for the seventy elders. There is, however, nothing in the Old Testament to indicate such additional "divine legislation". Nor could there be, for the Kabbala is of much more recent origin. Its two oldest works, the "Sepher Jezirah" (Book of Creation) and "Sohar" (Light, Radiance) show clearly that their sources originate in the period of Babylonian captivity. That was the last opportunity for the Jews to become familiar with the learning of the Chaldeans and with the religious beliefs of other nations, especially that of the Persians. They sought to bring all this into harmony with their own teachings of Jehovah. But as the Jewish sages had a considerable respect and awe of the Pentateuch, they tried to solve the metaphysical riddles which impressed them so greatly with the aid of the Holy Writ—by employing a complex system of combining letters and numbers.

The Kabbalistic methods were based on the peculiarity of the old Hebrew alphabet whose twenty-two letters are all consonants. Vowels are indicated by dots under the lines. Thus the Lord of Israel is simply written IHVH—the so-called *tetragrammaton*. The version 'Jehovah' was put forward by the Franciscan Galatin, confessor of Pope Leo X in the sixteenth century; while Ewald, in the eighteen-thirties, argued for 'Jahve' (more recently there have been other spellings and pronunciations of the same word.) Hebrew, like almost all ancient languages (for instance, Latin) has no numerals. Every letter also stands for a number—every word is a number and every number a word. If two words having the same numerical value are exchanged, the meaning is immediately altered. The Kabbalists sought by permutations to solve all the mysteries of the world; without any logic, with a feckless imagination, with thoughts that have no connection with anything preceding being presented as axioms which must not be touched for "they are based on the Holy Writ."

The Kabbala was a specifically Jewish work, using the Old Testament as its foundation; but in reality it was nothing but the Jewish version of the ancient "learned magic", a monument of cultural history but in no way a cultural, a religious or a legal document.

Our modern astronomy developed from the astrology of the ancients just as modern chemistry did from alchemy. The process though complex had a clear enough direction: ancient astrology and alchemy in which the belief in gods and demons was at first mixed with the steadily evolving pure natural science became first an astrology and alchemy of the learned. This was no longer based on a pure Chaldean, Egyptian or Arab magic; it was cleansed, improved and reformed by the science of Alexandria, modified by Occidental thinkers and philosophers. The creators of the European secret sciences gave their works a mystical character—but only because very often they did not realize the true sense of their own experiments; they suspected demonic influences behind them—powers in opposition to the Christian faith.

The first real dawn of science became noticeable in the thirteenth century—though it lasted only up to the fifteenth. In this period popes and princes patronized scientists and founded numerous universities. This was the epoch in which a number of great natural scientists appeared—though they were only accounted as "European magicians". Roger Bacon, Arnold Villanova, Raymond Lully, the Abbot Johann von Tritheim, Albert von Bollstatt were the most outstanding. Roger Bacon, the English monk, the "Doctor Mirabilis" (born about 1214) knew how to make gunpowder, invented magnifying glasses, offered an ingenious explanation for refraction and perspective, the apparent size of objects, the growing size of the sun and the moon on the horizon; he discovered the errors of the Julian Calendar and rectified them. But he wrapped himself, according to contemporary conventions, in such obscurity that he was regarded as a magician and clashed again and again with the Church, spending a not inconsiderable part of his life in prison. Yet in his *Opus Tertium* he formulated the basic tenet of experimental science: explore Nature in order to dominate her through herself and make her useful for yourself—in other words: "knowledge is power".

The most outstanding among these forerunners of modern natural science was Heinrich Cornelius Agrippa von Nettesheim (born 1456). His significance lay in his endeavour to transform the entire magical knowledge of his age into physics, mathematics and theology. His famous book *"Magia Naturalis"* was balanced by a *"Philosophia Occulta"*—it was he who coined the word "occult" for use in this context. He said: "Magic operations are no secret arts but only the natural application of these sciences." His "Occult Philosopy" is based on Aristotelian physics, on the astronomy of Ptolemy, on Neo-Platonic philosophy and the Jewish Kabbala. Agrippa's mystical elements consisted above all of the Kabbala with some additions of Christian theology and of the demon beliefs woven into the ancient "learned magic". Otherwise it simply mirrored the conception of the universe in the European Middle Ages—that is, medieval natural science. (In his *Philosophia Occulta* Agrippa speaks of telepathy: "I understand this craft and have tried it often; the Abbot of Tritheim also understands it and has executed it." Suggestion he treats as a magical agent of faith.) It is easy to understand that with the heroic discoveries of Copernicus, Galilei and Kepler this whole colossal edifice—of which Agrippa's Occult Philosophy was the crowning dome—had to collapse abruptly.

The medieval "secret scientists", sought to hide their knowledge from the masses. This was mainly due to their fear of informers and charlatans (they called themselves theurgists or theosophs while the conjurers adopted the title of "professors of magic"—harmless enough as they claimed only to entertain.) Hippocrates had already complained that the medical and philosophical "arts" were discredited by amateurs and demanded from all his disciples the swearing of a solemn oath and the full knowledge of the rules he established. The Hippocratic Oath has survived into our days and a modified form is still used in the medical profession.

Agrippa was the "last great magician". The independent seekers for knowledge had torn down the rooftree of the medieval temple of magic and separated, step by step, the mundane world, from the heavenly, intellectual world. The Church began to realize that a new age had dawned and started to support the new scientists. The art of conjuring and incantation, previously carefully guarded, became popularized; various magic operations were physically and chemically explained—in other words "profaned"—and thus, through the intensive work of enlightenment by the humanists the nations lost their taste for ancient occultism which sank into limbo as despised and ludicrous "curiosities". Soon we find occultism more or less relegated to Old Moore's Almanac and the "Egyptian dream books".

But the secret sciences, even the most ancient magic, were to experience a renaissance; it came in the eighteen-fifties through spiritualism. Considerably simplified, the fundamental ideas of spiritualism claim the immortality of the soul; after the death of the body it is possible for the spirit to establish contact with the world of the living; the soul or the spirit is able to produce various phenomena, partly psychical, partly physical. As a link between the two worlds persons of special qualifications are needed—these are the "mediums".

All these ideas were by no means new. The immortality of the soul is a Christian dogma. The possibility to consort with the dead was already believed in ancient times as the many incantations and conjurings of the priests prove. Mediumship was also known in the form of ecstasy or mystic trance; it was accepted that mediums had to be trained to achieve a special state. The attraction of spiritualism was not in its essential ideas but in the new form in which they were expressed and their combination with social ideas. The new religion with its semi-scientific trappings would not have spread so quickly if it had been unable to count on mystical instincts unsatisfied by materialism.

The most important influence on the belief in mediumship was exercised by Emanuel Svedberg (or Swedenborg, after he was ennobled). Born January 29, 1688, his clairvoyant talents impressed even Immanuel Kant. Kant relates how Swedenborg described on September 1, 1759 in Göteborg the great fire of Stockholm—though authentic details did not reach the port from the capital until two days later. It is outside the scope of this summary to discuss Swedenborg in detail; it might be sufficient to mention that his followers split into two sections. The purely religious faction founded the "Church of the New Jerusalem" (built upon the fantasies of the "Northern Seer" about Heaven and Earth) and became sectarians; the others created a scientific school in which "German Pneumatology" or Spirit-Teaching was studied. The "pneumatologists" were the first scientists who occupied themselves critically with spiritualism—at its contemporary level. They were composed of physicians, lawyers and theologists and contributed their investigations with true German thoroughness. The most outstanding pneumatologist was Johann Heinrich Jung-Stilling (born 1740, in Nassau). He taught that man consisted of body, nervous spirit (soul) and spirit and that the spirit, once liberated, was able to attract matter with the help of the nervous spirit and appear in another place as a *doppelgänger*. This was a theoretical explanation (two decades before Anglo-American spiritualism), of the so-called "materializations". Among other important German pneumatologists Georg Conrad Horst (1767-1838), a preacher, was well-known for his researches in the field of superstitions. Among others he published books called "Demonomagia," "Magic Library" and "Deuteroscopy."

While Swedenborg established the connection between man and

the spirit world more on a religious basis, the pneumatologists developed it scientifically. The phenomena of clairvoyance and materialization were interpreted by them in the terms of the "Northern Seer." However, the theoretical dissertations of the pneumatologists lacked all physical proof. They sought desperately a so-called "physical medium"—some being who would produce physical phenomena. They found one in Friederike Hauffe (née Wanner), the "Seeress of Prevorst." She owed her comparatively short-lived world fame to the physician Andreas Justinus Kerner (1786–1862) who held more than a thousand séances with her (the details of these experiments are contained in Kerner's work, "Die Seherin von Prevorst", 1829.) With the detailed discussion and analysis of Friederike Hauffe German pneumatology practically exhausted all the facts and theories which some time later, in a watered-down and sensational form, were to be exploited by American spiritualism.

American spiritualism began in the small towns of Hydesville and Stratford. In February 1848 poltergeists began to manifest themselves in the Hydesville home of the Rev. Mr. Fox. When the "hauntings" or "infestations" continued in spite of a committee that examined them, the great "discovery" of "table-rapping" and "table-turning" was made. It was not only in Rochester and the neighbouring towns that tables moved and raps sounded but all over America. Lectures were organized at which various objects flew through the air. Some claimed that these phenomena could be explained only by Spiritualist teaching while others branded them as "hypnotic swindle".

In the midst of considerable publicity came news of extraordinary events at Stratford, in the house of Preacher Phelps. True, the citizens of Stratford proved most unsympathetic. They chased the Phelps family from the town—and that was the end of spirit-rappings. But before that Mr. Andrew Jackson Davis had appeared in the Phelps home "to study the phenomena" and to exploit the "haunted house" for his own ambitious plans. After his investigation he declared: "I have discovered that the alleged haunting was partly the work of some boys who did it for fun and partly that of some unforgivably malicious people who were complete strangers to the family,".

Davis, later called "the Swedenborg of the New World", was born August 11, 1826, on a small farm in Blooming Grove (County Orange, New York State) the son of a drunken cobbler and a superstitious, neurotic mother. After a shiftless childhood—he did not start school until he was ten and soon quit to become a shepherd, employed by a fanatically pious farmer's wife—he returned to the city to educate himself at evening classes. In 1843 he fell under the influence of Mr. Levingston, a mesmerist who found him an ideal subject for hypnosis and with whom he travelled as a faith healer or medium through the States. Later Davis associated himself with the Reverends Smith and Fishbough, studied medicine and natural science in secret and in 1845 made himself "independent" with his own hypnotist and reporter. He began a series of lectures, delivered ostensibly in a state of trance.

Davis wanted to found a new religion; he wanted to become a "super-Messiah". From the beginning he showed himself an opponent of the Christian churches; he denounced in a subtle fashion the dogmas of original sin, salvation and eternal damnation, promising *all* spirits, even those of the most abject sinners, the kingdom of heaven. He championed the poor far more radically than Christ. But his teaching differed from all others by the circumstance that he could, in a manner of speaking, guarantee the supernatural revelations, the achievements of mediumship. "Table-turning", invented in America, became his most successful means of propaganda throughout the world. As early as 1849 a lady who returned from America to France started to popularise this mystical parlour-game. By 1851 the first Spiritualist review, *La table parlante* (The Speaking Table) was launched and an extensive specialist literature developed.

The true pioneer of French Spiritualism was Hippolyte Denisard Rivail who wrote under the pseudonym Allan Kardec. He proclaimed the rejection of the doctrine of eternal damnation. Kardec believed that through the trials and tribulations of the world human souls were purified and ennobled. But human life was too short for this process —therefore it was necessary for the soul to be re-born; and this re-birth occurred as often as the lofty purpose demanded it. But progress in the reincarnations was constant. The completely purified spirit enjoyed in the end the highest bliss of eternal life. The knowledge which the spirit acquired, the moral achievements, were never lost. Kardec called Spiritualism an "imperfect science". The German idea of a "*Nervengeist*" (nervous spirit) he turned into the French "*perisprit*."

Spiritualism (imported from America) became fashionable in France and this was a sufficient springboard for the conquest of Europe. Anglo-American Spiritualism was a religion, an organized faith from the beginning; but through its cunning and commercial admixture of occult matters it produced numerous phenomena. These could be divided into three main groups: physical, psychical and intellectual. The first group included table-turning, the second table-rapping (which was replaced by the planchette, a miniature table with a pencil attached to each of its three legs) the third the writing and oral mediums.

A great deal of publicity was accorded to various mediums and in 1869 the Dialectical Society, founded in London, decided to set up an investigating committee to examine spiritualist phenomena. After eighteen months and interminable arguments the Society declared that while certain mediumistic phenomena did exist, they must be due to some still unknown natural forces. This supported the aims of modern scientific occultism rather than Spiritualism. In spite of this, Spiritualists like to refer to this "first scientific acknowledgment" of a committee consisting entirely of scientists. As the report did not satisfy the intellectuals, the distinguished British chemist, Sir William Crookes undertook a special investigation. His aim was to unmask the most outstanding medium of his age, Daniel Dunglas Home; but instead he became if not a Spiritualist at least a believer in some aspects of unexplored and unexplained "psychic power". Crookes who conducted especially interesting experiments in trying to measure this force, constructed some brilliant control apparatus and was never suspected of any deception. Yet when the representatives of official, orthodox science examined his diaries, they declared that Home had duped the distinguished scientist in many ways. Another highly respected scientist, the Leipzig astrophysicist Friedrich Zöllner examined chiefly the "flying objects" using the American medium Henry Slade. He came to the conclusion that it was not the "penetrability of matter" that made these "wonderful phenomena" possible but the fourth dimension. Slade, like practically all famous mediums, was occasionally caught cheating; this led to violent attacks on Zöllner; in turn, he was trapped into extremely wild and abusive outbursts in his "Scientific Essays" (published 1878–79 in Leipzig, in three volumes) which discredited considerably the value of his work.

An endless series of spiritualist séances produced even more incredible things: spirits turned into solid by semi-solid bodies (materialisations) which the sitters were allowed to touch and photograph. Unfortunately, as in the case in Slade and so many others, mediums were again and again caught in trickery; the orthodox scientists proved hallucinations by the sitters (which seemed to provide new support for the old materialistic and mechanistic concept of the world). The spirit photographers, like Hudson (1872), Parkes (a little later) and Buguet (1873) were unmasked as common impostors who used prepared plates. Some of them were taken to court as criminals. The plaster-casts of "spirit hands" turned out to be equally fraudulent. In those cases which were carefully investigated either the participants had been misled by hallucinations or the mediums had been cheating; in the end a good many of the scientifically orientated spiritualists decided to forego experiments with physical mediums. They restricted to only a small part of the phenomena any explanation that involved the mani-festation of "unearthly" forces (the so-called "intelligences") and thus approached the attitude of the scientific occultists most of whom had come from the ranks of orthodox science. These succeeded in finding psycho-physical explanations for phenomena which had been held as occult and brought them into the domain of official science (for instance, suggestion, hypnosis.)

There are still spiritualists who believe in revelations and whom we should consider as members of a sect, disciples of a religion. There are the scientific spiritualists who ascribe some of the still unexplained phenomena to the intervention of spirits. Finally there are scientific occultists or psychical researchers who accept extrasensory or even supra-sensory powers but reject anything supernatural. Infrequently, the three categories sometimes overlap; though between the first and the last there is—even today—an unbridgable gap and much bitter animosity.

Yet the work of psychical researchers in the last fifty years—the achievements of men like Baron Schrenck-Notzing, Gustav Geley, Professor Rhine, Dr. E.J. Dingwall, Fritz Grunewald, Ubald Tar-taruga, Charles Richet, Harry Price (in spite of recent attacks since his death) and scores of others—seem to point to the future belonging to the scientific occultists, the psychical researchers. They are bound to absorb the scientifically inclined spiritualists and the orthodox scientists alike in the fullness of time. It is, of course, not their task to fight with the faith of the believers. Spiritualist dogma is like any other—you either believe or do not believe it; you demand proofs or allow yourself to be persuaded of scientific truth when you no longer possess faith.

★   ★   ★

Even the most scant historical outline of occultism would be incomplete without reference to the three associated or parallel fields of animism, theosophy and antroposophy.

Animism was evolved by Alexander N. Aksakof, the distinguished Russian philosopher and psychical researcher (1832–1903) who was Russia's principal exponent of parapsychology and spiritualism. He worked in his native country, in England and other parts of Europe. He wrote and translated many works and sat with the principal mediums of the day (D.D. Home, Mme. d'Espérance, Eusapia Palladino, Henry Slade, Eglinton and others). He left about £4,000 to the British Society for Psychical Research. Animism was a theoretical interpretation of occult phenomena and in opposition to the spiritualistic theory. It is more comprehensive; the animist maintains—until the contrary has been proved—that his theory embraces all occult phenomena while the spiritualist divides them into those that can be explained animistically and those where in his opinion such explanation is insufficient and therefore the spiritualist hypothesis is the only answer. Dr. Tischner writes: "Spiritualism is the interpretation of occult facts that claims survival after death and the possibility of communicating with the spirits of the deceased while other occultists deny this or at least do not consider it the only possible explanation of these facts. There are still others who maintain that one must assume the origin of some phenomena can be traced to 'spirits' without claiming that these are the spirits of the dead. This was for instance the view of Sir William Crookes. Belief in spirits and in their communications with our world has existed in every age but this belief has only become an organized religious conception of the world through Spiritualism that developed in the United States. It is both a reaction against the materialism of our age yet it is very much a child of our own times; instead, as in earlier centuries, trying to reach the ultimate mysteries by faith, it tries to prove them by experiments; an attitude which to my mind appears to ignore the very essense of any faith. This experimental religion is a counterpart of Haeckel's Monism which also attempts a kind of religion based on knowledge and experiment. We scientists only occupy ourselves with Spiritualism to the extent of it being an interpretation of experimental knowledge which serious researchers gather in séances."

Theosophy was the imaginative creation of an extraordinary woman, Elena Petrovna Blavatsky—daughter of a German nobleman, General von Hahn, granddaughter of Princess Helen Dolgoruki. She was born in 1831 at Ekaterinoslav (Dnepropetrovsk) in Southern Russia. She was a neurotic, unusual child, a sleepwalker and dreamer. At seventeen she married the aged General Nikifor Vasilievich Blavatsky but the marriage was never consummated and she soon left him (later she married a Mr. Betanelly, stipulating that he would never attempt to claim his conjugal rights; this marriage was also short-lived.) After leaving her first husband, Mme. Blavatsky travelled extensively in Europe and Asia, visiting Tibet and India. In 1870 she appeared in Cairo as a trained medium; she claimed to have spent seven years with the 'Mahatmas' in the Himalayas. These were "men of wisdom", dwelling in the fastnesses of Tibet who, by their holy life, had obtained divine power and knowledge, were accomplished mind-readers and were able to "dissolve material objects", transporting them "by occult streams or currents" over considerable distances. These "adepts" were people who had discovered the Philosophers' Stone; Mme. Blavatsky claimed to have been trained as an adept herself. Now she returned to the civilized world at the command of her teacher "Mahatma Koot Hoomi" in order to propagate theosophy, that is, the innermost essence of the religious and philosophical systems of all ages. In 1873 she went to America and in 1875 organized the Theosophical Society with the spiritualist Colonel Henry Steel Olcott. A branch was also set up in Bombay; an official journal, *The Theosophist* was established and Mme. Blavatsky published her first book "Isis Unveiled" (1877). Her followers increased rapidly; by the time of her death in 1891 they were estimated at over one hundred thousand in various parts of the world. Her books, "The Secret Doctrine" (1888), "The Key to Theosophy" (1889) and "The Voice of Silence" (1889) added to her reputation and many distinguished men, philosophers, journalists, scientists, even prelates, accepted her claims and treated her with considerable respect.

At the same time there was no lack of sceptics and opponents. The British Government and the Society for Psychical Research asked the distinguished Orientalist and Indian civil servant, Brian Houghton Hodgson to examine Mme Blavatsky's so-called miracles. His careful report was a devastating exposure. She had to confess that her "miracles" were tricks performed with the aid of two fakirs, that the "Mahatmas" were pure invention. In 1885 she settled in Italy; when she died, she was poor, forgotten and discredited.

Yet her work survived. Mme. Blavatsky had transplanted Buddhist teachings into the Western world; and the dogmas of Karma, the law of inescapable consequences and effects of all actions, of reincarnation had a great attraction for many world-weary Westerners. Nor was there any lack of enthusiastic followers who tried to whitewash Helena's memory. Richard Wefer, who published his "A Noble Woman and Her Antagonists" after the First World War was fairly typical of them. He tried to prove that Mme. Blavatsky possessed occult talents which made any trickery quite unnecessary. On the other hand she could not be made responsible for Olcott's manipulations even if she had played a few practical jokes on some fools!

Madame Blavatsky's organisation after her death soon found a new leader in her disciple, Mrs. Annie Besant—though she completely changed its principles. Annie Besant was born in 1847, the daughter of an English doctor named Wood and his Irish wife. She was an extremely pious Christian but her Celtic heritage inclined her to mysticism. In 1867 she married the Reverend Frank Besant, brother of Sir Walter Besant, the novelist. In her autobiography she said: "In my childhood I only had two ideals: my mother and Christ." As the wife of the vicar of Cheltenham she wrote a number of tracts; but after a while she felt religious doubts rising in her, separated from her husband and began to study Eastern religions. She became associated with Charles Bradlaugh (under the pseudonym 'Ajax') in propaganda for free thought and the limitation of population. In 1889 she joined the Theosophical Society and developed into a devoted pupil of Mme. Blavatsky. At their first meeting Mme. Blavatsky, who never stopped smoking Russian cigarettes, received her with the words: "My dear Mrs. Besant, I've longed to see you for such a long time." Soon Mrs. Besant was kneeling at her feet and pleading: "Will you accept me as your disciple and grant me the honour to be your witness in front of the whole world?" Thereupon Mme. Blavatsky placed her hand majestically upon her head and accepted her with the words. "You are a noble woman. May Koot Humi Lal Singh bless you!"

From 1907 until her death in 1933 Mrs. Besant was president of the Theosophical Society—besides being a zealous champion of Indian independence and in 1917 president of the Indian National Congress. She introduced the elements of Hinduism into theosophy, replacing Buddhism. She published a whole series of books on reincarnation, on Karma, on theosophy and psychology, on the religious problem in

India; she also published a remarkable autobiography. She founded the "Order of the Rising Sun" and later the "Order of the Eastern Star."

Mrs. Besant was devoted to the cause which she had adopted after a somewhat eclectic, experimental career; she was honest and sincere. But she was also something of an autocrat. She soon clashed with Dr. Rudolf Steiner, the general secretary of the German theosophists. Their arguments led to a split. The School for Theosophy was founded in 1875. Dr. Steiner joined it in 1902 and for eleven years he represented Mrs. Besant's views. But in 1913 he left, taking some 2400 members with him. He invented the name *Antroposophy*. He founded the *Anthroposophischer Bund* and a number of institutions for the teaching of his doctrines, such as the Goetheanum at Dornach, near Basle. Even though he had an independent interpretation of theosophy from the beginning, to reconcile it with the Germanic spirit and Christianity, his ideas still remained by and large the original theosophy of Mme. Blavatsky.

It is not easy to sum up all that Dr. Steiner (who died in 1925) meant by his "*Geisteswissenschaft*". The basic idea of all the various branches of theosophy is perhaps reducible to the aim of exploring and developing all unexplained laws of Nature and all the latent powers in human beings. "There is no limit to knowledge" (or cognition, perception). Thus the field of activity includes both the entire universe and the single atom. The Indian teachings were "Christianized" in several ways. Steiner added two more to the five Indian "egos". He differentiates between the physical, the ethereal, the astral bodies, the ego (lower *manas*), the spirit itself (higher *manas*), the life spirit (*buddhi*) which is the spiritualized astral body and finally the *atma* (the spiritual man.) Thus we would possess three physical, three intellectual and three spiritual links or members. The more the human spirit develops, the more he becomes a "spiritual man", a clairvoyant. Steiner's *Karma* was also "Christianized" for he argued that Karma was not compatible with the venerable idea of grace. A Buddhist might wish to be liberated from the almost endless chain of reincarnations in order to reach Nirvana; but a Christian cannot return to earth often enough in order to shape a richer life, to reach a higher level and to penetrate into the inexhaustible mystery of Christ. If this is not a matter of faith—or, according to one's ideals, pure theosophy—then there is no scientific occultism. The tenets of theosophy cannot be explained or accepted rationally—like any other dogmas they must be believed or rejected with no alternative. But psychical research cannot get involved with articles of faith; it must deal with facts so far as they are to be ascertained and interpreted.

There has been a great deal of argument about the "proper study" of psychical research, of scientific occultism. There have been controversial views as to how far its field should extend and what divisions should be made within it. At one time there were four main groups—telepathy, clairvoyance, telekinesis and materialisations. In 1922 the Psychological Society of Berlin, headed by Dr. Albert Moll, elaborated these four groups in more popular terms by posing the following questions:

(1) Is there a clairvoyance involving space or time?

(2) Does telepathy exist—i.e. thought-transference without any means of the generally accepted means of communication?

(3) Does telekinesis exist—i.e. are there individuals who are capable of moving objects without any of the known mechanical forces?

(4) Do dead people materialize? or are there any other materializations? Do individuals exist from whose fingers or mouth tangible or visible matter evolves which can take the shape of limbs, heads or even whole bodies?

More recent research seems to indicate that the four divisions can be reduced to two main groups. Dr. Waldemar von Wasielewski who was a highly respected authority in the fields of telepathy and clairvoyance claimed that these two were only different branches of the same psychical talent. He defined them under the collective names of "direct perception" or "panaesthesia". At the same time Baron von Schrenck-Notzing (whose monumental "Materialisation Phenomena" is still a standard work) put forward the view that telekinesis was only a preliminary stage of "teleplastics"—the term he used for tangible and visible materialisations.

Dr. Ubald Tartaruga who combined the functions of a high police official in Vienna with psychical research, formulated the following system for occult phenomena:

I. Supranormal psychology
  (a) telepathy
  (b) clairvoyance

II. Supranormal physiology
    (a) telekinesis
    (b) teleplastics

The division of psychic phenomena into psychological and physical, those of the mind and of the body, is fairly general. But the dividing line between supranormal psychology and physiology is not always clearly defined; if we only spoke of supranormal "physics", it would narrow the definition of telekinetic and teleplastic phenomena with their overwhelmingly biological character. The two main groups which Dr. Tartaruga championed must be evaluated collectively.

*   *   *

We might now ask: what are psychic phenomena, what is the nature and essence of mediumship? Phenomena and mediums have been investigated by serious and competent scientists under conditions of strict, scientifically validated control. What happens usually to provoke such investigations? Objects 'fly' around or hover in the air, changing their place without any human agency—or so it seems! The mystery is invested in the inexplicable movement, in the apparent defiance of gravity, in loss of weight. William Crookes, Friedrich Zöllner, Charles du Prel, F.W.H. Myers, Harry Price, James Henry Hyslop, Professor E. Morselli, Dr. Julian Ochorowicz, Baron Schrenck-Notzing, Fritz Grunewald, Dr. Gustav Geley, Professor W.J. Crawford were but some of the physicists, psychiatrists, physicians, engineers and natural scientists who have investigated such phenomena. Several of them designed ingenious and sensitive control apparatus; many of them claimed that they had excluded all possibility of fraud.

Their experiments were initially concentrated on differentiating between telekinetic and teleplastic phenomena—though Schrenck-Notzing came to the conclusion that these were but different facets of the same process. The most outstanding achievement of telekinesis was the levitation of tables or other heavy objects (or of the medium himself); these objects often remained for more than half a minute in the air. The greatest reported success of teleplastics was the "psycho-dynamic replacement of a stereoplastic creature" (here we again become involved in the unavoidable jargon of psychical research: this means simply materialisation of a tangible, three-dimensional human body.) In other cases such materialisations, emerging from the body of the medium, were flat—two-dimensional.

Dr. von Schrenck-Notzing's huge work "Materialisations Phenomena" and the shorter but comprehensive "Physical Phenomena of Mediumship" are still the standard references in this field. (Physical mediumship, by the way, has become much discredited in recent years and such mediums are now rare. But this does not detract from Schrenck-Notzing's work or the work of his contemporaries and predecessors.)

Schrenck-Notzing described the substance that emerged from the body of the medium: it was cold, reptilian to the touch, usually invisible but could be repeatedly photographed. This substance or material was shaped according to the conscious or unconscious will of the medium into "teleplastic forms" whose task it was to grasp and move solid objects. (While Eduard Hartmann declared these phenomena as "simple forces of pull and pressure" Schrenck-Notzing opposed this theory for it did not account sufficiently for the more complex actions of telekinesis.) During his experiments, he claimed, there were clear cases of a definite volition, a discernible purpose, the force could be localized, there was a co-ordination of motional and tactile sensations, of concepts of pressure and touch. The telekinetic motions were precise as if carried out by invisible fingers and "are, to a certain extent, subject to the general laws of the physiology and biology of the human organism." Bottazzi, a professor of physiology at Naples University, called them "medianistic limbs" while Professor E. Morelli, a Genoese physiologist and psychiatrist named them "neoplasm" (others have spoken of them as "pseudopods.") These telekinetic shapes are created according to biological principles, are sometimes and partly reminiscent of human limbs—but often enough are of fantastic and bizarre forms. Sometimes the medium "externalises" this mysterious mass (which is also called ectoplasm) only for a "creative purpose"—to create "phantoms"—which finally retire into the medium's body. The xenologists therefore speak of an "emission and absorption" of matter. Sir Oliver Lodge observed as early as 1895 such "pseudopod-like growths" during his experiments with the Italian medium Eusapia Palladino. Researchers at Columbia University also found "limb-like formations" in her materialisations.

It was at this time generally agreed that the actual limbs of the mediums "performed similar motions when the objects were pulled or pushed". Schrenck-Notzing, always cautious in his deductions, called this "either a necessary, constant condition.. or only an accompanying phenomenon, making the effort easier; something that habit has made unavoidable." He pointed out that the mediums *really* performed work involving considerable effort (if not with their actual limbs); practically all of them showed much exhaustion and muscular tiredness after the séances. Far more interesting seemed the fact that the weight of the medium increased exactly by the weight of the "levitated" objects—which could not be explained by any other theory. (Of course, if a medium were cheating his weight would also increase by the weight of a table or chair which he lifted—not with his "pseudopods" but with his own, material hands.) Most psychical researchers insist on placing the medium on carefully balanced scales during séances. Fritz Grunewald used as a counter-check a very ingeniously constructed "phantom coach." In cases where the medium levitated himself, it was assumed that he supported himself with his "dynamic arm". Professor Crawford evolved his own theory of "beams" and "rods" —but their essence was the same as the "pseudopod" or "dynamic arm" theory. The medium's willpower was supposed to be transformed into matter; this was the best demonstration of the (Einstein's) theory of matter being simply a form of energy. (J. Erik Nordberg, an Austrian psychical researcher wrote some thirty five years ago: "Materialisations are emissions shaped by the medium's organism. The teachings of the Aristotelian-Thomistic school had already declared that the soul possessed the power of shaping matter, being the essential form of the body. Not bound to the body, the psyche rules matter, is able to dissolve whole groups of cells and to change bodily matter into a different aggregate state. There is no stronger argument against materialism.")

Physical mediums have been much discredited by the numerous frauds of which they were guilty. But in our own century they have become once again subjects of psychical research. From the point of view of exact science it is only to be welcomed that most of the re-researchers and experimenters are *not* spiritualists. Psychical research has, among other things, considerable historical importance; it may well provide an explanation for the ancient belief in witchcraft (witches were supposed to be recognizable by losing weight without any apparent physical cause)—not to speak of hauntings, poltergeists, every kind of "spook". It can clarify for us the meaning of Eastern religions, so long wrapped in mysticism—the religions whose apostles had reached, purely intuitively, the conviction that the spirit, the psyche, was something primary and matter something secondary. In other words, whether we call it soul, spirit, psyche, idea or even energy —it is such a force that creates matter.

But scientific occultism, psychical research—the often unspectacular and unrewarding experiments—show us something else. We have earlier examined areas of investigation—the *terra incognita* between the scientifically explored and the scientifically still unexplored into which the borders of all exact sciences merge. Xenology cannot be considered a waste of time; it is a specialist science like crystallography or biochemistry with all the controls and techniques such disciplines involve. Medicine, both clinical and psychiatric, has recently advanced into the borderland of psychical research through its examination of the causes of hysteria, of hallucinations, of extrásensory perception and associated subjects. The results are by and large systematic although there is considerable argument about nuances and details. It cannot be denied that paranormal or supranormal or extrasensory (whichever term is most acceptable) psychology and physiology have been established and that research from within these subjects has illuminated a purely metaphysical area.

It was known long before the Christian era that some persons possess special psychical faculties. The idea of mediumship is expressed more or less clearly in the most ancient writings; though the word "medium" is only about a hundred years old in its present sense. The Anglo-American Spiritualists who coined the term (or rather, gave it its special meaning) intended it to describe a person who provided the means of communication with the "spirit world". It is claimed that all people possess mediumistic qualities, in lesser or greater degree; but that even the most brilliant inborn talent must be perfected by training. This last statement has often been perverted into the ridiculous by sceptics—whenever a previously "trained" professional medium was caught cheating. By "training", destructive sceptics simply implied a thorough schooling in conjuring tricks and ways of "cheating without being found out".

Ubald Tartaruga who as a high police official did much interesting work with clairvoyant mediums had little love for spiritualists for, as he put it, "you cannot accept the *deus ex machina* in the natural sciences." Yet after many years of theoretical and practical studies he came to the conclusion that *all* human beings had inborn mediumistic faculties and that these could be more or less developed—just as inborn intellectual faculties may be refined. Mediumship may decrease or disappear completely—as with other psychological talents, for instance, artistic intuition. Tartaruga was willing to accept Allan Kardec's classification of mediums into physical, sensitive, auditive, visual, oral, writing, somnambulistic, healing (among others)—categories according to their different activities or "means of expression".

Mediums, of course, are *not* the links, the mediators between the living and the spirit world; yet the name "medium" has been generally accepted by psychical research for mediums provide the "catalyst" by which phenomena which are still occult, that is, unexplored can be induced and manifested.

A great deal of psychical literature is devoted to the vexed problem of frauds, but such cases do not deter the scientific psychical researchers. They state that all professional mediums, wanting to earn money, are vulnerable to the (understandable) ambition to "produce" something. It is up to the scientist to devise fool-proof controls, to make fraud impossible. No one would refuse to accept money just because there are counterfeit coins or notes in circulation. A chemist would not give up his work because some of the substances he has to investigate are poisonous. Examples are quoted of "unconscious fraud", an impulse of the subconscious; a favourite case is the confession of Mrs. Finch, a famous medium who said: ". . .it was a real struggle between the subconscious desiring the phenomena and my normal self which was put by this into a strange, highly disadvantageous position. In my predicament I finally prayed to the Powers to Whom I was subject and with the silent cry for help to be saved from fraud I lost consciousness. . . Now I understood the psychology of fraudulent mediumship better than years of observation could have taught me . . ."

All this might be granted—and even the fact that suitable mediums (especially for physical phenomena) are extremely rare and psychical research must be content with whatever human material it can find. But I still feel that any medium caught cheating should be excluded from the work of scientific occultism—in the interests of psychical research itself. Or at least his or her work should not form part of xenologist literature. Psychical research will always be derided and denounced if it uses questionable proofs and fraudulent mediums. Fraudulent mediums should be disqualified—just as a jockey is warned off the course when he has pulled a race; or a boxer is banned from the ring if he has thrown a fight. No jury would accept the testimony of a witness who has been convicted of perjury. Unfortunately psychical researchers expose themselves again and again to the justified attacks of their opponents, by using discredited mediums as if nothing had previously happened to disqualify them—using them both for experiments and for the basis of their theories and deductions.

It is a stubborn misbelief that mediums can only be employed in a hypnotic or trance condition. There are many clairvoyants who work in a completely conscious state.

To sum up: Most if not all human beings have mediumistic qualities but not all are suitable experimental subjects. Most people have little or no idea of the processes in their subconscious. Mediumistic faculties can be trained and the person can show special aptitude for a particular branch of mediumship. The phenomena are essentially similar whether they are being produced at the demand of or within the framework of spiritualism, theosophy or psychical research. But the *interpretation* of these phenomena is vastly different. In order to produce the phenomena neither hypnotism nor a trance condition are necessary.

★　　★　　★

Since Freud and Joyce, Adler and Jung, Ferenczi and innumerable other pioneers, the existence of "the subconscious"—in psychology and medicine, in literature and art—has become an accepted fact. Yet only sixty years ago it was still part of the "occult" and Dr. Alfred Lehmann, director of the psychophysical laboratory at Copenhagen could write in his standard work: Superstition and Witchcraft: "The subconscious is a ridiculous chimera; there is not the slightest proof of its existence." But even Dr. Lehmann was unable to explain lapses of memory or the sudden remembering of names that had been forgotten. "How this happens," he wrote, "we cannot say with any certainty. . ." but then he added: "Thus a sharp line has been drawn between the actual conscious life, the 'upper consciousness' and the unconscious, the 'lower consciousness'. . . This is a retrograde step, a return to the old mystic psychology of Schindler; in psychological life the pole of the day is being balanced by a pole of the night. . . only the names are new... though for various reasons the word 'subconscious' would be preferable here, I still use 'unconscious'—because I do not want to create the impression that I accept this modern and ludicrous teaching about the psyche's light and darkness, day and night polarisation which has insinuated itself under the invidious name of the subconscious."

This is a typical semantic confusion of orthodox science—though the term "subconscious" would have been far more convenient, the learned Dr. Lehmann refused to use it lest he antagonize "officialdom". But to-day not even the anti-Freudian would deny that the subconscious exists.

It is also generally accepted that our real psychical (or psychological) life functions in this subconscious. Consciousness is divided from it by a "threshold" and has been repeatedly and aptly compared to a searchlight. It always illuminates only a certain sector of ideas or perceptions—those upon which our attention is concentrated. The intensity of this light is blurred near the edges. Consciousness has been called "a subsidiary phenomenon of psychological processes which are essentially purely passive"; it has also been compared to a thin layer which covers an immense variety of subconscious processes, until recently unsuspected and hidden in the immensely complex, tangled thicket of our minds. Psychoanalysts and psychiatrists agree that whatever we have once experienced (even without our being conscious of it at the time) can emerge on the surface at a given moment. Today, thanks to Freud and his successors, we know that the significance of the subconscious is immense—that inhibitions, phobias, neuroses are all rooted in former experiences which we have seemingly forgotten. Freud spoke of "alien bodies in the life of the psyche", comparing them to something within the body that causes inflammation and suppuration, upsetting the balance of organic life. As for subconscious memory, its limits have never been totally explored nor can its extent be overestimated.

The mass of subconscious ideas seems to be chaotic until it becomes grouped around some nucleus or centre which then represents the consciousness of the ego. There are people in whom several such centres or nuclei exist which Tartaruga has called "psychic solar systems". He classifies cases of split personalities—cases well known to medical history. Three, four, five such "egos" or "personalities" have been observed which are completely unaware of each other. It has happened that Ego No. 1. has, for instance, entered into correspondence with Ego No. 2.

Genius is manifested through the subconscious. Creative, artistic talent is the best proof of this. Goethe or Mozart have more or less observed by their own examples that their creative work was completely alien to their conscious egos. That is why skills and crafts can be acquired—but no study of prosody will make a great poet or no teacher, however inspired, can turn a dauber into a great painter. It has happened to almost everybody that suddenly, while studying some subject which has remained in spite of the closest application, dark and confused, the answer emerged simply and clearly across the threshold of consciousness. The work had been done deep down, in the "mystical" regions; the subconscious has been at work while our consciousness struggled in vain.

The mysteries of occult, psychical phenomena cannot be explained by any other reference than the subconscious. Of course, we must consider here the clearly marked difference between intellect and psyche; for we must not forget that the subconscious is merely an effect of the psychic apparatus—of that unknown, unexplored force we call, for want of a better word, the soul.

Memory is a most unreliable faculty. It has been established that only those details are retained in our memory of any happenings which have caught our attention in the decisive instant of time—regardless of their importance or triviality. That is the explanation of the gaps or contradictions in witnesses. Often it is the deep impression of an event which etches only this or that single phase into the memory. Certain states of excitement, fear, expectation, hope, have a decisive influence on the receptive powers of the intellect; so that we either sense the facts wrongly or forget quickly even correctly observed circumstances. In the same way suggestion, both during the experience and its reproduction, can be an important factor. This suggestive falsification of memory, and the adjustment of memory plays a considerable part in many stories concerned with clairvoyance, prophetic dreams and telepathy—and must always be taken into consideration by investigators. But these limitations apply only to the functions of our conscious memory. Psychoanalysis has shown that we store numerous sensual impressions in our subconscious which have never penetrated into the full light of the conscious but have immediately "sunk" under its threshold. These emerge repeatedly in dreams, under hypnosis and in trance. To use the analogy of the searchlight—these are the impressions which had reached only the edge, the outer limits of the immensity of our consciousness.

One technical term for the emergence of such not completely conscious impressions is *cryptomnesia*—the hidden memory.

But if something apparently long forgotten rises into the consciousness, we speak of *hypermnesia*. Sometimes a person carries out an action without knowing why he acts—for instance, under hypnotic or post-hypnotic suggestion. This is ascribed to the so-called "latent memory".

While conscious memory is unreliable, the subconscious memory is clear and exact. It seems that our subconscious memory retains all experiences with complete faithfulness to the end of our lives—so that it has been called, with some justification, "absolute memory". "Total recall", of course, is impossible for this "absolute memory" is not governed by the conscious mind.

Sensitivity to various stimuli varies greatly—not only in the different species of animals but also relatively between animal and human being and between different types of men. The acuteness of our senses decreases in direct proportion to the progress of civilization. This might be considered as additional proof that the main task of the intellect was originally to defend Man from the dangers of life. Cultural advances have repeatedly demanded considerable sacrifices of physical qualities; the blessings of culture of which the civilized nations are so proud robbed not only the human body but also the human psyche of many faculties. In view of our evolutionary history it is in no way surprising that some individuals—who could be called atavistic exceptions—possess a hypersensitivity far above the normal average.

This hyperaesthesia is frequently observed in hypnotised subjects in whom a far more acute sense of hearing and a considerably heightened awareness of light stimuli occur. But this is based on the essential nature of hypnosis.

It is within our own ability to direct our attention to any object or process—to concentrate. Our thoughts, our consciousness determine their direction deliberately. But very often this happens without our volition—by outside stimulation or through other people. Suggestibility is not restricted to persons with mediumistic faculties; it is a completely normal condition. (By "suggestion" we mean the outside stimulus itself which attracts and fixes our attention.) Too little heed is paid to the numerous suggestions constantly assailing us. Everything that influences us is suggestion: the maternal word, the teacher's word, the opinions expressed in magazines and newspapers, the radio or TV, the "message" of a play or film, religion, superstition, prophecy—the list is endless.

Physiologists have pointed out that by prolonged concentration it is possible to fix the attention, to visualize so perfectly some image of memory or fantasy that in its effect it becomes a real, sensual perception. Thus the "visual and auditive hallucinations of suggestion" come into being—which accounts for innumerable "miraculous visions" and "ghosts".

The mere expectation to see or hear something definite is sufficient to create the visual or auditive effect provided one is suggestible. Whether it is auto-suggestion or comes from somebody or something else, makes no difference.

There are many physical processes within our body over which our "ego" has no power at all. It is therefore natural that inner, organic changes can also depend upon our state of consciousness, modified by suggestion. It is possible to influence the heart-beat, the digestive processes. The power of the "psychic healers", of "healing by prayer" depends on suggestion. We know how many psychosomatic diseases can be cured by suggestive power. Lourdes and other places of pilgrimage and "miracle cures" depend on the psychical influence of religious faith.

By suggestion we can induce a strange, sleep-like state which James Braid, the British surgeon and writer first called "hypnotism".

For thousands of years "crystal-gazing" has been employed to produce visions and hallucinations artificially. Modern occultism has also employed it. Many mediums use the crystal in order to affect their subconscious. Crystal balls are simply mechanical aids to achieve a trance-condition. The same condition would be produced by using the glass of a pocket-watch, gazing into a mirror, at a magnifying glass with a black background or a pool of water. According to what they used to produce visions, the ancient and the medieval sorcerers and fortune-tellers were divided into hydromancers, capnomancers, crystallomancers, cleromancers (who divined the future by throwing dice, bones, etc. or casting lots), pegomancers (diviners by means of fountains) and a score of others. Another method was to listen to the "sound" of empty shells. The "dreams of numbers", the visionary forecast of winning lottery tickets as seen on the surface of "fairy wells" belongs to the same category.

The medium may use any of these objects to produce a peculiar dream-like state which may be a preliminary hypnotic condition that can easily pass into hypnosis. According to the talents or faculties of the person involved, more or less sharply defined pictures are produced—sometimes in colour—pictures of human beings, words, letters, numbers, etc. These correspond to the subconscious images rising to the surface. The essence of this phenomenon is in the deliberate exclusion of the normal consciousness by concentration—for example, on the crystal ball in the expectation of seeing something. "Staring into a crystal ball," Dr. Wasiliewski explains, "usually excites the subsubconscious sphere and represses consciousness." "With some mediums," Dr. Tischner points out, "visions are produced which are connected with purposeful intellectual processes within their subconscious; but quite often true occult facts are brought to light. . . this method facilitates the emergence of images and facts from the subconscious. . ."

Hypnotism was known in ancient Egypt. In India, China and Greece hypnotic trance was used by the priest-healers—although without understanding of its real processes. The methods of inducing it were the "laying on of hands" or stroking parts of the body with the fingertips. In the Middle Ages the belief in witchcraft was based mainly on misunderstood and misinterpreted hypnotism; while the successes achieved by "white magic" were venerated as "miracles". The priest-healers, the physicians, acquired a mystical glory—but so did many "lay hypnotists"; among them the Emperor Claudius and Vespasian, King Francis I of France, Elizabeth of France, James II of England practiced this art—without knowing what they were doing.

It was only towards the end of the eighteenth century that scientific investigation began although initially it was still mixed with superstition and error. Franz Anton Mesmer, the "discoverer" of the so-called "animal magnetism", a strange mixture of pioneer and charlatan, was followed by Charcot, Lavater, Dupotet, Puységur and several less eminent physicians and scientists. They followed Mesmer's lead, accepting his theory that some "fluid" was exuded by the body of the hypnotist; this was supposed to be produced by "animal magnetism". Mesmer wrecked his own career by a number of mistakes and failures —some of his experiments ended in the death of his subjects—and hypnotic experiments ceased for some time. (He attempted such forcible cures that he caused serious disturbances in people with weak nervous systems—hysteric cramps and spasms sometimes resulting in death.)

It was in the mid-nineteenth century, in 1843, that interest in hypnotism revived. James Braid, the Scottish physician, had worked in India and used his studies to good effect. He explained artificially produced hypnotic sleep as "an exhaustion of the senses through one-sided mental concentration." His contemporaries had no idea how close this brilliant forerunner of modern medical hypnosis had come to the heart of the problem; he was denounced as the worst kind of charlatan. The Paris Academy of Sciences subjected his theories to an "expert examination" and delivered a shattering opinion. This was the end of Braid's work; he died, embittered and forgotten.

Yet his work was destined to bear fruit. In 1866 Dr. Ambroise Auguste Liébault, a physician from Nancy, investigated again and came to the conclusion (which is the generally accepted theory today) that hypnotism had nothing to do with "fluid"; it was simply a matter of suggestion. He also established the fact that suggestion was the precondition of hypnotism—and not the reverse as was at first believed. Mesmer's "animal magnetism" theory has still some champions though no scientific or factual basis exists for it.

The popularisation of hypnotism was not the work of any scientist but of the Danish businessman, Hansen (1880). It was his propaganda that aroused the interest of the public, the press and the scientific world.

Hypnotism is *not* a state of sleep though it resembles it. In normal sleep all external senses cease their special activities, while under hypnosis certain sense-areas not only remain sensitive to stimuli—but even acquire a hyperaesthesia. These are the areas to which attention is directed. A hypnotic trance can only be a partial sleep.

The *depth* of hypnosis, however, can vary considerably. There are at least three degrees—a light state, an intermediate and a deep state. The borderline between the three is not always clearly recognisable and only qualified physicians or trained, professional hypnotists should be allowed to practice any of them.

The first faculty which the hypnotized subject loses is that of conscious control over his body. The hypnotist can command him to be unable to open his eyes, loosen his clasped hands or move his temporarily paralysed limbs, to remain in a posture which he could not maintain in his normal, waking state. The sense of sight, smell and taste can be modified—a glass of water can be "turned" into wine and under suggestion produce alcoholic symptoms. Scientists devised an apparatus called the pletysmograph which recorded the sensations of pleasure when a hypnotised subject was told that a glass of water was the best Burgundy. The regular symptoms of hypnotic trance are today familiar even to laymen. Insensitivity to pricks and cuts, the temporary disappearance of knee and other reflexes can all be induced in deep hypnosis; sight, smell, taste, muscular sensation can be temporarily "disconnected"; the last to be eliminated are the senses of touch and hearing. In the deepest hypnosis "an isolated contact" is established; the subject becomes totally dependent and concentrated on the hypnotist; he feels only whatever the hypnotist suggests. The whole normal exterior world is excluded.

Today the most frequently used method to induce hypnotic conditions is verbal suggestion. The hypnotist "persuades" the subject that he is, for instance, unable to open his eyes. Verbal suggestion is far more frequent in ordinary life than might be imagined. Persuasion seeks to convince, admits the possibility of criticism and contradiction, only trying to weaken and overcome them. Hypnotic persuasion aims at creating obedience, to establish a relationship of master and slave. If we follow it, we do so blindly and uncritically.

The use of glittering, shining objects or of "magnetic passes" is simply the employment of similar, prolonged stimulation of the senses which usually has a somniferous effect. The monotonous sound of the rain, the murmur of a stream, the buzz of the hairdresser's clippers, the ticking of a watch all have under certain circumstances a sleep-inducing power.

The main source of the legends about "black magic" lay in the circumstance that the "sleeping" senses become completely anaesthetized; while those "kept awake" show hyperaesthetic faculties. Somnambulists, so superstition proclaimed, possessed "magic powers". But scientists, once they had penetrated this, discovered that no medium was capable of displaying any knowledge in a hypnotic state which he had not possessed before; a person, for example, who had never studied Russian could not suddenly speak it under hypnosis. Spiritualists have consistently tried to prove the opposite in order to demonstrate the "intervention of the spirits". Today these apparent miracles are known to well up from our subconscious memory, with telepathic influences or with the clairvoyance faculty which often becomes intensified under hypnosis. Here hypnotism is an aid—a liberating of the subconscious —not a miraculous, magic power. By disconnecting the "disturbing" outer senses a psychological concentration is achieved.

Here we should also consider auto-hypnosis, auto-suggestion which is practised usually by people who have been often hypnotized. Self-hypnosis differs little from the "trance-condition" of spiritualist mediums of whom it is said that their "spirit has left the body and therefore is totally unreceptive to the outside world." Yet in self-hypnosis there is no dependence on another hypnotist, the consciousness is usually less limited, passivity not so marked; there are various intermediary states right up to the extremes of split personality—from which the trance condition differs only in its shorter duration.

There are movements and gestures we perform without being conscious of them. It is quite easy for women to knit or embroider while carrying on an animated conversation; doodling is compatible with close concentration on some discussion. As no physiological or psychological explanations could be found for this, such actions were called in earlier time "magic movements". Today we talk of "automatism" and trace them back to the activity of the subconscious; especially as it has been proved that all ideas can be transposed into some movement under proper circumstances. Carpenter spoke of "ideomotoric gestures or movements." The dowser's stick, twig or wand, the so-called Siderian pendulum, a great deal of ancient necromancy all employ or employed this "automatism".

In the case of a well-developed mediumship, the subconscious may also reveal itself through the planchette, the ouija-board, automatic writing. Automatism has been called, quite aptly, the "megaphone of the subconscious" though here we must differentiate between the normal and the supranormal subconscious. Automatism also aids the images created by telepathy or clairvoyance to reach the surface of the consciousness.

The subconscious, memory, hyperaesthesia, suggestion, crystal-balls and shells, hypnosis and automatism—all these are essential elements, aids and factors of mediumship. In the following pages the lives of a representative selection of mediums is portrayed. The reader must make his own judgment. I have sought to present them as they were, to be truthful to the facts and my own vision of the events.

★   ★   ★

CHAPTER ONE

Hanussen: The Devil's Prophet

LATE IN April, 1933, the farmworker Mathias Hummel had the unpleasant experience of finding a corpse in a small wood about fifteen
miles from Berlin. The body, riddled with bullets, had been hastily
buried in a shallow grave; but the spring rains had washed the topsoil
away and a well-shod, large foot was sticking out of the mud.

Hummel ran to tell the police. Seven hours later *Kriminalrat* Mölders
faced a slim, fair-haired young man in his office at police headquarters
in the Alexanderplatz.

The young man's name was Dzino Ismet, a Bosnian of German
origin.

"I need your help," Mölders told him. "It might be unpleasant. . .
but I can't spare you the trouble. We've found a corpse. We have reason
to think that it might be Hanussen."

Dzino, his face haggard, nodded silently. A few minutes later, in
the basement morgue of the huge red-brick building, a uniformed
policeman lifted a coarse sheet from the body. Dzino gave it a quick
glance, then turned away.

"Give me a cigarette," he asked the *Kriminalrat*. "That's him."

"Are you sure?"

"Yes. I recognize his teeth."

After the *post mortem* the corpse was released for burial. But it was
not claimed. Erik Jan Hanussen, who less than three months before
had packed the huge *Scala*, Berlin's leading variety theatre, every night,
owned newspapers, cars, jewels, a fabulous villa and a yacht, ended
in a cheap pine-wood coffin, in a pauper's grave. Not a word of his
murder was published in the German newspapers. Mölders was told
to close the case. The bullets extracted during the autopsy were not
examined by ballistic experts. No witnesses were heard. These were
the orders—given by Goebbels, the all-powerful head of Ministry of
Propaganda of the Third Reich, then not quite six months old.

Only very few people discovered where Hanussen was buried. In the first weeks after his funeral, a young woman with soft brown eyes, a delicately tilted nose and long, reddish-brown hair visited the grave several times. She brought flowers. But after a while her visits stopped. Hanussen was forgotten. His very grave has disappeared. His villa, yacht, diamond rings and gold bracelets; his platinum tie-pins and cuff-links, his bank balances—confiscated for the benefit of the Nazi Party— the Party he served; the Party that liquidated him as if he had been a stray mongrel, only fit to be destroyed.

It is not easy to discover the true facts about this extraordinary man. Truth and fancy, legend and slander, genuine psychic gifts and blatant charlatanism are inextricably mixed in the record. For much of it he was himself responsible. He loved to mystify, shock, attract and repel people. Beyond doubt he was a little mad—or more than a little in his megalomania. He had a practically insatiable sexual appetite. He wasn't handsome or even particularly good-looking. Of medium height, with thick, black, oily hair, bushy eyebrows that almost met over the bridge of his slightly aquiline nose; his eyes were dark and not too large, with deep half circles under them; he always wore a dead-white make-up on the stage. His mouth was ordinary and his rounded chin cleft. Only his hands were remarkable—white, expressive, with long fingers, always exquisitely well-kept. He used them like the instruments of an orchestra—cajoling and commanding, threatening and caressing.

His real name was Heinrich Steinschneider. He was born the son of the caretaker of a synagogue. He left school when he was fourteen, running away to join a circus. He spent his adolescence on fair-grounds, in booths and tents. He was a knife-thrower and a fire-eater; when times were bad, he would play the role of a three-legged virgin or a two-headed bushman. He was even a professional strong man, though a phoney one—he burst cardboard chains and would readily work as a clown or a fake Hercules.

When did Heinrich Steinschneider become Erik Jan Hanussen? Among the few witnesses whom Kriminalrat Mölders was able to question, was a Viennese businessman named Fritz Holdt. He and the murdered "seer" had served in the same company during the first World War.

"At first he was always playing tricks in our quarters," Holdt said. "He would put out burning matches in his mouth, he spread ashes on the ersatz honey that was part of our rations—and ate it. We all thought he was crazy. Until one day—I think it was in Flanders— we were cut off. It was very hot and we were terribly thirsty. We hadn't a drop of water for thirty-six hours. Then Steinschneider sud- denly pointed to the ground. He dug a small hole with his boot-heel. 'There's water here,' he said. All we heard was 'water'. We hadn't talked about anything else for almost two days. Steinschneider was crazy—but still, we dug and we found water. A natural spring. That was the beginning. Steinschneider died and Hanussen was born. You see, the story got around. The general heard about it. He sent for Hanussen and he liked him. He was transferred to headquarters. . . to entertain the troops. Once he appeared in front of the Kaiser. He got something nice out of it. Then I lost sight of him. But after the war I heard of him again. He had joined a tiny itinerant circus. And one day he eloped with the owner's wife—after pawning most of the equipment."

For a while Hanussen disappeared completely. Then one morning he called on the manager of the Ronacher Circus in Vienna. The Ronacher was doing badly—because Breitbart, the "Strongest Man on Earth" was drawing all the crowds to the chief competitor. Breit- bart burst chains, bent thick iron bars and forced open triple locks.

"I have the biggest sensation in the world for you. You want to bet?"

"I never bet."

"You've got a pretty girl in the outer office!"

"Is that supposed to be news?"

"Tonight she'll break chains twice as thick as Breitbart!"

"You are mad!" the director replied.

But he changed his mind as Hanussen began to explain. He agreed to give his visitor fifty per cent of the net profits. What a fantastic attraction! A nineteen-year-old, fragile blonde—with the strength of a giant!

The Ronacher was sold out every night, until the underpaid staff went on a strike and out came the truth. Hanussen had used light- weight imitation chains and fooled the public. (A couple of weeks later Breitbart was also unmasked as a cheat.)

But by then thousands had paid good money and Hanussen had collected his share. He disappeared again for a few months—and then made his debut at one of the smaller music-halls. And he was a fan- tastic success.

He wore immaculate tails and his chalk-white, strong face, his deep-set dark eyes, his sensitive hands, seemed to dominate the spellbound audience. Women were by far in the majority. They appeared to love his arrogance, his superb self-confidence.

"And now it's your turn, madame," he addressed a rather fulsome blonde. "Let me tell you something of your life. . .Your first husband was killed in the war."

"That's right," the woman said, leaning back, feeling herself the centre of attention next to the clairvoyant.

"Your second divorced you."

"That's correct."

"The third was killed in a car accident. . ."

"I. . .I think that's all I. . ." the plump lady started to protest.

"I haven't finished yet," Hanussen cut her short. "The man *you* want to marry now is eight years younger than you are. But he won't marry you. Your fourth husband will be much older than you. I can see him. . .he's short and a little fat and has a carefully trimmed beard. No, you haven't met him yet, madame. But I could tell you his name. Only—it isn't so urgent, is it?"

The audience laughed. Hanussen moved on among the rows, stopped in front of an elderly man, told him that he was a professor of mathematics—and that his son had failed in the very same subject. . . He gave similar demonstrations of his "clairvoyant" powers—the usual, not-too-original tricks. But then his arrogance and his frivolity seemed to drop from him like a cloak. The lights dimmed. A violet spotlight illuminated his face. He looked eerie now, his face haggard, his brow deeply furrowed. He spoke in a broken, hoarse, almost panting voice.

"Seven days ago. . .a baker was murdered. . .in the Gänsemarkt. No one knows who did it. . .no clues. . .Too many possibilities. . .too few probabilities. . .You all know the case, ladies and gentlemen. I. . .I am going to solve it. Right here. Tomorrow you can read it in the papers —the confirmation. . .Give me a little time to. . .to concentrate. . ."

There was breathless silence in the audience now. They all stared, fascinated, almost hypnotized, at the man with the heavy black eyebrows, the sensitive hands which seemed to pluck the words from the air.

"I see the murderer. He is young, tall, blond. I see him quite clearly now. His name is Walter. He isn't far from here. He's left the town. I see his shadow. . .there. . .on the railway embankment. . .The train comes. . .twin lights. . .they approach. . .And there is Walter. . .he's climbed up the embankment. . .he's on the rails. . ."

Hanussen cried out violently. "It's happened," he panted. "The train's crushed him. . .The murderer is dead. Look at your watches, ladies and gentlemen. It is forty-six minutes past nine. Compare my description with the newspaper reports—tomorrow. . ."

His face relaxed, his voice became steady; again he was arrogant and self-assured.

"And now. . .if you permit me. . a fifteen minute interval. . ."

There was no applause; people were too shaken by the performance. Most of them crowded into the corridors and lobbies of the theatre, discussing excitedly what they had just witnessed. Some spoke of psychic powers, others of charlatanism. But even in the most sceptical there was a little shiver of anticipation, a tiny element of doubt— what if Hanussen was truly a seer? Would he have stuck his neck out if he hadn't been sure that the coming day would justify his "clairvoyant" description?

A few people remained in their seats. Among them a woman— well-dressed and beautiful with soft brown eyes, a delicately tip-tilted nose and long reddish-brown hair. The interval wasn't yet over when Hanussen re-appeared. He descended the stairs leading from the stage into the auditorium, hesitated for a moment, then made straight for the woman and sat down in the empty seat next to her. She received him with cool amusement as he told her that he wanted to talk to her. "Are you trying to collect material for your next production?" she asked as he stared at her.

"I don't need that," he said. "I know almost all I need. You are twenty-two, married to a man you do not love. His name is Baron Prawitz.

You have no children—nor do you want any. You love tennis and dancing. You have the not entirely undeserved reputation of being rather frigid. Do interrupt me, Baroness, if something is wrong. . ."

"Almost everything is right," she replied calmly. "Your detectives have done excellent work."

"The only detective I have is my brain."

"And your business is the stupidity of mankind, megalomania, cheap tricks! I'd have nothing against it if you didn't pretend to be genuine! If you told the people—all this is just skill and clever illusion, amuse ourselves, but do not take it seriously. . ."

Hanussen got up and stared into the eyes of the contemptuous baroness as if to hypnotise her.

"Let me tell you something, madame—to prove that I am no trickster. You'll have to pay for your doubts. Look at me, Baroness. Do you see my black, oily hair, the straight parting, the yellow skin of my face? Can you smell the tobacco. . .the odour of a chain-smoker? Can you imagine falling in love with such a man?"

"You're crazy—or drunk. . ."

"Within four weeks you'll become my mistress. You'll leave your husband. We're going to have a wonderful love affair. You'll follow me to Berlin. But it won't last long, our long nights and short days of happiness. I'm not cut out to stick to one woman in my life. You'll go through hell. I'll have other mistresses. I'll abandon you. . .Go on, Madame. . .hurry! Try to escape your fate! I wish you luck—I, Erik Jan Hanussen who is going to wreck your life!"

The Baroness got up abruptly. She stared at Hanussen for a moment, her beautiful face contorted in anger and disgust. Then she turned away. It was a retreat that bordered upon panicky flight. Hanussen made no attempt to follow her. His face remained set, his eyes half-veiled. Then slowly, almost painfully he made his way back to the stage to give the second half of his performance.

★   ★   ★

About a month later Hanussen was facing a judge in the small Czech town of Leitmeritz. He was accused of trickery, of extracting money under false pretenses. The case had awakened tremendous interest. More than a hundred journalists came to the small Bohemian river port on the Elbe; the pressure of the crowd was so great that the court held the trial in the ball-room of the biggest hotel. It was a clash of two worlds —the world of reality, of law, represented by the State Attorney of the Czechoslovak Republic and the world of the occult (the intangible and inexplicable) of which Hanussen was the protagonist. His whole career was at stake—for if he was proved an impostor, the journalists would proclaim it to the world and he could never again make a public appearance in any reputable place.

The first rounds seemed to go all to the prosecution. Hanussen's real name, his origin, his early career were mercilessly exposed. He made a very unimpressive figure, sitting huddled in the dock, his arrogance, his masterful irony apparently stripped from him. On the fourth day of the trial he awoke from his strange lethargy and then came a sharp clash with the State Attorney.

"You told an old woman that her son was still alive though he had been missing for ten years. There is no proof for your statement."

"Nor is there any proof to the contrary."

"But you took money for your so-called clairvoyant prophecy."

"You are also being paid for your so-called accusations."

The presiding judge reprimanded Hanussen for his remarks and threatened to fine him for contempt.

"Do you deny that you have accepted money for your pretended forecasts of the future?" the State Attorney continued.

"I deny nothing."

"Well, you see. . ."

"I see very well," Hanussen interrupted angrily. "I am a clairvoyant. That is my profession. An honest profession. Just like that of a State Attorney—except that one cannot learn it by study like jurisprudence. That's why there are fewer clairvoyants than state attorneys; though I don't deny that it would be a good thing if all state attorneys were clairvoyants."

There was laughter, and when it subsided, the state prosecutor said, "You heard the expert witnesses. Science denies quite definitely the existence of anything called clairvoyance. This has nothing to do with telepathy which has been accepted by psychologists as an established fact. If there is no such thing as clairvoyance, anyone calling himself a clairvoyant must be an impostor."

"You have yet to prove a single case of imposture on my part," protested Hanussen.

"A single case? I'll prove a dozen."

There was a fidgeting, uneasy commotion in the room. But by now Hanussen had completely recovered his poise.

"Very well," he said. "Let me provide proof—against the prosecution. . .Listen, Mr. State Attorney. You have two hundred crowns in your wallet, a bus ticket and an unpaid tailor's bill. . ." There was laughter as Hanussen continued: "In the attache case of the presiding judge there are two sandwiches and a book. . .a commentary on criminal law. But let me continue. The sergeant at the door has left his handkerchief at home—and borrowed his wife's. His wife is sitting in the centre of the last row. The sergeant has a small snuffbox and a comb in his pocket. Three teeth of the comb are missing. Would you please check all this. . ."

"This is not a music hall," the judge intervened. "You are facing a court of law. Your freedom is at stake. Please, take this more seriously. . ."

"I ask the court to have the statements of my client checked," Hanussen's counsel rose. "They would provide full proof for his clairvoyant talent."

"That's just telepathy," protested the prosecutor. "It has nothing to do with clairvoyance."

"Is it? Then let me give you other proof," Hanussen continued. "At the railway station at Leitmeritz, Platform Two, there is a man standing. He wears a green hat. Ten minutes ago he burgled the Commercial Bank. His train is arriving at Platform Two in four minutes. The money he stole is in his briefcase. If you act at once, you can still arrest him. . ."

Hanussen was right. They caught the bankrobber at exactly the spot he indicated. Hanussen was triumphantly acquitted. In the judgment the court expressly acknowledged his clairvoyant powers, ignoring the medical and scientific experts. It was this court judgment that was to help Hanussen to conquer Berlin in the late twenties.

Outside the hotel, temporarily turned into a courtroom, he ran into an elegant pretty woman. It was Baroness Prawitz.

He greeted her with an arrogant smile and said: "The four weeks are almost up, Baroness. Do you remember our talk in Vienna?"

"I do. But I forgot to give you a proper answer."

She swung out her hand and slapped him—once, twice, very hard. Hanussen stood there, silent and dazed.

"Why are you so startled?" she asked. "Aren't you a clairvoyant?"

★　　★　　★

It was late in 1929 that I saw Hanussen perform for the first and last time in the *Scala*, the great variety theatre of Berlin. As a young journalist I had heard much about the "great clairvoyant", had caught a glimpse of him late one night in his favourite coffee-house, the Romanisches Café which the Berlin wits had baptized "Café Megalomania". (Too many egos, successful or on the skids were flaunted here —it well deserved its nickname.)

I was taken to the *Scala* by one of my colleagues, a reporter on the "Nachtexpress" (a late evening paper) a middle-aged, hard-bitten journalist. As it happened he was one of the three men whom Hanussen picked for "subjects" that night. And he told a good many things about my friend which I certainly hadn't known—that he was two months overdrawn with his salary, that he spent practically all his money playing the horses, that eight days previously he almost lost his job because he kissed the chief sub's fiancée, that originally he wanted to become a lawyer but failed his finals—and so on. All this, my colleague protested, was childish stuff, anyone on the staff on the "Nachtexpress" could have provided the information. "What about the future?" he demanded. Hanussen told him to come to his office—the future was no joke but (as he put it somewhat fancifully) "a cold grey spider stretching its ugly, long tentacles after its victims. . ."

His second "victim" that night was a rotund little gentleman in a dinner jacket. And Hanussen, after a brief pause, told the past not of the man—but of the clothes he wore. He described colourfully and wittily the history of the dinner jacket—"which has lived through sixteen weddings and twenty-one funerals"—and disclosed at the very end that its present wearer was a tax-inspector having come to control the entertainment tax which the *Scala* had to pay on the box-office receipts. He told the embarrassed civil servant: "Your visit was quite unnecessary, my friend. The Scala has two thousand seats. It is sold out every night. You could not have got in tonight if you hadn't come in your official capacity. Now you'd better go. . ."

All this was good if not necessarily responsible fun. But the third "experiment" jolted me, I must confess. Hanussen was a superb showman—he always built up to a climax.

For those in the know there was another thrill about his performance—his assistant, whom he introduced as "Jane, my medium and my helper." In a brief, close-fitting costume, her long, beautiful legs in net-stockings, she was strikingly beautiful—but strangely unprofessional and almost clumsy as she gave the audience a shy, brief smile and a half-hearted bow. I did not know until my colleague told me that she was the Baroness Prawitz who had deserted her husband, her family, her home—to become Hanussen's mistress. His "prophecy" was fulfilled—even though it had taken two months and not four weeks before the lovely lady "succumbed to his will." And now here she was, moving as if in a trance, being exhibited to the sensation hungry Berliners many of whom knew by now who she was and what had happened to her.

It was with his third subject that night at the *Scala* that Hanussen really demonstrated his clairvoyant powers. I still can offer no other explanation—unless it was a remarkable coincidence or unless he had prepared an elaborate plot, involving some extraordinarily efficient arsonists. The third man was the head of a well-known private bank; a stiff, elderly gentleman with a Prussian crew-cut and student duel scars across his left cheek. Hanussen looked at him and proclaimed: "For heaven's sake. . .I see a house. Four stories. . .in a main street. Wait a moment! It is near the Alexanderplatz. Four stories—many rooms. A bank. . ." He paused, taking a deep breath. There was nothing ironic or playful about him now. "Call the fire brigade!" he shouted. "At once! Otherwise your bank's going to burn down tonight. You've exactly four minutes. Thank your lucky stars for the new engines of the Berlin firemen! You have now three minutes and fifty seconds. I mustn't delay you. There's been a short circuit in your strongroom. There are 360,000 Marks in cash in the safes. . .Hurry—if you want to save the money. You still have three minutes and twenty seconds. Why do you hesitate?"

The audience became uneasy. The tall, stiff man hesitated. Hanussen called an usher and told him to take the man to the nearest telephone. The banker followed him, his face expressionless. He picked up the phone, asked for a number, spoke briefly. A few minutes later sirens screamed outside. A three station alarm. They found the strong room in flames but were able to put them out before any serious damage was done. The bank was securely locked from the outside and no trace of any entry could be discovered. The cause of the fire, as Hanussen had foretold, was proved to be a short circuit.

Berlin was split into two camps. One said that Hanussen was a true clairvoyant, a man with supernatural powers. The other said that the bank manager and his staff had been his accomplices—that the whole thing was carefully prepared and staged. But who could offer a reasonable and acceptable motive for a conservative and rich banker to get involved in such a fantastic scheme? The bank was solvent, did excellent business—and continued to do so. After a few months, of course, the whole affair was forgotten—except by those whom Hanussen now and then reminded of it.

*　　*　　*

He was now riding high on the crest of the wave. The *Scala* paid him a thousand marks a night plus a share of the profits. His private clients paid him huge sums for a consultation. The Baroness was no longer his "assistant". As he had foretold, they separated. She had been trying to break from him but in the end it was he who sent her on her way—with brutal suddenness.

A few weeks later Hanussen found another assistant—far more efficient and clever than the Baroness. His name was Dzino Ismet, an ex-officer of Yugoslav origin. The clairvoyant met him in a night club where Dzino was enjoying himself with two very young and pretty twin girls called Marion and Margot. Hanussen "clairvoyantly" decided that two women were too many for one man—especially when that one man was practically broke. He made Dzino an offer: he would pay his debts if he became his confidential secretary.

"What does a secretary working for you have to do?" the ex-officer asked.

"A great deal. To see much and talk little, that's the first rule. The strangest people ask to see me, Dzino. They all have to wait their turn —even if they are cabinet ministers. Some wait half an hour or two hours, others two or several days. Before they are admitted, I must know their names, whether they have money, whether they deceive their wives, what party they vote and what they want—or do not want—to hear. I need a bright man without scruples. I think you are the right one. . .What do I expect you to do? Eavesdrop on conversations. Go through the pockets of their overcoats. Pump their chauffeurs. Put a pretty woman on to them. Or private detectives. Make them drunk! Tell me what illnesses they had and of what they are afraid. Everything's grist to the mill. Do what you like but get me information. Don't look so startled! Even a clairvoyant can't know everything. I need someone who saves me the drudgery. You can make a couple of thousand marks a month to start with—twice as much—and before long ten times! You'll drive your own car. You'll marry the prettiest woman in Berlin."

He shook the other man's shoulder as Dzino still stared at him.

"Well, what is it? You're near the bottom now, aren't you? You've even considered marrying a greengrocer's fat widow, haven't you?"

"That's quite true," the ex-officer relaxed and laughed. "Why do you need an assistant if you know everything?"

"Yes or no?"

Dzino said yes.

He moved into Hanussen's palatial villa on the Lietzenburger Strasse. He became the clairvoyant's manager, assistant, and confidant. He made arrangements with Hanussen's discarded mistresses and provided new ones. He became the magician's apprentice, his faithful servant and his unscrupulous accomplice.

And it was Dzino who introduced Hanussen to Count Helldorf.

Helldorf, a degenerate and dissolute aristocrat, was the commander of the SA, the brownshirt Nazi private army in Berlin. This was, of course, before the *Machtergreifung*, Hitler's coming to power. Nazis and Communists were still battling in the cities of Germany; Hindenburg hadn't yet yielded his place to the "Bohemian corporal". Helldorf was always in financial difficulties—and he didn't mind where he got his money from. What was far less likely: Hanussen, the son of the Viennese synagogue-caretaker, the non-Aryan, a member of the race the Nazis were pledged to exterminate, was quite ready to provide the cash. Even more, he told Helldorf:

"You are close to victory, Count. My prophecies are always fulfilled. The National Socialist Party is going to win—soon, within months. I can see flags waving and signs rising. *Ein Volk, ein Reich, ein Führer!* I see a whole nation on the march. I see the Führer make his entry into the Chancellor's Palace...Whatever I can do for you, Count—just let me know. You are my guest—my friend."

"Thank you."

"Perhaps you, too, can do me a service one of these days. . ."

"Anything," replied Count Helldorf.

And an hour later the SA-flag was waving from the bonnet of Hanussen's huge, gleaming, supercharged limousine. He became the first "honorary Aryan" of the movement. As Will Berthold wrote in his posthumous biography more than twenty years after his violent death: "The adviser of the rich bankers, of filmstars, of politicians, the fabulously successful attraction of the *Scala* became the devil's prophet."

And at first all went well. Hanussen made subtle and assiduous propaganda for Hitler—advising all his clients to vote for him. When the astrologer and clairvoyant Möcke set himself up as Hanussen's rival, trying to discover mistakes in the "great man's" horoscopes and predictions, Hanussen simply asked Count Helldorf for another "little favour"—and Möcke, a quiet, modest, self-effacing man, was beaten up by SA thugs. Hanussen paid well for such "services rendered"

—a whole SA squad was equipped with jackboots and brown shirts at his expense.

As if blinded by his own success and totally unaware of the threatening danger, Hanussen's colossal arrogance and self-assurance seemed to grow daily. He charged his clients fabulous sums—not just for his prophecies but for the influence he flattered himself he had won with the future rulers of Germany. As for women—his "harem" included some of the loveliest actresses, dancers and ladies of the aristocracy. Not one lasted long. He drove himself and others at a mad pace—as if he wanted to squeeze everything out of whatever years or months remained of life.

One of the strangest cases of his clairvoyant powers (this is well-documented) was connected with a girl called Grace Cameron; an English girl who had won a beauty competition in Belgium and later drifted to Berlin where she was one of the hostesses at the huge Palais de Dance, a barn-like dance hall which Hanussen loved to visit late at night.

Grace was one of the few women whom Hanussen was apparently unable to bring under his hypnotic influence. She was polite but totally unimpressed by him. Night after night they sat together, drinking champagne, talking very little. After a week or so the clairvoyant gave up any attempt to make Grace his mistress. But she still attracted and fascinated him. And one night he told her:

"You'd like to get away from all this. . ."and he indicated the dancing crowd, the couples in the small alcoves, the whole sleazy, meretricious atmosphere.

Grace Cameron nodded. She was afraid of Hanussen, and always sensed something menacing and inhuman in him. Yet she went on listening to the hoarse, staccato voice:

"You won't remain here long. You'll marry—a rich and good-looking man. You'll meet him here, under this crystal chandelier. Right here. . ."and he pointed to a spot on the dance-floor a few yards from the table. His voice was getting low now, he was breathless and his eyes had a glazed, absent look. He seemed to be fighting a nameless, irresistible power that gripped him. Grace Cameron was shivering. "Beware, Miss Cameron!" Hanussen went on, his voice barely audible. "The man. . .you are going to marry. . .will also be. . .your murderer. I. . .hear shots. . .bullets hit you. . .you collapse. . .You are dead. . ."

A couple of months later Dzino Ismet faced his boss over the breakfast table. Hanussen had a bad hangover and wasn't in a very sociable mood. He began by scolding his assistant for becoming less and less efficient, for making silly mistakes. "Are you getting old or are you in love?" he asked at the end of his tirade.

"Both," replied Dzino who never lost his temper. "And I want to get married."

Hanussen jeered at such "middle-class sentimentality". But his curiosity was roused. He asked: "Who is she? what's her name?"

"She's a hostess at the Palais de Dance," Dzino replied. "Her name is Grace Cameron."

Hanussen stared at him, his hangover forgotten. "That's impossible he said. "I won't let you do it."

There was a violent argument. The clairvoyant told his accomplice what he had told the English girl—that he would become her murderer if he married her. But Dzino did not believe his boss. After all, he knew too much of Hanussen's methods to take his predictions seriously—at least so far as he was himself concerned. In the end Hanussen shouted at him: "Go to hell, Dzino! Go to hell in your own way! I told you—you'll end as a murderer and a suicide. But I can't *make* you believe me. . ."

Indeed, he couldn't. Though Grace was far more impressed by Hanussen's sinister prediction than was Dzino Ismet, she was too deeply in love with the ex-officer to refuse to marry him. "Believe me," Dzino told her, "it was just bluff. He wanted to give a propaganda performance—to impress you or some other people in the Palais de Dance. It is all the same to him *what* he prophesies. Don't you notice his trick? He predicts so many different things that some of them must be fulfilled. People forget whatever is unpleasant or gloomy in his predictions. Basically we only believe what we *like* to believe. The rest we forget—within seconds or hours. . ."

This sounded logical enough—and Grace, in any case, was not an intellectual, she could not out-reason her lover. Three weeks later they were married.

In 1937, more than four years after Hanussen's death, an unemployed croupier shot his wife and child dead in Vienna and then committed suicide. His name was Dzino Ismet.

★   ★   ★

Hitler came to power; the brownshirts became masters of Germany.

Hanussen celebrated their victory as if it were his own. He gave lavish parties for his political friends and allies. He felt himself not only absolutely safe—he had Helldorf's I.O.U.s in his pocket—but an equal of the Nazi leaders. Pem, the mordantly witty Berlin journalist wrote: "Hitler and Hanussen have one thing in common: they base their careers on the suggestion of great promises. Hitler brought 'clairvoyance' into politics. Hanussen introduced politics into clairvoyance."

Then came the evening in the palatial villa in the Lietzenburgerstrasse that was to lead directly to Hanussen's downfall and death. The clairvoyant had acquired a new medium—a charming blonde actress named Maria Paudler. The guests included a dozen journalists, about the same number of SA leaders, and a few pretty, elegant women.

After a sumptuous supper at which champagne proverbially flowed like water, the séance began. Miss Paudler sat in a chair; Hanussen slowly stroked her temples. She was soon in a quite genuine trance. The blonde actress was no accomplice of the clairvoyant. It was the first time that she had collaborated with him.

A few minutes passed. The guests sat in a large circle, some stood leaning against the walls. There was silence but not much tension or expectation. The SA-leaders, the journalists, Hanussen's admirers and sycophants had attended a dozen such gatherings. The room was in semi-darkness; only the cigarettes and cigars glowed. With a curt gesture, Hanussen demanded attention.

The actress began to speak. At first the sounds were inarticulate. Gradually the staccato syllables combined into words, the words into sentences. But it was still unintelligible, as if she spoke some strange, foreign language. Only slowly, gradually did her speech become clear and normal.

At first it was the usual trance-medium's production. She described objects which some of the guests held hidden in their hands. She predicted places, names, connections of the future. She answered questions, unhesitantly and correctly. Dozens of mediums could do that—it was sheer telepathy. But near the end of the séance something strange and unexpected happened.

"I can see it," Maria Paudler whispered brokenly. "A disaster. . . The enemies of Germany strike. . .they want to destroy the movement. . .I see a house. . .a big house. . .it is burning. . .it burns down. . . It is meant as a signal for a. . .a revolt. . ."

The SA-men stirred uneasily. The journalists became restless. What

was Hanussen up to? Was this a political prediction? A daring forecast?

"But Hitler will triumph. . ." Maria Paudler cried suddenly.

"Lights! Put on the lights!" someone else shouted. It was then
quiet in the big room.

"Ladies and gentlemen," Hanussen said when Maria Paudler came
out from her trance, "we want to keep quiet about this part of our
séance, don't we? You have to promise me that, won't you?"

On the night of February 27, 1933 the Reichstag was partially destroyed by fire.

All those who attended the party in Hanussen's villa realized now
what the prediction meant. Hanussen had triumphed again. For the
last time. Those who were intimates of Helldorf and Ernst, the SA-
leaders, knew very well about the plans for burning the Reichstag
and using the incident to destroy the final vestiges of civil liberties
in Germany (the freedom of speech and press were abolished the next
day throughout the Reich.) Hanussen was an intimate friend of the
arsonists; they made no secret to him of their plans. It was Hanussen
who suggested to Maria Paudler the "vision" during the trance. But
the story of Hanussen's séance could not be kept within the four walls
of the luxurious villa. Rumours and whispers spread rapidly.

And somebody somewhere pressed a button. Hanussen knew too
much. Hanussen was a Jew. Hanussen had abused the confidence that
had made him an "honorary Aryan."

★　★　★

Kriminalrat Mölders succeeded in piecing together the story of the
last hours in the clairvoyant's life—at least up to the point where he
disappeared. Much later, after the collapse of the "thousand-year Third
Reich" others added the final details.

On that morning in March, 1933, Hanussen woke up in excellent
mood. At eleven he visited his bank. He was publishing an astrological
newspaper which sold well. Now he wanted to expand—to use his
Nazi connections in order to buy several newspapers and magazines.

The great Mosse newspaper organisation was in trouble. Its owner
had left Germany, leaving his deputy in nominal charge. The real
master, however, was the commissioner whom the Nazis had installed.
His name was Ohst. Hanussen went to see *Herr* Vetter, the temporary
and nominal managing director. He asked him bluntly how much the

"Berliner Tageblatt", the once flourishing liberal daily of the Mosse Verlag would cost? *Herr* Vetter smiled and told him: "I have great esteem for you, Hanussen. But I think you overestimate yourself."

Hanussen replied calmly that he and his friends could easily raise the purchase price. Vetter told him to telephone him next day; then, as the clairvoyant left, he reported to Commissioner Ohst the gist of the conversation. Ohst hurriedly passed on the information to his superiors. Within an hour Hermann Goering, then Prime Minister of Prussia, sent for Count Helldorf. "This is an impossible situation," Goering told the Berlin commander of the SA. "The Party cannot remain involved with this Jewish charlatan. I expect you to deal with the matter at once—before there is a scandal."

Helldorf nodded. He no longer needed to borrow money—the Nazis were masters of Germany. Whatever gratitude he owed Hanussen, he certainly could not risk Goering's or the Führer's displeasure.

At noon that day Hanussen drove slowly along the Unter den Linden and the Kurfürstendamm. Near the Friedrichstrasse he stopped his car suddenly. He caught a glimpse of a woman who looked familiar. He got out and told the chauffeur to follow him slowly. Then he walked up to her. It was the Baroness Prawitz. At first she was reluctant to talk to him—but within a few minutes she agreed to take him to her apartment. She was still beautiful—but poor. She lived by modelling and carving small animals—does and stags and hares—which were charming and life-like enough to sell quite well. She had a small, almost bare but strikingly clean and neat apartment at the back of a bleak tenement house. She seemed calm, at peace. She prepared a simple lunch and they talked. Gently she reproached him for the company he kept. He told her that Hitler was the future—and that he had simply backed the winning side as he would back a horse, without worrying what colour it was. Then he suddenly offered her help. This was no life for her—wouldn't she come back to him? Let them make a fresh start! But she refused, without anger or resentment. No one could go back, she explained. No one could make a fresh start with the same man or the same woman.

Abruptly, Hanussen's mood changed. He became pale, he shivered. "I'm afraid," he told the Baroness. "I know one thing: the end is terrible. It is always terrible. But my end is worse than that. . ."

She tried to calm him, reminded him that he had been wrong before about the fate of others—why shouldn't he be about his own?

"Yes, I have been wrong—often," he admitted. "But not about this. I am convinced that my fate will be exactly as I foresee it. There is no escape."

"But why don't you go away? To France? to England? anywhere. . ."

Hanussen did not answer. He stayed another hour with the Baroness —hardly speaking, haggard, in a state of near-collapse. Then he left. He drank four brandies in a café. He went into a flower shop and sent a dozen orchids to the small flat at the back of the tenement house —a last gesture, a final message to the woman whose life he had wrecked. Then he returned to his villa, sent his chauffeur to fetch the car. He slept an hour, then summoned Dzino. He asked him how his wife was, whether he still liked being married. Dzino replied coolly. They discussed next day's appointments; then the ex-officer told his chief that a woman had telephoned—she would only give her Christian name: Hedi. She would ring again. Yes, Hanussen would speak to her. Hedi had been his girl-friend for a few months in Vienna. They had parted good friends. Now she was working as a secretary at SA Headquarters.

Half-an-hour after his return she called again—in a state of great excitement. He could barely make out at first what she was trying to say. But then she calmed down a little.

"Listen, Erik. . .pack your bag at once! Get all the money you can from the bank! Then take a taxi—and the first train out of the country. to-night! D'you hear me? To-night!"

"You're crazy, Hedi."

"No. This is very serious. My God, what can I do to make you understand? You're in danger, Erik! They'll do something to you. . ."

"What can they do to me? And who are 'they'?"

"I can't tell you. I don't know yet—not all of it. But it is certain. I heard it with my own ears—they talked about it to-day. I can't tell you more. I must be careful, Erik. I can't come to see you. They're bound to keep a watch over your house. . .Go away, Erik! Leave at once!"

Then she rang off. Hanussen put down the receiver, annoyed. His forebodings, the sense of approaching doom that had shaken him in the apartment of the Baroness—all that had faded away, was forgotten. Hedi must be mad, he thought. These hysterical women! He had another brandy, dressed and set out for the *Scala*. On the way he called in at the "Green Branch", a favourite rendezvous of theatrical and show

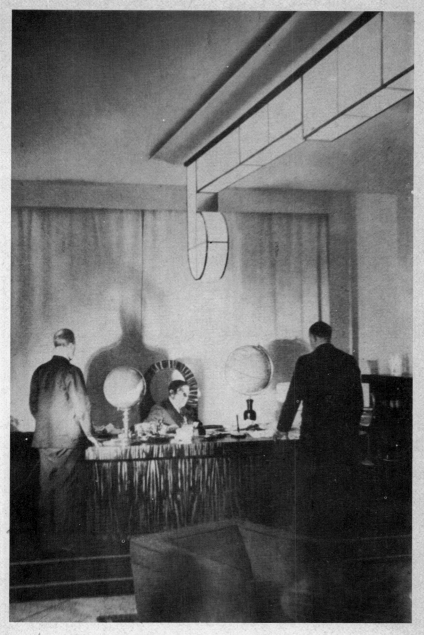

Hanussen

business people. And here he was given another warning—this time by Toni Ott, another Viennese woman whom he had known for several years. She told him that SA-men had been asking for him the night before. She told him to be careful; she advised him, like Hedi, to take a trip abroad. Hanussen grunted: "Nonsense!" Then he glanced at his watch. He was due at the theatre in eleven minutes. He decided to walk.

On the way, a dozen yards or so from the "Green Branch" he was stopped by a man who asked for a light—then demanded to know whether he was Hanussen, the clairvoyant.

"Yes, I am. But I haven't time for autographs now. . ."

A car drew up slowly to the kerb. Two other men emerged from the shadows. They told him they had to talk to him—it was important—and invited him to get into the car.

And Hanussen obeyed—without any protest. He assumed that it was Helldorf who had sent for him. He warned them, though, that he hadn't much time—in half an hour he was due to go on at the *Scala*. The three men laughed. Then the car drove off.

On the way Hanussen must have realized that he was being taken for a ride—in the tradition of the Chicago gangsters. He pleaded, he offered bribes. It was all in vain. The car left the city behind, travelling at speed along the highway to Breslau. About twenty miles out of Berlin, it stopped. The three SA-men dragged Hanussen from the car, drove him with blows and kicks across a ploughed field, through a small copse, another field and into a larger wood. There they fired five bullets into his quivering body—and then seven more to make sure that they had finished him off. They dug a shallow grave and left him to rot; the clairvoyant who foresaw his own end and yet refused to try and escape his doom.

★   ★   ★

In 1955 a German film company made a picture about Hanussen's life. O.W. Fischer, the brilliant actor played the part and also directed the film. It was a highly romanticized and eulogistic affair which turned the "Devil's Prophet" into an anti-Nazi martyr, the film was too kind to a man who was a strange mixture of charlatan and genuinely gifted clairvoyant, an unscrupulous hedonist yet a generous benefactor of many poor and unhappy people. No scientific examination of his work has ever been made nor is there likely to be one—so many of the people involved are dead or disappeared in the war and its after-math; few written records exist and those are highly contradictory. The production of the film established one unknown fact—that Hanussen had been married as a young man in Vienna but separated from his wife long before he began his brief triumphant career in Berlin. His widow and his daughter Erika both lived in Meran where Mrs. Hanussen (she has changed her name) is a partner in running the Hotel Excelsior while Erika, a pretty, darkhaired woman works both as an actress and a writer. *She* claims no clairvoyant powers.

★   ★   ★

CHAPTER TWO

D.D. Home: The Medium of Kings

"He spoke in a whisper, as though the spirits were arranging something. He then said to us: 'Do not be afraid, and on no account leave your places;' and he went out into the passage. Lindsay suddenly said: 'Oh, good heavens! I know what he is going to do; it is too fearful.'

Adare: 'What is it?

Lindsay: 'I cannot tell you, it is too horrible! Adah says that I must tell you; he is going out of the window in the other room, and coming in at this window.' We heard Home go into the next room, heart the window thrown up, and presently Home appeared standing upright outside our window; he opened the window and walked in quite coolly. 'Ah,' he said, 'You were good this time," referring to our having sat still and not wished to prevent him. He sat down and laughed.

Charlie: 'What are you laughing at?'

Home: 'We were thinking that if a policeman had been passing, and had looked up and seen a man turning round and round, along the wall in the air he would have been much astonished. Adare, shut the window in the next room.' I got up, shut the window and in coming back remarked that the window was not raised a foot, and that I could not think how he had managed to squeeze through. He arose and said, 'Come and see." I went with him; he told me to open the window as it was before, I did so; he told me to stand a little distance off; he then went through the open space, head first, quite rapidly, his body being nearly horizontal and apparently rigid. He came in again, feet foremost, and we returned to the other room. It was so dark I could not see clearly how he was supported outside. He did not appear to grasp, or rest upon, the balustrade, but rather to be swung out and in. Outside each window is a small balcony or ledge, 19 inches deep, bounded by stone balustrades, 18 inches high. The balustrades of the two windows are 7 feet 4 inches apart, measuring from the nearest points. A string-course, 4 inches wide, runs between the windows at the level of the bottom of the balustrade; and another 3 inches wide at the level of the top. Between the window at which Home went out, and that at which he came in, the wall recedes 6 inches. The rooms are on the third floor. . ."

The time: December 18, 1868. The place: Ashley House, Victoria Street, London. Those present: Viscount Adare, the future Earl of Dunraven, the Master of Lindsay and Charlie Wynne. And of course, the central figure of this extraordinary demonstration—Daniel Dunglas Home, the most famous of all nineteenth-century mediums.

Few men have aroused such fierce controversy, won such fervent and famous partisans and acquired such vituperative and articulate enemies as the son of William Hume (the spelling was changed later), who was himself an illegitimate son of the tenth Earl of Home. Few men of such birth rose to hobnob with kings and emperors, the cream of British and Continental aristocracy, the most outstanding scientists, artists and writers of the Victorian era. And certainly no medium, however much attacked and derided, had such a spotless career—for no critic could ever offer any proof of fraud against him or, alternately, provide any valid explanation of the fantastic variety of phenomena Home produced—consistently, year after year, more often than not in broad daylight or in well-lit drawing-rooms; in the majority of cases in places which he had never entered before.

The bibliography of Jean Burton's beautifully-written and well-documented "Hey-day of a Wizard", Home's most recent biography, runs to five pages. Horace Wyndham in his *"Mr. Sludge, the Medium"* acknowledges over twenty volumes as his source material. Home himself published two long books ("Incidents in my Life", and "Lights and Shadows of Spiritualism") while Sir Arthur Conan Doyle edited "D.D.Home, His Life and Mission" by the "wizard's" second wife. So there is certainly no lack of material even for the most detailed study of this fascinating character. Yet just because of the abundance of the available data, the thousands of articles, the innumerable references in memoirs and diaries, it is almost impossible to reduce Home to a clear-cut, normal-size figure. The approach of his biographers varies immensely. Miss Burton treated him as a psychological puzzle, a social phenomenon and a dramatic theme—and she found him slightly ridiculous. There is an undertone of amused condescension in her book—the smiling contempt of the mid-twentieth century intellectual for the sentimentality, the posturings and the naivety of the Victorian age. Horace Wyndham was frankly hostile—a fact shown by the very title he chose for his biography—*Mr. Sludge, the Medium*. Sir Arthur Conan Doyle, as a fervent spiritualist, went to the other extreme when he wrote: "He came as one of the first and most powerful missionaries who have set forth upon the greatest of human tasks, to prove immortality, to do away with the awful mystery of death, to found religion upon positive knowledge, and to break down the dense materialism which was as great within the Christian Churches as outside them... He was admirable in every relation of life..." Harry Price, though sceptical of some of Home's phenomena, accepted him as genuine and wrote: "I consider Home to be the greatest physical medium of whom we have any record, and he was never exposed."

Consider the list of some who shared the occult experiences connected with D.D. Home: Viscount Adare; the Hon. Alexander N. Aksakoff, the famous Russian psychist, an Imperial Councillor; Alexander II, Tsar of Russia; Sir Edwin Arnold; Princess Marie of Battenberg; Lord Henry Brougham; Elizabeth Barrett Browning; William Cullen Bryant, the American poet; Professor William Crookes; Alexandre Dumas; the Empress Eugénie and Napoleon III; Sir Edward Bulwer Lytton; John Ruskin; W.M. Thackeray; Wilhelm I, King of Prussia. There were others, less eminent or famous. On the other hand Home also had his share of violent opponents among the great or the celebrated. Robert Browning was certainly the most determined of them and in his *"Mr. Sludge, the Medium"* (which title Wyndham took for his biography), he used all his brilliance and power to paint Home in the blackest possible colours. Charles Dickens also hated the very name of Home. Michael Faraday refused to attend any séances with the "wizard" or, for that matter, with any medium. In fairness, it must be added that among those who investigated personally Home's powers, there were very few doubters and that his most virulent denouncers were those who would not take advantage of repeatedly offered opportunities to sit with him. Thus he remained, throughout his life and remains in the seventy-odd years after his death "an unsolved enigma" (Encyclopaedia Britannica) and a "curious and as yet unsolved problem" (Dictionary of National Biography) while Miss Burton summed up her own opinion quite non-committally:

"Home gave no clues during his lifetime and he took his secret with him. No one could say whether or to what extent he believed in his own legend. All that was certain was that he had given a brilliant and marvellously sustained performance; and sometimes great actors who play one role for many seasons almost forget where the role ends and their own personality begins."

★   ★   ★

Daniel Dunglas was the third child of William Hume, an engineer and his wife, Elizabeth McNeal (who was reputed to have second sight). He was born, one of eight children, on March 20, 1833 at Currie, a small village near Edinburgh. He was one year old when a childless aunt, Mrs, Mary McNeal Cook, took him under her care. He was seven when his family emigrated to the United States and settled in Connecticut; two years later the Cooks followed, taking Daniel with them. Though he continued living with the Cooks, he frequently visited his family who lived near by and his relations with his mother were especially close and warm. Of his sisters and brothers, Christine seemed to be the most intimately linked with him; she was the survivor of the Home twins, her sister Mary Betsey dying at the age of twelve.

Daniel was a delicate, nervous child, suffering at an early age from the tuberculosis that was finally to kill him. Spoiled because of his precarious health, something of a show-off (he loved music, was a fair singer and elocutionist), he had little regular schooling and took no part in the games and sports of his contemporaries. "Visions and apparitions"—mostly connected with the death of friends or members of the family—were an early experience for the boy. And he was seventeen when a most distressing outbreak of poltergeist and telekinetic phenomena upset his aunt so badly that she turned him out of her house, throwing his Sunday suit out of the window after him.

But the young man had many friends and never lacked support and hospitality. Wealthy farmers, prosperous merchants, doctors, editors, the more liberal clergymen of New England rallied to his side. So did their womenfolk who found him much to their liking. "He is but seventeen years old," one of them wrote to a friend, "tall for his age, fair complexion, hair neither red, brown, nor auburn, but like a three-coloured changeable silk, rather inclining to curl. . . Lively grey eyes, nose not remarkable, handsome mouth and teeth—easy manners; very intelligent for his age, perfectly artless, and very affectionate. . ."

In 1851 Dr. George Bush, Professor of Oriental Languages in New York University, a Swedenborgian, offered the young man the opportunity to study for the ministry. Home at first accepted—but within a short time changed his mind, offering as an excuse that his mother had told him: "You must not accept this kind offer, as your mission is a more extended one than pulpit preaching." About six months later, while staying with the well-to-do Elmers family in Springfield, Massachusetts he had a séance with a delegation from Harvard University, headed by the poet William Cullen Bryant and consisting of Messrs. B.K. Bliss, William Edwards and David A. Wells. They experienced raps, energetic movements and levitation of furniture, not to mention powerful shocks. They issued a glowing testimonial to the young medium:

> "In conclusion we may observe that Mr. D.D. Home frequently urged us to hold his hands and feet. During these occurrences the room was well lighted, the lamp was frequently placed on and under the table, and every possible opportunity was afforded us for the closest inspection, and we admit this one emphatic declaration: *We know that we were not imposed upon nor deceived.*"

This high praise had immediate results. The Elmers offered to adopt him and make him their heir if he changed his name to theirs—an honour which Home politely declined. Mrs. Clark, the wife of the Bishop of Hartford, made a similar offer. The Reverend S.B. Brittan, a New York parson, took Home to Manhattan, where he was received with flattering acclaim. A group of investigators, organized by Dr. Bush, conducted a series of séances with him. They included Dr. John Gray, a pioneer in homoeopathic healing, Dr. Robert Hare, Professor Emeritus of Chemistry at Pennsylvania University, Judge John W. Edmonds of the New York Supreme Court, and Professor Mapes, the noted agricultural chemist. Telekinetic phenomena and manifestations "of a distinctly electrical nature" were observed. Edmonds later wrote:

> "I went into the investigation originally thinking it a deception, and intending to make public my exposure of it. Having from my researches come to a different conclusion, I feel that the obligation to make known the result is just as strong."

In December 1852 W.M. Thackeray, on his first American lecture tour, attended a Home séance at the house of George Bancroft, the historian. He exerted himself in every way to detect any possible fraud; he got down on his hands and knees to examine the floor, asked innumerable questions—and was quickly converted for life to belief in Home's powers. When his angry and sceptical friends later taxed him with being duped, the author of "Vanity Fair" replied imperturbably: "Had you seen what I have witnessed, you would have held a different opinion. . ."

Shortly afterwards Home returned to Connecticut. It was in South Manchester, at the home of Mr. Ward Cheney, a silk manufacturer, that he first levitated himself. F.L. Burr, the editor of the *Hartford Times*, recorded this new and startling feat at some length; it occurred suddenly and without warning. "I had hold of his hand at the time and I felt his feet—they were lifted a foot from the floor!. . .Again and again he was taken from the floor; and the third time he was carried to the lofty ceiling of the apartment, with which his hand and head came in gentle contact. . ."

Home's repertoire, as Jean Burton pointed out, remained pretty well the same throughout his life. Raps, the movement of various objects, the playing of an accordion, the levitation or violent agitation of often very substantial pieces of furniture, cold breezes, "spirit messages", the elongation of the medium's body and his own levitation —these, with some variation, were the "stupendous phenomena" which he produced. There were one or two special "attractions" which he developed later—and his audiences never accused him of monotony. Nor did anybody ever manage to duplicate all this by mechanical means or suggest any *acceptable* explanation as to how it could be done by trickery—though hundreds of people tried to do so. As for Home himself, whenever he was questioned about the phenomena or his own powers, his answer was invariably: "I don't know."

The months he spent in New England were like a triumphal tour. Crowds followed him everywhere; scores of people travelled hundreds of miles to catch a glimpse of the "miracle-worker". He usually though not invariably went into a trance; and on such occasions his "spirit-controls" (speaking through him) always referred to him in the third person singular as Dan or Daniel—as if "they" wanted to separate clearly the conscious D.D. Home from the entranced medium. Psychiatrists might find this evidence of schizophrenia—but there was nothing of the madman or even the neurotic about the self-possessed young man.

For a short time he toyed with the idea of studying medicine (Dr. Gerald Hull of Newburgh on the Hudson, a member of the New York group which investigated him suggested this) but he soon gave up the plan. His left lung was found to be badly diseased and he returned to Hartford and Springfield. Later he visited Boston where his power suddenly waxed "in a manner which surprised me not less than other witnesses." Complete figures began to materialize. "Spirits were seen distinctly by all present in the room, and more than once they kissed persons present so as to be both felt and heard."

Once more in New York, Home gave a séance for Horace Greeley, the editor-in-chief of the *Tribune* who was impressed. Then, as his doctors advised him to seek a milder climate, he decided to leave America. Mr. and Mrs.D.Jarves, rich and cultured patrons of art (they were friends of the Brownings, too) paid for his passage and— though his choice for a sunnier land was odd enough—in March 1855 he sailed for England.

★   ★   ★

Poor, in indifferent health and practically friendless, Home reached London—and within a few weeks found partisans and supporters of "the highest quality". Lady Waldegrave, Lady Combermere, the Marchioness of Hastings and Baroness Grey de Ruthyn were among the society hostesses who welcomed him; Sir Edward Bulwer-Lytton was his host both at his Park Lane mansion and the great stately home of Knebworth. Lytton, somewhat guardedly, acknowledged "the extraordinary phenomena which are elicited by your powers." At his London home he met the aged Robert Owen, the great social reformer and utopian who, in turn, introduced him to Lord Brougham, one of the most die-hard materialists and sceptics. Brougham, almost ninety, took along Sir David Brewster of St.Andrews "to assist finding out the trick."

They found no trick; but Sir David developed an elaborate theory on how Home *could* have done it all. Home resented this implied charge of fraud and challenged Brewster to have another séance with him and take any precautions he liked. Sir David declined; however, he found himself by chance at another sitting at the home of Mr. John S.Rymer, a prosperous solicitor of Ealing—together with Mrs.

Fanny Trollope, the famous traveller and authoress and her younger son, Thomas Adolphus, brother of the great novelist. They had both come from Italy for the express purpose of meeting Home. Mrs. Trollope did not like him and the séance produced only modest phenomena—the levitation of a table, with rather violent movements. T.A. Trollope's account was rather characteristic of the sceptics' reaction to such manifestations. He and Sir David Brewster hurled themselves under the table.

> "I said to Sir David," Trollope wrote, "as our heads were close together under the table, and we were on 'all fours' on the floor. 'Does it not seem that this table is raised by some means wholly inexplicable?' 'Indeed, it would seem so!' he replied. But he wrote a letter to the *Times*. . .in which he gave an account of his visit to Ealing, but ended by denying that he had seen anything remarkable.

Sir David refused to believe his eyes and ears—because if he had done so, it would have wrecked his whole system of scepticism. "I don't know," he admitted later, "But spirit is the LAST thing I will give in to!"

Dr. J.J. Garth Wilkinson, London correspondent of the New York *Tribune*, was, on the other hand, completely convinced by the various séances he had with the young man. He wrote a long letter to the *Morning Advertiser* about Home, describing the various phenomena and ending:

> "Considering that it requires a large apparatus for the greatest wizards to effect the smallest part of what we saw on this evening, one might have expected that Mr. Home would have had rather bulging pockets, but I can assure my readers that he was as meagre and unencumbered as the scantiest dresser need be: he had no assistants and no screens . . ."

The most famous sitters at Ealing were the Brownings. The séance held in July 1855 gained for Home one implacable enemy and one lifelong—though more private than public—champion within the same family. Robert Browning declared that he had "never seen so impudent a piece of imposture in his life." His wife, then acknowledged as the foremost poetess of England, had a completely different opinion. As to the celebrated occasion, here are two versions of what happened—and they disagree just as much as the Brownings did:

"When the Brownings reached England, they were invited to make a pilgrimage to Ealing, to test the mediumship of Mr. Rymer's protégé. Full of hope, Mrs. Browning, having induced her husband to accompany her, accepted. But the séance which they attended there was marked by an awkward happening and one that led to regrettable results. The Rymer children had, in honour of the distinguished guests, picked a bunch of clematis, which Home had fashioned into a wreath and deposited on the table before the business of the evening began. As soon as the lights were obscured, there was the customary shower of raps, followed by mysterious touches on the arms and legs of the gathering. Presently, the atmosphere being 'sympathetic', Home went into a trance; and while, in this condition, he was delivering a long and disjointed address (of which nobody could understand a word) the wreath rose in the air without being touched, circled round the room, and finally settled on the head of Mrs. Browning. A delicate compliment to genius. Still, this sort of thing being rather more than he had bargained for, her husband refused to stop any longer, and insisted on leaving the house and taking his wife with him." (Horace Wyndham.)

". . . we were touched by the invisible, heard the music and raps, saw the table moved, and had sight of the hands . . . At the request of the medium, the spiritual hands took from the table a garland which lay there, and placed it upon my head. The particular hand which did this was of the largest human size, as white as snow, and very beautiful. It was as near to me as this hand I write with, and I saw it as distinctly . . . I was perfectly calm! not troubled in any way, and felt convinced in my own mind that *no spirit belonging to me* was present on the occasion. The hands which appeared at a distance from me I put up my glass to look at—proving that it was not a mere mental impression, and that they were subject to the usual laws of vision. These hands seemed to Robert and me to come from under the table, but Mr. Lytton (Sir Edward Lytton's son) saw them rise out of the *wood of the table*—also he tells me . . . that he saw a spiritual (so-called) arm, elongate itself as much as two yards across the table and then float away to the windows, where it disappeared. Robert and I did not touch the hands. Mr. Lytton and Sir Edward *both did*. The feel was warm and human—rather warmer in fact than is common. The music was beautiful." (Elizabeth Barrett Browning in a letter to her sister Henrietta.)

Though Browning was furiously angry (he thought that the spirit hands were either "the scoundrel"'s naked foot" or contrivances attached to it) he wrote and asked for a second séance. Home, scenting trouble, excused himself with another engagement. And when he called on the Brownings a little later (he said it was simply a courtesy visit before he left London), the poet was abominably rude to him. As a matter of fact, Home became something of an obsession, a *bête noir* for Browning; he never ceased to denounce and abuse him and, in due course, transformed this dislike into his vitriolic portrait of "Mr. Sludge, the Medium." On the other hand, Elizabeth Barrett remained his staunch champion to the end of her life.

★   ★   ★

But this was only an unpleasant episode in Home's triumphant European progress. In Florence, his next stop, he was the guest of the Villino Trollope. Society hostesses competed hotly for his company. The Countess Orsini, the Prince of Saxe-Meiningen, Baron Seymour Kirkup (the artist), Princess Lubormirski, Countess Cotterel, Count Branicka and his mother were among his aristocratic sitters. So was Hiram Powers, the great American sculptor and Mrs. William Burnet Kinney, wife of the American Minister to the Sardinian court. All of them were deeply impressed with his powers—and indeed, as Home himself recalled later "the manifestations while I was at Florence were very strong." On the other hand Dickens, stopping on the Arno during his Italian journey, firmly refused to go near the young medium. And there were gathering storm clouds—feminine jealousies, slanderous tongues, anonymous, threatening letters and even a mysterious attack in which he was slightly wounded. But the three most important things that happened to him during his stay in Italy were to influence his whole future life. The first was the flat announcement by the "spirits", made in the evening of February 10, 1856 that his mediumistic powers would leave him for exactly twelve months. The second was that some of his friends—among them the Trollopes—cast him off. This was the Victorian age and the lady-authoress objected strongly to Home recuperating from another bout of tuberculosis at a villa belonging to an Englishwoman who was separated from her husband—though there was not the slightest hint of any sexual relationship between her and the medium. And thirdly—in what Miss Burton calls "perhaps the obscurest episode of his entire career"—he became a Roman Catholic.

Home himself thought, with commendable self-censure, that it was because he had not behaved properly that his spirit guides and controls deserted him—as a warning and a punishment. He accepted it humbly. The Trollopes and other former friends were speedily replaced by the Branickas who engaged him as a tutor and took him with them first to Naples and then to Rome.

Rome was a dangerous place for Home to visit. Only fifteen years had passed since the Inquisition had decreed the strictest measures against all "unbelievers, Jews and magicians." But the danger was removed by Home's decision to be received as a member of the Catholic Church. This was done in less than three weeks. With Monsignor Talbot as his instructor, Count Branicka and Countess Orsini as his sponsors, he was baptised on Easter Monday by a Jesuit father in the chapel of the English College at Rome. Pope Pius IX received him in audience, asking him numerous questions and dismissing him with his blessing. A short time afterwards he left with the Branickas for Paris.

There were still eight months to go of his "year of punishment". His Polish friends left him stranded without any money. He was seriously ill. It was, perhaps, the lowest ebb of his fortunes,—as if, indeed, his invisible masters and companions had decided to teach him a thorough lesson—to chastise him for his snobbery, his love of finery, his undeniable vanity. His confessor, Father Ravignan, was almost his only friend in Paris during these long, dreary weeks. Yet at the same time scores, perhaps hundreds of people were ticking off the days on the calendar. On the morning of the 11th February 1857 the Emperor Napoleon III sent the Marquis de Belmont to pose the momentous question: "Had Monsieur Home recovered his occult powers?" The answer was, happily, "yes". On the stroke of midnight a spirit hand had touched his forehead and a voice whispered: "Be of good cheer, Daniel, you will soon be well."

To the distress of the kindly Père de Ravignan who had hoped that his spiritual child had forsaken for ever "sorcery and witchcraft", Home resumed his mediumship. Old and new friends rallied around him. He became the house guest of Count Alexander de Komar. His very first séance was given at the Tuileries and though it started badly (Home insisted that only a small circle should be present and the Empress left in high dudgeon) within less than an hour Home had overcome this initial handicap (the Emperor had the Salon d'Apollon cleared of all but a few people and the Empress returned.) The next two séances were just as brilliant—and though the Emperor consulted both the professors of the Sorbonne and Robert Houdin, the famous magician, nobody could offer an explanation for the raps, the spirit hands, the luminous vapours, the tinkling shiver of the crystal chandeliers. After this it is understandable why the highest court circles, the entire aristocracy paid tribute to Home. The Duchess of Hamilton, Prince Joachim and Princess Caroline Murat, Count Felix Bacchiocchi, the Court Chamberlain, Prince Richard and Princess Pauline Metternich all followed the lead given by Napoleon III and his beautiful Empress. But, as throughout his life, Home did not lack enemies. The Duc de Morny and Count Walewski (Napoleon I's illegitimate son, Foreign Minister of the Second Empire) were the most important; the Emperor's favour gained him the undeserved reputation of sinister political influence. Many neo-Gothic horror stories were invented about him.

All this was crowded into six weeks; for on March 20, Home sailed for America. But he parted from the Imperial family on the most amicable terms and with the promise to return soon. Lord Cowley, the English Ambassador, reported: "He (Home) has gone to bring his sister who, he says, is more wonderful than himself, and who is to be educated here at the Empress's expense. . ."

Back in America, Home had a mixed press (the New York *Herald* published a Paris dispatch according to which the young medium had been banished from France because he had stolen £30,000)—but his old friends received him with delight. In May, together with his sister Christine, he was back in Paris. Lord Cowley's information was correct; she was sent to the Convent of the Sacred Heart in Paris, a most distinguished institution where the Empress herself had been educated two decades earlier. Here she was to spend seven years without showing any talent as a medium and grow up to become a devout Catholic.

The séances at court were resumed. Home "performed" in the presence of Grand Duke Constantine of Russia, of Maxmilian II of Bavaria (who was most alarmed by a mysteriously moving table). His social life was one busy whirl of engagements. He made friends with Balzac's Polish widow, with the Marquise de Boissy (who, as Teresa Guiccioli, had been Byron's mistress), and the dramatist Victorien Sardou and many celebrities in the arts and letters.

There was a plan—discarded like so many others involving too much effort—to visit Turkey "as a way was opening by which I might be the means of bringing light there,"; but instead Home visited the Grand Duke of Baden-Baden (his patroness, the Duchess of Hamilton, was the Grand Duke's daughter) at whose court his august sitters included the King of Wurttemberg, the Prince Regent of Prussia and the Prince of Nassau. But Eugénie, who had an "entire belief" in him. summoned the young man to Biarritz where the French court was spending the summer. Unfortunately, Home fell seriously ill soon after his arrival and was treated by Dr. E. Barthez, the court physician of the infant Prince Imperial. Dr. Barthez did not like him at all and later (using the secondhand evidence provided by a M. Morio de l'Ile) accused him of downright fraud. Temporarily, at least, he seemed to fall out of favour with Napoleon III and his wife; but this breach was soon mended and the Empress retained her unshaken faith in him, to the end of her long life.

$$\star \quad \star \quad \star$$

A chateau near Bordeaux; Paris; The Hague (where he gave séances for Queen Sophia and was rewarded by a royal ring); Brussels; Paris again, were the next stops on his peregrinations. In the spring of 1858 Home spent a few days at Pisa and Florence. Elizabeth Barrett Browning wrote in some excitement:

"Now let me tell you, Home, my protégé prophet, is in Italy . . . An English woman, who from infidel opinions was converted by his instrumentality, to a belief in life after death, has died in Paris and left him an annuity of £240, English. On coming here he paid all his wandering debts, I am glad to hear, and is even said to have returned certain *gifts* which had been rendered unacceptable to him from the bad opinion of the givers. I hear, too, that his manners, as well as morals are wonderfully improved . . ."

It was in Rome that Home met seventeen-year-old Sacha de Kroll, younger daughter of the late General Count de Kroll and a god-daughter of the late Tsar Nicholas. It was mutual love at first sight. Twelve days later their engagement was announced. Four months later they were married—in St. Petersburg. Home's best man was that lusty giant of French romantic literature, Alexandre Dumas. Alexander II, the recently crowned Tsar of Russia, showed the most kindly favour to bride and bridegroom and became the medium's warm, lifelong friend. He was represented by two aides at the wedding and Home was again and again invited to Peterhof or Tsarkoe Selo, the Imperial residences. The honeymoon was spent touring the extensive estates of Count Kotcheleff, the bride's brother-in-law and included visiting large tracts of the interior of Russia and the Crimean coast.

Sacha had not been allowed to witness any of her husband's phenomena; but when the time came to listen to the raps and gaze on apparitions, she seemed to take it all in her stride. Among the high-born friends his marriage brought to Home were the Grand Duke Constantine, Count Schouvaloff, the poet and writer Count Alexis Tolstoy and Baron Nicholas Meyendorff, commander of the Imperial Horse Guards. Indeed, his occult power had brought the boy from Currie a very long and brilliant way.

The only child of the union, Gregory or Gricha, was born on May 8, 1859; his birth attended by a number of signs and portents, brilliant spirit-lights and the song of invisible birds. He was baptized into the Roman Catholic Church; but later, he was re-christened into the Greek Church, when his sponsors were the Tsar of Russia and the Grand Duke Constantine—an exalted enough brace of godfathers.

Home was generally accepted as an exemplary husband. He and his charming wife reached England in November 1859, after visiting Paris and Switzerland. No longer a penniless adventurer without background, Home's old and new friends received the couple with flattering attention. Séances were held in the homes of the Duchess of Somerset, the Duchess of Sutherland, Lord Lyndhurst (the Lord Chancellor) and many of the peerage and most of the notables in art and literature flocked to them. Thackeray came again and so did Bulwer-Lytton; Mrs. Thomas Milner Gibson made him the lion of her famous Monday at-homes. There was a brief interruption when Home made a sentimental journey to his birthplace; but soon he was back in the London whirl. While his Russian friends clamoured in vain for his return, Count Alexis Tolstoy and two others came to the British capital and recorded two "most impressive séances". The first Tolstoy called "overwhelming" and about the second he wrote: "I would have gone a thousand leagues to see these things . . ."

Through most of his life, Home had to pay for success and serenity with sorrow and misfortune. This period was no exception. His young

D.D. Home

wife had become infected with tuberculosis and was rapidly reaching the incurable stage of the disease.

She died in the South of France in February 1862. It was what the Victorians called a "beautiful death". Mary Howitt, a Quakeress and the English translator of Andersen's fairy tales, wrote her moving obituary. ". . .Her meekness, her playful, winning ways, the joyfulness with which she anticipated her removal, almost cast into shadows the wonderful gifts and powers of her husband. She had long been in daily communication with the spirits of her departed friends, and felt the life opening to her was certain and beautiful beyond conception —the bright spirit world had become a calm reality. . ."

Eighteen months before Sacha's death Thackeray's famous literary monthly published a long anonymous article about Home, written by the Irish journalist and critic Robert Bell. It described in detail a séance held at Mrs. Gibson's home—and, the most sensational part, Home's levitation. The article caused an immense storm. Thackeray was strongly attacked but refused to desert his contributor. Half-a-dozen theories were proffered as to how Home did it—all of them by people who were not present—and Dickens recorded that he took the liberty of regarding Home as an impostor. "Afraid of the truth, of course," wrote Home's staunch believer, Mrs. Browning, "having deeply committed himself to negatives. Dickens, too, who is so fond of ghost-stories, as long as they are impossible!"

Poor Sacha's death was followed by a vexatious lawsuit involving her estate and, until its settlement, Home's income was stopped. He returned to England in August 1862. In January 1863 he paid another visit to Paris, once again a welcome visitor at the Tuileries and many fashionable salons. He started work on his autobiography; the first volume was published in 1863, the second in 1872. Most of the actual work was done by William Wilkinson, a solicitor, and the result was somewhat querulous and flat. Perhaps this was necessary to balance the unavoidably sensational material. The reviewers received it either with abuse or with courteous scepticism; but it went into two editions in England and five in America; it was also translated into French. Not content with literary laurels, at the end of the year Home went to Rome to take up the study of—sculpture. But his career as an art student in the Eternal City did not last long. After a questioning by Pasqualonni, the Chief of Police (interrupted by a burst of "spirit-raps") he was expelled from Rome on January 5, 1864. The Governor of Rome had been willing to permit him to stay if he gave a solemn promise to "desist from all communication with the spirit world." This Home was unable to do—for, as he always maintained, he had no control over his powers. The most he could undertake was not to give any séances while in Rome and "avoid, as much as possible, all conversations upon spiritualism." This was not sufficient for the authorities and, accompanied by many and distinguished supporters, he passed through the gates of Rome, travelling first to Naples and then to Nice. When he returned to London in April, Home lodged a formal complaint with Lord Palmerston about the expulsion incident. It became an international affair—and Home's cause was hotly championed by a strange alliance of die-hard, anti-Catholic Protestants and rabid Spiritualists. John Bright, the great Free Trader, had a séance with him at the home of Mr. and Mrs. Samuel Carter Hall (he was the editor of the *London Art Journal* and she of the *St. James Magazine*) and recorded in his diary: "Mr. Home, the great medium, there. Manifestations as usual, except one thing new to me . . .Curious and not explained. All hands on the table at the time." And, again, he noted about a second séance: "Very wonderful." Home's partisans arranged for Mr. John A. Roebuck, the Radical Member of Parliament for Sheffield, to ask a question in the House about his expulsion from Rome—but A.H. Layard, Palmerston's Under-Secretary, returned an evasive answer and no diplomatic action was taken.

Shortly afterwards Browning's *Mr. Sludge, the Medium* was published. The model for this nauseating, cringing, unscrupulous cheat was, of course, the poet's *bête noire*, Daniel Dunglas Home. Except, however, Home never made such a confession as the cynical Sludge:

"Now for it, then! Will you believe me, though? You've heard what I confess; I don't unsay a single word: I cheated when I could. . ."

And Home himself refused to believe that he was Browning's "inspiration". Years later he made some comparatively restrained comment about the poem—but even then it was the *cause* and not his own person which he defended. He called it "an offensively coarse attack" and "an insult to the memory of his deceased wife, who lived and died a believer in Spiritualism. . ." Nor did it really hurt Home's reputation. Almost nothing did. And as if to compensate for Browning's searing attack, John Ruskin had a series of séances with him and soon the author of "The Stones of Venice" was writing to Home: "I believe you are truly doing me the greatest service and help that one human being can do another in trusting in me in this way, and indeed I hope I so far deserve your trust, that I can understand noble and right feeling and affection. . ."

This was the *cri du coeur* of a lonely, disillusioned, tormented man, finding a little comfort in regaining a particle of faith. Shortly after receiving this letter Home returned to America arriving towards the end of the bitter Civil War. Harriet Beecher Stowe and her brother the Reverend Charles Beecher welcomed him although Mr. Stowe did not like him personally, even though he thought that "some of his doings are as real as they are strange." During his visit Home gave several public readings and proved to be a brilliant elocutionist. Returning to Europe in May 1865, he collected his sister Christine from her convent, was again warmly received at the French court and met such celebrities as Mustapha Pasha, brother of the Viceroy of Egypt and the great, irrepressible Rossini. From Paris he moved on to Russia where the Tolstoys were delighted to entertain him at their country seat and he was the guest of the Grand Duke Constantine, ending up with a several weeks' stay at Peterhof—during which his friends wrote to him "c/o H.I.H. the Emperor of Russia." Home was laden with diamonds and emeralds by his Imperial patron and the aristocracy (even his best friends had to admit that he "loved glittering stones dearly"); but he also obtained, as a favour, the release of a political prisoner. He was greatly exhausted by Russian hospitality, however splendid, and he rested at Nijni-Novgorod before returning to England. His power seemed to weaken and for a considerable time he restricted himself largely to lectures and public readings with fewer séances than before. One of his lectures was disturbed by the challenge of a magician ("The Great Wizard of the North") who demanded that Home should "prove his words!" and when Home did not oblige him, called him "a swindler and a humbug." This did not seem to throw Home off his stride. In 1866, to add still another area to his ways of self-expression, he became an actor, appearing at Worcester and receiving kind, even glowing notices—though he did not pursue his plan of acting the title-role of "Hamlet" in London.

Instead he was, within two years, playing a much less pleasant part —that of the defendant in a sensational and unsavoury lawsuit. The plaintiff was a rich, vulgar and eccentric lady, Mrs. Mary Lyon, seventy-five year old illegitimate daughter of a Newcastle factory-owner and widow of Charles Lyon, a kinsman of the Earl of Strathmore. In January 1867 Home had become the resident secretary of the Spiritual Athenaeum, the intended headquarters of the Spiritualist movement. Here Mrs. Lyon discovered him. She adopted him, gave him £24,000 as an "entirely free gift", added another £6000 when he changed his name by deed poll to Daniel Home Lyon, made over another £30,000 to him—only to turn against him within a very short time. Home used the money to pay his debts, bought a cottage for his aunt, Mary Cook (the same who had turned him out of her Connecticut house) and settled annuities on various members of his family. But by February 1867 Mrs Lyon had changed her allegiance to another "true or pretended medium" named Miss Nicholls; in May she sought legal advice to recover the last £30,000 and in June she took steps to get *all* her gifts back. The case was heard in April 1868 and not only was the court packed with people but all over England people were betting feverishly as to the outcome of the trial. It was spiritualism that was on trial —just as much as Home himself. And the Vice-Chancellor, Sir George Markham Giffard, after ten days, ordered Mrs. Lyon to pay all costs —but, in a reserved judgment, Home was ordered to return the entire £60,000 he had received. And of course, his enemies and critics, had ample opportunity to tear his reputation to pieces.

Even so, he was not left without friends. To recoup his losses, he undertook a tour of public readings in fifty cities of England and Scotland which was highly successful. He continued giving séances which produced "signs and wonders...of nightly occurence." The Countess of Caithness, the learned Patrick Proctor Alexander, General and Mrs. Boldero, Lady Gomm were some who witnessed these. One of the most remarkable occasions was at the Northern Hotel, Aberdeen, where, according to Mrs. Boldero:

"The table quivered so violently and the plates rattled and moved so much that General Boldero was obliged to stop eating...A large arm-chair near the fire-place rushed across the room and up to the table, placing itself near one of the reporters... General Boldero states that all felt this to be a most remarkable manifestation, as Home had not been into the coffee-room where they were at supper till they had entered it together, and no thread or trickery of any kind could have moved the chair with the precision and velocity with which it left its place and abruptly joined them..."

Some months before the painful law-suit, and towards the end of 1867 Home had made the acquaintance of Lord Adare, a Guardsman in his early twenties who was also an occasional but by no means amateurish journalist (he covered the Abyssinian War for the *Daily Telegraph* and was to cover the Franco-Prussian War in the company of Home.) The two men became firm friends. Adare recorded 78 séances and a good many of his private experiences of Home's powers. This he did in a series of letters to his father, the Earl of Dunraven. The letters were privately printed in 1870; more than fifty years later, Adare (who by then had succeeded his father) permitted the Society for Psychical Research to reprint them. The original edition was introduced by Adare's father who had attended several of the sittings and who very firmly vouched for Home's genuine powers, though he was rather doubtful about the spiritualist claims to base a religion on the occult phenomena. A full list of the participants was given and the phenomena included an accordion "played, with no one touching it", an arrow brought through the air, a glass of brandy emptied and filled, clairvoyance, flowers deprived of their scent and brought through the air, the remarkable fire-tests (with Home handling red-hot coals apparently unscathed), a harp played by "spirit-hands", elevation, elongation, levitation, faces and hands becoming luminous, second sight, 'other-worldly music', luminous objects, furniture and other objects moving without any physical agency, a pencil writing by itself, a piano raised off the ground, various raps, sounds, visible and tangible spirit hands, spirit voices and spirit laughter—a variety to satisfy the most voracious appetite. Horace Wyndham hints that Adare wrote his record with his tongue in his cheek. But the young man says in his introduction seriously and sincerely enough:

"I have witnessed many persons make, at their first séance, every effort to account for the phenomena by trickery and mechanical contrivance, and failing that, to reduce them to the effects of some unknown force. I have invariably found them (provided of course that the séance was successful) very soon obliged to admit that these phenomena cannot be accounted for, except on the supposition that they are caused by an unseen but active and reasoning intelligence."

This was his opinion and he stuck to it—for at the age of eighty when his letters were published for a wider readership, he was still firm in his belief in Home's genuine power—and just as little able to account for them as the medium himself.

Adare's was the longest association with Home's mediumship and though in April 1869 the heir of the Earl of Dunraven married and gave up attending séances, they remained friends and frequently met.

Together they reached the German headquarters a few hours after the decisive battle of Sedan—Home as the correspondent of the *San Francisco Chronicle*—and covered the long, bitter siege of Paris. Home turned out to be a competent and assiduous reporter. He was also a privileged one: the King of Prussia, the future Emperor, recognized him (Wilhelm I had attended one of his séances when he was Prince-Regent); he had a safe-conduct and was able to come and go far more freely than most of his colleagues.

After the fall of Paris and the terrible, gory days of the Commune, Home was glad to accept the invitation of Baron Meyendorff to visit Russia again. He found that six years had made no difference in the affection and friendship of his high connections. The Tsar called him to the Winter Palace; he found new friends in the distinguished psychical researcher, Alexander N. Aksakoff, an imperial councillor and in Professor A. von Boutlerow who held the chair of chemistry at St. Petersburg University. Through these two he met Julie de Gloumeline, a delightful, dark-haired girl who became his second wife. She was Aksakoff's cousin and von Boutlerow's sister-in-law.

A series of experiments, organized by the Russian Academy of Science and led by Dr. Karponitch, took place with good results; and even finer phenomena were obtained in Boutlerow's home. Several sceptics —among them Dr. N. Wagner, Professor of Natural History—were apparently "converted". One séance was held with a glass-topped table under which Home's feet (which he was supposed to use for his "tricks") were clearly seen securely wrapped in a plaid (he was suffering from one of his periodic bouts of illness.)

As with his first wife, Home's courtship was a whirlwind one. He and Julie de Gloumeline became engaged within a few days of their first meeting, though they were not married until October 1871. In March of that year Home had returned to England in order to submit himself to a series of investigations by William Crookes, the young but already famous physicist and chemist. Everybody (including the press and his fellow scientists) expected Crookes to proclaim either fraud or, because of the stringent test-conditions, the failure of the medium. Instead, much to the dismay of everybody, Crookes gave Home an enthusiastic testimonial:

"The phenomena I am prepared to attest," he wrote in the *Quarterly Journal of Science* which he co-edited, "are so extraordinary and so directly oppose the most-firmly-rooted articles of scientific belief —amongst others, the ubiquity and invariable action of the force of gravitation—that, even now, on recalling the details of what I witnessed, there is an antagonism in my mind between *reason* which pronounces it to be scientifically impossible, and consciousness that my senses, both of touch and sight . . . are not lying witnesses . . . "

Crookes stuck to his opinions for the rest of his life—and, however much he was derided and assailed, went on to become President of the British Association for the Advancement of Science. He was also the last man to conduct scientific experiments with Home. For after Home's second marriage which provided him with financial independence (he also won the law-suit over his first wife's estate) Home retired, finally and completely, at the age of thirty-eight. He was received into the Greek Orthodox Church and any séances he gave for the rest of his life were in small private circles. His second marriage was just as happy as the first although it lasted considerably longer and Mrs. Home survived her husband by many years. In 1872—when his daughter Marie was born prematurely and died after a few days—he published the second volume of "Incidents in My Life" and in 1877 he brought out his "masterpiece", "Lights and Shadows of Spiritualism." It was a long and reasonably well-written survey of ancient and modern spiritualism, tracing the subject from before the Bible to his own days; it was also harshly denunciatory of "the follies and knaveries" disgracing the occult. He spoke of "brazen and unblushing" impostures—and, unavoidably, compared his own work with that of his successors. The book was a considerable success even though some spiritualists "insatiable for marvels" were sorely hurt.

The last years of Home's life were spent in Russia and in the South of France with occasional trips to Florence, Paris and London. He died on June 21, 1886 at Auteuil, at the age of fifty-three. His son Gricha is believed to have entered the Russian army when his stepmother returned to her native country in 1890. Home's grave is in the Russian cemetery at St. Germain-en-Laye where he rests together with his infant daughter.

★   ★   ★

Millions of words have been written about this extraordinary Scotsman—but none have really solved the riddle of his powers and of his life. The attempts of scientists, psychologists, imaginative writers have all failed, whether they started with the assumption that he was a genuine medium or with the premiss that he was a fake. He is a classic case of the dilemma we meet again and again in the vast field of the occult—he and his phenomena have disappeared, even the most painstaking record of them can be questioned by the sceptics and there is no possible way of separating truth from falsehood. But certainly the world has not seen his like in all the generations since he died.

★   ★   ★

CHAPTER THREE

The Schneiders: A Psychic Family

BRAUNAU or Braunau am Inn is a fair-sized town in Upper Austria, about thirty miles north of Salzburg. The town has a rail junction, breweries and tanneries and has one of Austria's biggest aluminium plants at Ranshofen (one of its suburbs). It was the birthplace of Adolf Hitler (a distinction which the Braunauers would prefer to forget). It was also the home of one of the most remarkable families in psychical research—the Schneiders.

The father, Josef Schneider, was a compositor, a very intelligent, much respected and quiet, exceptionally well mannered man. His wife, a gentle, unassuming woman, had borne twelve children of whom six—all of them boys—had survived. They were named Karl, Hans, Fritz, Willi, Franzl and Rudi. Four of them were mediumistic, though Hans and Karl possessed this faculty only in a very slight degree while Willi and Rudi were destined to become two of the most famous and most discussed mediums in Europe if not in the world.

No one has offered any valid explanation why the Schneider boys should have developed psychic faculties. No traces of abnormality could be found on either side of the family. Yet Willi showed signs of mediumship at the age of fourteen and Rudi at eleven.

"One evening," Harry Price writes in his Rudi Schneider monograph, "Herr Schneider's friends were holding a séance with Willi when 'Olga', *the trance personality who then spoke through Rudi's brother* said that the power was not good and that she wanted Rudi to 'assist.' But the boy's parents objected on the grounds that Rudi was only eleven years of age. Rudi was then asleep in bed. 'Olga' said nothing but a few minutes later the door opened and Rudi, deeply entranced, entered the room and took his place in the circle."

Willi, not yet sixteen, was adopted by Baron von Schrenck-Notzing who conducted a long series of experiments with him. In his monumental "*Materialisations-Phaenomene*" (the second edition was published in Munich in 1923) he devoted forty pages to these experiments and published a page of photographs showing a number of "teleplastic manifestations".

Schrenck-Notzing's work with Willi began in October 1919 with a series of séances in five different homes; some were held at the Baron's laboratory. After finishing school, Willi was apprenticed to a dental technician and undertook to work for a year exclusively for Schrenck-Notzing. He moved to Munich where he lodged in the home of a lady, greatly interested in occult phenomena. "Thus it was possible. . ." wrote Schrenck-Notzing, "to keep any harmful influences away from him and to follow closely his psychological development and the occasional, spontaneous psychic phenomena during his stay in Munich."

Schrenck-Notzing subjected Willi to a regular and thorough medical examination which included intelligence tests and psychological checks. He gave a detailed analysis of the young boy's character:

"Lively reflexes. Psychogenic squint, especially when depressed. Field of sight shows normal limits. No disturbances in the area of sensibility and motility. School record and general development correspond to social milieu; it must be emphasised that his father's intellectual interests and knowledge—especially with regard to the history of his home-town and occultism—are far above the usual lower middle-class standards.

Willi's general knowledge is normal considering his schooling. His memory is good average. A soft, kind-hearted character, obedient, modest; he easily gains the affection of those who get to know him well. His work as dental technician has been highly praised both by his former and his present employer; a diligent and trustworthy worker. Will-power underdeveloped. Easily impressionable; irritable. Changeable moods; unmotivated, over-sentimental sadness and nostalgia changing suddenly into gay abandonment. Inclination to masquerades, dancing and acrobatic performances. Love of nature. Abstract thinking rudimentary but imagination lively. Great ambitiousness. Strongly marked sympathies and antipathies towards people which play a great part at the séances. His self-importance strongly stimulated by earlier séance-successes in spiritualist circles. Some capriciousness; idiosyncratic dislike of certain kinds of food. Frightened by his own phenomena. Lack of self-discipline combined with stubbornness. Inclined to be spendthrift, desire of easy-going, expensive way of life. Actions more influenced by emotions than by reasoning. Deep, dreamless sleep, especially after séances. Often day-dreams. While fully conscious but somewhat absent-minded he sees sometimes clouds and head-like formations; also full figures in white garments and veils; i.e. similar to those observed during séances. No actual hallucinations. . ."

I have quoted the Baron's long analysis of Willi's character and psychological make-up at some length (it continues for several pages in his book) to show how thoroughly he enumerated the young boy's good and bad qualities. He was equally thorough in organizing the sittings, keeping records, establishing the most rigorous control, doing everything humanly possible to exclude all fraud. During five months there were never less than five, usually seven to ten participants at the sittings, including university professors, physicians, writers, psychical researchers. The conclusion Schrenck-Notzing reached concerning 56 séances held between December 3, 1921 and July 1, 1922, in which 94 people took part, was clear and definite:

"No single participant noticed the slightest suspicious manipulation by the medium or anybody present and the collective impression of all witnesses can be summed up by saying that Willy Sch. could not have produced the phenomena through the known mechanical means, i.e. fraudulently. Doors were locked before the sittings so that there was no possibility of any accomplice gaining access during the darkness to the laboratory. In addition, the most important ma-terialisation processes took place in the centre of the semi-circle, immediately under the eyes of the observer, at a distance of 40 centi-meters to one meter, in the light of a lamp with a red bulb standing on the table. Any person separated from the site of the manifesta-tions by the circle of participants would have been unable to influ-ence them in any way. Finally, in the case of many phenomena the nature and evanescence of their appearance, their flowing, chang-ing and fantastic shapes and their mode of development until they reached their final form argue against any possibility of a fraudulent production of them—even if one would assume that one of those present would have tried to deceive his fellow-observers. . ."

Professor Schrenck-Notzing believed firmly in Willi's mediumship and so did those who participated in the séances; at least no voice was raised questioning the method of controls or alleging any fraud. Yet the phenomena were greatly varied—raps, cold winds, black shapes, materialisations of heads, hands, arms, levitating of various objects—the whole range of the usual séance phenomena.

In May 1922 Harry Price, the British psychical researcher and Dr. E.J. Dingwall, then Research Officer of the London Society for Psychical Research were invited by Baron Schrenck-Notzing to visit Munich and take part in sittings. The first séance was held on May 29, Price and Dr. Dingwall examined the séance room and the adjoining apartments and carefully checked the control methods. Willi was held by two persons who controlled both hands and feet. There were five red lights and these, with luminous pins and bracelets which were stuck all over the medium, enabled the sitters to see all his movements.

In his "Rudi Schneider" Harry Price wrote about the three séances he attended with Willi:

> "These séances were, to all intents and purposes, under our own control. We examined everything, affixed our seals to the séance room door, etc. etc. After the séances Dingwall and I signed statements to the effect that we had witnessed genuine phenomena, which included many telekinetic movements—starting and stopping of a musical box in a gauze cage—to order. The box also wound itself up. A pseudopod or hand-like form picked up my handkerchief several times. Loud raps inside the cabinet were heard; the 'hand' or pseudopod showed itself against a luminous plaque, etc., etc. And all these phenomena occurred at a distance of some feet from the medium, who was controlled by two persons. At the fore-control Willi was searched and put into black tights, which were outlined with luminous bands and buttons. It was a wonderful display of phenomena, produced in really excellent red light. . ."

There were two other, equally successful séances and the English visitors returned to London, fully convinced that Willi Schneider had genuine psychic powers. In December, 1922, Price delivered a lecture at the London Spiritualist Alliance at which he paid public tribute to the young medium. This lecture and his subsequent articles led to a long essay published in the Journal of the American Society for Psychical Research, headed "The Conversion of Mr. Price." Certainly Price considered Willi one of the most important mediums of the world;

he was greatly impressed by the stringent controls and the "amazing phenomena."

Following the Munich visit of Dingwall and Price, Willi was invited to England at the end of 1924 by the Society for Psychical Research and gave a number of séances; but though a few striking telekinetic phenomena were witnessed, the visit was not particularly successful. Price thought that this was because "the strangeness of the country, or the people, or the unfamiliar surroundings of the séance-room, may have had a deterrent effect upon the phenomena."

Not long afterwards Schrenck-Notzing and Willi parted company through one of those arguments or misunderstandings common enough between a medium and his "patron". Willi went to Vienna and put himself under the guidance of Dr. E. Holub, head of the famous Steinhof asylum. During the brief period the well-known alienist worked with Willi a new phenomenon, levitation, was witnessed in addition to materializations, telekinesis and the usual "repertory". Dr. Holub died suddenly and left Willi at a loose end. But Frau Dr. Holub offered him a home, the experiments continued and in April, 1925, Harry Price was invited to take part in them. He reached Vienna in June and attended three séances. He described them in considerable detail in his "Account of Some· Further Experiments with Willy Schneider" in the Journal of the American S.P.R. (August 1925) and gave a summary in his "Fifty Years of Psychical Research" fourteen years later; nothing much happened at the first sitting, but that of June 8, with Professor Hans Thirring and Professor Ludwik of Vienna University among the sitters, was quite spectacular:

"A two-sided gauze screen, twenty-eight inches high, was placed round a strong wooden oblong table, on which was a cloth. The screen was between the medium and table, on which were placed various articles, including a rubber squeaking doll. A sitter and I controlled Willi, who had been examined and was dressed in a two-piece pyjama suit, to which were sewn luminous buttons. In a few minutes Willi was in trance, and by the light of a red lamp (by means of which all the sitters could see one another) the following phenomena were experienced: the tablecloth was lifted; the table was moved and swung round; the luminous rubber doll squeaked several times (proving that something was pressing it); the table turned completely over on to the sitters. These manifestations were witnessed several times. The 'doll' phenomenon was particularly striking. Willi was five feet eleven inches from it, the other sitters being more than six feet from the toy. No doubt exists in my mind that we witnessed genuine phenomena, during the production of which Willi was breathing heavily and rapidly (200 cycles per minute). . ."

A promise by Willi's "control", an "entity named Otto", that he would produce levitation, was not fulfilled at the third and last séance but Price returned to London well satisfied with his visit. A short time afterwards Schrenck-Notzing and Willi made up whatever differences they had and Willi signed a two years' contract with the Baron, undertaking to continue the experiments with his original sponsor. In October, 1925 Harry Price found him at Braunau when he visited the Schneiders for the first time.

During this visit Price met Captain Fritz Kogelnik who was the first to discover the "psychic family." Apparently it all began one night when the family were amusing themselves with a ouija board. They discovered that "requests to the intelligence operating the board were carried out even to the extent of the displacement of objects at the far side of the room, on demand." At a séance which Kogelnik attended in the early spring of 1919 at the Schneiders' modest home in the main street of Braunau, a tablecloth was slowly raised from the table though no mortal hand was near it and this "miracle" was seen in a light "strong enough to recognize distinctly every person in the room." Willi was then fourteen, Rudi (who was not present) was only eight years old. At this early period Willi did not go into a trance —but was merely an amused and puzzled witness of the proceedings.

Soon, however, Willi was developing into a medium and acquired as his own the "control" or spirit entity supposed to be responsible for the manifestations. This "control" was called "Olga"—a lady who later transferred her allegiance to Rudi while Willi acquired another called "Minna". Most mediums, of course, have such "controls"— it is almost an obligatory tradition. No psychical researcher took "Olga" seriously; she, like all other "controls" was supposed to be the "trance personality" or "secondary personality" of the medium. Yet she was accepted (again as other "controls" are) in order to humour the medium—or, if the pun can be forgiven, for "appearance's sake". This, too, is traditional in mediumship. On one occasion "Olga" declared that her full name was Olga Lintner, known previously as Lola

Montez, the dancer and adventuress. In Price's opinion "Olga" was "merely a conventional name. . .manufactured in trance from material deep. . .in (the) subconscious mind. . ."

Captain Kogelnik was convinced of the genuineness of the phenomena and attended hundreds of séances with Willi at which many telekinetic phenomena and materialized limbs were seen, under good conditions of control.

Gradually the news of the advent of "Olga" spread, causing much excitement in the little town and provoking sensational stories in the local papers. Crowds of people, eager for "wonders" besieged the modest home of Herr Schneider—and the manifestations decreased. At this time, according to Kogelnik, Willi began to "help" the phenomena. So the captain persuaded his father to permit him to take the boy to his home where control could be more satisfactory. Here, with only Kogelnik, his wife and two ladies present, Willi produced the first of the very rare full-form materializations recorded in his career:

"In the middle of the room a sofa was placed, and adjoining it three chairs, so as to give the general effect of a circle. The room was lighted by a red lamp, hanging from the ceiling. On a table near me was placed a phonograph. Willi was comfortably seated on the left corner of the sofa; at his right was my wife, whom he liked best of all. She took both his hands, and after about one minute he was in deep trance. His head sank on to her left shoulder. I asked: 'Olga, are you here?' A slight tapping of the medium's foot answered, 'Yes.' I continued: 'I know, Olga, that you are very fond of music. Would you perhaps like to materialize yourself and dance a tango?' 'Olga' agreed, with the same tapping of Willi's foot. The phonograph was ready to play; I only had to throw the lever. I did so; and at the first note of the music a phantom was visible, standing among us. It danced the tango very correctly and gracefully. It was about five feet tall, and one got the impression of a slim figure, covered all over with cobwebby veils. As the dance proceeded these veils waved about, and I leaned back in my chair as they nearly touched me. It was a most impressive sight; the gracefully and mutely dancing phantom, while the medium lay in my wife's arms, absolutely motionless. At the last note of the music the phantom disappeared like lightning, just as it had come. . ."

The difficulty with this "most impressive sight" was the same as with all spirit manifestations—apart from those present only convinced spiritualists believed that it ever happened. And of course, there was always the unconscious humour, the slightly or broadly ridiculous aspect of an "apparition" dancing the tango. The trivial, the vulgar, the comic are often present at séances and are one of the main reasons why men of science are repelled by them. "Olga", once she transferred herself to Rudi Schneider, insisted on the participants at the sittings singing her favourite song—a popular hit called "Katharina"—and the spectacle of philosophers and physicists, psychical researchers and eminent writers singing unharmoniously together was difficult even for them to accept. Yet "Olga" and all the other "controls" had to be humoured—or they turned sulky and there were no phenomena at all.

In any case, after meeting Kogelnik and learning about the early history of the psychic family, Harry Price and his companions had three séances at the Schneider home. These were held in the principal living room which they examined minutely. More than thirty feet long and eleven feet wide, it had two double windows overlooking the main street, twenty-two feet below. A pair of light curtains were suspended from the ceiling across a corner of the room, enclosing one of the windows and these formed the familiar "cabinet".

The sitters included Professor Karl Gruber and Professor Hildebrand and the séances were most successful.

". . .The following were amongst the phenomena which I recorded during or immediately after the séances, held under perfect conditions of control of the medium," wrote Harry Price. "Swaying and billowing curtains; cool breezes; telekinetic movements of a handkerchief, lamp, bell, fan, and other objects; the appearance of pseudopods, or hand-like 'terminals,' stumps, and fully-materialized hand; tug-of-war with handkerchief, between the 'hand' and sitters, etc. These manifestations were repeated time after time, giving the sitters ample opportunity to study the conditions of control during the actual appearance of the phenomena. . .The two professors, Willi and I, adjourned to a nearby cafè after the last séance, which we agreed was the best the medium had ever given under test conditions."

Not long after these sittings Willi Schneider practically retired from mediumship. His powers had began to wane and although there was another series of experiments with Baron Schrenck-Notzing, it was

Rudi Schneider (left)
with his brother Willi.

Willi Schneider

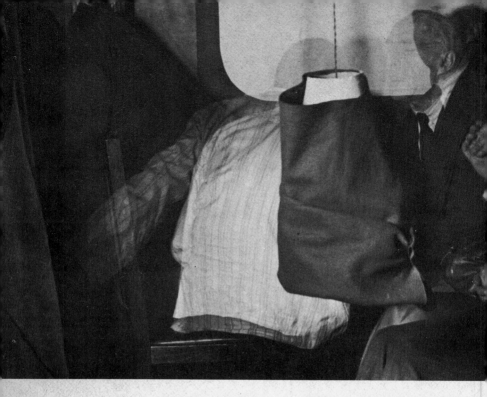

(above) Automatic photograph of Rudi evading control at a seance April 28th 1932: Harry Price is shown in double exposure at right.

Harry Price demonstrating the electrical control apparatus used for experiments with Rudi Schneider

evident that his psychic talents were almost exhausted. He worked hard at his dental studies, and his mediumship became a secondary consideration. His "mantle" had now fallen on his younger brother, Rudi.

★   ★   ★

Like Willi, Rudi had also been more or less "adopted" by Schrenck-Notzing who worked with the boy with shorter or longer interruptions until his (the Baron's) sudden death in January 1929. Rudi was a healthy and robust youngster, more interested in cars, football and, later, his sweetheart Mitzi (who became his wife) than in psychical research. Yet his work with the Munich researcher produced excellent results, more or less on the lines of Willi's. In December 1925, not long after Price's second visit to Braunau, Herr Schneider himself wrote with pardonable parental pride that Rudi had been producing phenomena "which very few mortals had ever got to see. In yesterday's sitting there were at least thirty appearances of an almost six-foot high phantom. At one time there were two such phantoms. One of them touched a member of the circle. Materialised hands were seen in innumerable profusion. Telekinetic phenomena were observed at a distance of more than two yards." Then he added, perhaps a little unfairly: "Compared to yesterday's séance, the one which you attended with Willi was completely negative..."

He asked Price to come soon and not wait until the spring when Rudi's power might be less spectacular. A few weeks later Professor Gruber who had attended some séances at Baron von Schrenck-Notzing's Munich laboratory, reported enthusiastically that "Rudi produced magnificent phenomena. A hand appeared and took a ring from Baron von Schrenck-Notzing's finger."

Price, accompanied by two personal friends and by Mr. E. Clepham Palmer of the London *Daily News*, arrived in Braunau late in April 1926. In his "Fifty Years of Psychical Research" he summed up this visit:

'We had two séances with Rudi, both divided into the usual two portions. The sittings were again held in the Schneiders' principal living-room, and the lighting and other conditions were identical as with Willi, except that there were now four of us to control the medium, family and room. The phenomena we witnessed were almost identical with those experienced with Willi a few months previously: telekinetic movements, cold breezes, materialized limbs (we saw a half-formed hand drag a bell off a table); pseudopods playing with handkerchief; knocks, raps, thumps, etc. Rudi's mediumship much impressed us. . .On his return to London Mr. Palmer wrote a series of articles in the *Daily News*, describing our experiences and admitted that he 'could imagine no means by which the phenomena could have been fraudulently produced...'

Others, however, were less enthusiastic. Four months later, in August 1926, Dr. E.J. Dingwall and an American journalist named W.J. Vinton, had a number of sittings with both Willi and Rudi. Vinton, in an article he wrote for "Psyche" in April 1927 accused the whole family with conspiring to produce false phenomena; but he did *not* detect any fraud, that is, he could not really say *how* the alleged conspiracy worked. In the same year Dr. W.F. Prince of the Boston S.P.R. had several sittings with Rudi at Stuttgart and Braunau; he also suspected collusion but could offer no actual proof. J. Malcolm Bird had a single séance at Braunau on October 11, 1927 and also accepted the Dingwall-Vinton-Prince hypothesis—while equally unable to discover the *method* of the alleged collusion.

Yet during the same period Schrenck-Notzing was observing good phenomena at Munich under perfect conditions of tactual control. Later the Baron introduced an "electric chair"—an idea which Harry Price had suggested some years previously—an armchair with electrical contacts for head, arms, feet, seat, and hands. Whenever any part of the medium's body was *not* in contact, a small red signal light would automatically switch off and the lack of control would be at once discovered. Schrenck-Notzing also made the medium and the controllers wear metallic socks and gloves which formed part of the circuit of an electric light. Again, if hands or feet of both medium and controllers were not in proper contact, the light would be extinguished. Schrenck-Notzing and Karl Krall, (trainer of the famous "talking horses of Elberfeld") planned to have a long series of sittings in their respective laboratories using this virtually fool-proof control. But within a few weeks of each other, both Baron Schrenck-Notzing and Krall died. Rudi Schneider was left without sponsors or fully qualified experimenters. It was at this stage that Harry Price became associated with the young Austrian medium. He had been anxious for a long time to get Rudi to London; but the first allegiance of the Schneider boys had been naturally to their generous patron, Schrenck-Notzing. In November 1926 it seemed that Rudi was on his way to England but at the last moment his father wrote that he could not go. His employer (he was apprenticed as a motor-mechanic) had fallen ill and Rudi was needed in Braunau. In the end nothing came of the idea for more than two years.

On March 20, 1929, Price arrived in Munich and Rudi met him, together with Dr. Gerda Walther, Baron Schrenck-Notzing's secretary who was a writer on psychical research and for several years had been the contact between Price and the Schneiders. Rudi was at the time employed occasionally by an electrical engineer, Karl Amereller, who was trying to find him a permanent position in the motor trade. There was a depression in both Germany and Austria and jobs were not easy to get.

Price found the boy in an unhappy mood—partly because of this uncertainty and partly because of the various attacks on his mediumship. However, Herr Amereller arranged a séance—the first since Schrenck-Notzing's death—and this convinced Harry Price that Rudi still had some power. It would certainly be worth while, Price decided, to get him to London.

There were difficulties; Rudi had received an invitation from Visby, on the Swedish island of Gotland and was in any case doubtful whether he wanted to continue his work as a medium. Early in April 1929 Dr. Gerda Walther wrote to Price: "Rudi isn't very much inclined to take up mediumship again even for a short time and a long journey rather seems to annoy him instead of alluring him. . .He abhors being called a professional medium." There was also the problem of finding a suitable person to accompany Rudi, someone who spoke English as Rudi would be unhappy as a stranger in a foreign country. In the end Herr Amereller volunteered. "Rudi can't go alone," explained Dr. Walther. "Even 'Olga' said so. He is always entirely dependent on somebody else. His own will is very weak, though he tries to be stubborn sometimes to show he has his own will." However, all the problems were solved; on April 11, 1929, Rudi and Amereller arrived in London. Price and his associates paid their expenses. The first séance was held on the following evening.

There were altogether five sittings. They were all successful, producing brilliant and varied phenomena.

"Floating, levitation, and intelligent movements of many objects such as waste-paper basket, toy zither, etc.; the tying of knots in hand-kerchief; writing on paper by pseudopod or 'terminal'; billowing of curtains; raps and knocks on table, chairs, etc., both inside and outside of cabinet, at command; production of teleplasmic masses resembling arms, legs, a 'snow-man', 'childlike form', etc., some luminous and all showing volition and intelligence; apparent fall in temperature of cabinet, cool breezes, winds, etc.; taps felt by sitters, and gentle tugs at their clothing; cognition of objects whose where-abouts were unknown to sitters. Most of the above phenomena were witnessed in the light of a sixty-watt red bulb, by ninety-nine sitters, twenty-one of whom assisted at controlling the medium."

A very impressive list; and Harry Price had persuaded such scientists as Lord Rayleigh, Prof. A.O. Rankine, Dr. William Brown, Professor F.C.S. Schiller, Professor A.F.C. Polland, Dr. C.E.M. Joad and Professor Nils von Hofsten to attend the séances. Furthermore, he improved the tactual-electrical control by providing *all* the sitters, controllers and medium with metallic gloves and socks forming part of an low voltage electric light circuit. These gloves and socks were securely taped on and could not be removed during a séance without instant detection. Unless a sitter tightly clasped the hands of his neighbour or kept his feet in firm contact with the metallic plates screwed to the floor, one of six lights was extinguished, instantly revealing the faulty control. Before each séance Rudi was thoroughly examined and donned a special suit. Thermal data, pulse-rate, respiration were recorded care-fully.

Harry Price published a detailed account of these séances in his "Rudi Schneider" (Methuen & Co., 1930) in which he had some harsh things to say about those who had attacked Rudi's mediumship in the previous two years. He was certain that at least so far as the London séances were concerned, fraud was out of the question.

Rudi received considerable publicity in the British Press. Though Professor A.M. Low was not quite convinced about the efficiency of the electrical control and suggested "the capacity method", Price proved that his own system was foolproof. Dr. Walther wrote happily from Munich that these séances would once and for all dispose of the charges made against Rudi of having a confederate. She asked Harry Price to describe the conditions of control in these sittings as minutely as possible "because certain German sceptics say one cannot rely upon your experiments because you never exactly describe how the mediums were controlled." Professor Grätz of Munich gave Price advice on eliminating two possible evasions in the electric control.

There were immediate plans for a return visit and the idea was proposed of getting Rudi a permanent job in London. Yet the séances apparently had taken a lot out of him. "Frau Amereller told me," wrote Dr. Walther shortly after Rudi's return to Munich, "that Rudi was frightfully nervous. . .and had not much bodily strength either —his blood-pressure is much too high and he is tired immediately if he runs fast a little..." His phenomena, she warned Price, seemed to be much weaker in summer than in spring and it would be best to arrange for a new series of sittings in the autumn.

"If Schrenck's theory is right," Dr. Walther offered some interesting suggestions, "that the forces used for the materialisation have something to do with superfluous sexual forces (generative powers), it might of course also be that both powers are strongest in rutting time (I don't know if that is the proper English word: I mean the time of germination, etc.) which is spring. . ."

In the meantime Price had to defend Rudi's mediumships against several attacks. The fact that Herr Amereller had accompanied Rudi and that he was an electrical engineer gave a certain support to the sceptics. "Naturally when you announce that you are convinced," one of them wrote to Price, "it does reflect a peculiar mentality, but a very usual one among occultists. Personally I doubt if you believe a word of it but use the fame of these mediums for the purpose of ordinary publicity. . .It is said that he (Rudi) brought over his control apparatus with him including the man to rig it up. . ."

This was quite untrue; Rudi had brought no apparatus and there was no reason to suspect Herr Amereller of aiding him. Amereller was more amused than angry at these accusations, pointing out that if *he* was a confederate, then Price and the sitters between whom he was placed were all accomplices, for they were all included in the electrical control of the circle. Amereller had co-operated with Schrenck-Notzing in the exposure of several mediums and was a man of unblemished reputation.

Meanwhile Rudi was more interested in playing football for the local team than in his reputation as a medium. He had enjoyed his

London trip. In a letter to Harry Price he thanked him for all "the kindness and understanding you have shown me." He asked for a little rest before discussing his return to London; he also had to consult Baroness von Schrenck-Notzing, who, with her husband, had been such a benefactor of the whole Schneider family.

All through the summer of 1929 letters passed between London and Munich and London and Braunau about arranging a second and longer stay of Rudi in England. Herr Schneider pointed out that the hot weather was bad for mediumship. Major Kalifius, the head of the circle which sat with Rudi in Braunau, explained that the boy had to make his way in "normal life" and wanted to find a secure job which he could take on after his return from London.

Though Harry Price was annoyed about the delays, he did not press the Schneiders, and Rudi was more delighted with scoring six goals out of the winning eight of his team than with the long articles the world's press was publishing about him. In July he celebrated his twenty-first birthday with a "jolly fun party". Early in August Dr. Walther reported that the young man was intending "to give up mediumship anyhow. . ." But he must have changed his mind for the long negotiations continued. Herr Schneider refused to let his son go to Stockholm for a series of sittings and invited Harry Price to visit Braunau and discuss the London trip. Price couldn't make the journey and a great many letters were exchanged about Major Kalifius who was supposed to accompany the young medium and stay in London for the first two weeks until Rudi had become used to the surroundings and the new sitters. This was "Olga's wish" and Dr. Walther warned Price not to disregard it. Baron von Schrenck-Notzing, she said, had done so once and all phenomena ceased forthwith until the Baron propitiated Rudi's "control".

Harry Price did not take her seriously but he could not betray his doubts or show his sceptical attitude openly to Rudi and his family. To them "Olga" was a very real person who took part in their daily life, influenced their decisions and whose presence was always felt (whether the Schneiders entered into this make-believe sincerely or with some mental reservations remains an open question). Price had to accept Olga: "we propose to have two séances weekly unless Rudi would be willing or desires to have an occasional extra one. Perhaps Olga would direct us in this matter." No quotation marks; Olga had to be treated as an actual and very much "alive" person. And when Rudi arrived in London on November 13, 1929, for his two months' stay, he was accompanied by Major Kalifius—as "Olga" had demanded. He gave twenty-two séances during this period.

"Most of them," wrote Harry Price in his *Leaves from a Psychist's Casebook*, "were productive of the same brilliant phenomena and all were held under the merciless electric control which I had imposed at the previous series of experiments. During the latter part of the experiments I divided the séance-room into two portions by means of a fine mosquito-net; the note-taker was on one side of the net, the medium and sitters were on the other. The latter were really in a sort of large net cage, each person being electrically connected up in a series with a number of red lamps, which were extinguished if anyone moved hand or foot. Under these conditions we obtained the most magnificent phenomena..."

Once again the papers were full of Rudi's name. Once again there were attacks and counter-attacks, letters to the press and lectures. On November 29, 1929 Mr. Noel Maskelyne, the famous magician, challenged Rudi Schneider to produce genuine psychic phenomena, offering £100 to Charing Cross Hospital if he succeeded "under test conditions imposed by us." Harry Price who had earlier issued a formal challenge to the *World's Pictorial News*, offering £1,000 "to any conjurer who can repeat the phenomena under similar conditions," now wrote to Maskelyne, turning the tables rather neatly on him:

"Now, sir, I am just as anxious as you to find fraud," he wrote, "If it exists. I am therefore going to ask you, in a friendly spirit to help me find it.

I extend to you an invitation to come to the National Laboratory of Psychical Research (the time to be mutually arranged) and produce the following manifestations under the identical conditions as we have imposed upon Rudi:

1. A steady mass of fog or vapour is to appear at the opening of a pair of velvet curtains, hanging our séance room.
2. From this cloud a human hand (or something resembling it) is to be produced. This 'hand' shall pick up and throw a handkerchief, after which both the 'hand' and the 'smoke' (I refrain from calling it teleplasm) shall disappear.
3. The 'smoke' is again to be produced, and from it two arms (or

foggy terminals—call them what you will) are to grow; then the two 'feelers' (or shall I call them pseudopods?) shall pick up a waste-paper basket and hold it above the heads of the sitters. All this to take place in clear red light.

4. Lower the temperature of the cabinet as registered by Negretti & Zambra's instruments, produce cool breezes developing into a wind. (These manifestations have actually occurred with Rudi Schneider as medium.)

So much for the phenomena. Now as to yourself, acting as a medium, you will be required to pant like a steam engine throughout the experiment, and your pulse rate will have to read as high as 112 beats per minute.

You will not be permitted to bring an accomplice. You will be searched before and after the experiment; the séance room will also be searched, both before and after the séance, for machinery or other apparatus. You will be required to wear the writer's pyjama suit. You will be held hand and foot on a chair at a distance of five feet from the curtained cabinet, your hands and feet will be encased in metal coverings, through which a mild current will pass (have no fear, you will feel no shock!) By means of these electrical controls a series of tell-tale lamps will disclose any effort on your part to break contact.

If you can, under these conditions, produce the phenomena that I have specified, I shall then know one very important fact, viz. that the phenomena can be simulated by some method of legerde-main. Up till now I have failed to find any such method—and I have tried very hard, believe me! . ."

Mr. Maskelyne replied that it was up to Rudi Schneider to prove his genuine powers, if any, and not up to him to reproduce the phenom-ena. Sir Arthur Conan Doyle entered the battle—which developed into a series of challenges and counter-challenges—taking up the cudg-els on Rudi's behalf. The basic controversy was simple enough. The conjurers claimed that they must be allowed to test Rudi Schneider in their own way and prove to their satisfaction that he was genuine. Harry Price replied that the young medium had been tested by dozens of scientists—what was questioned was the magicians' statement that they could produce the same phenomena. It was a complete deadlock.

In December 1929 Price made one last dramatic attempt. He went to the Coliseum where Noel Maskelyne was putting on a "magic act" called "Olga". The psychical researcher managed to get on the stage as a member of the "committee" to control what he described as "a very old principle of trap-door effect dished up in a pseudo-psychic dress." When the act ended, Price walked up to the footlights and, stopping the orchestra, addressed the audience for five minutes. He explained the work of his laboratory and told the story of Rudi's mediumship; then he repeated his personal offer to Noel Maskelyne if he came to the Laboratory and duplicated Rudi's phenomena, under the same conditions and before the same independent group of investigators.

Price's unexpected appearance on the Coliseum stage was widely reported in the newspapers; but the deadlock continued. "Mr. Price wants Mr. Maskelyne to try to reproduce the Schneider phenomena," one newspaper wrote, "under the conditions which have been imposed on Schneider. Mr. Maskelyne wants Mr. Schneider to reproduce the Schneider phenomena under conditions imposed by Mr. Maskelyne. Neither shows any disposition to give way."

But apart from the sceptical magicians, serious scientists like Professor A.M. Low though Rudi "worthy of every possible consideration." Major Kalifius returned to Braunau after the first fortnight. The Schneiders were delighted to find that their son enjoyed London. Herr Schneider asked Price to "find Rudi some work in your laboratory after the Major's departure so that he should not be bored and feel homesick." Dr. Walther wondered what the sceptics would say when phenomena were produced without any of Rudi's so-called "confederates" being present—as some of the finest phenomena *did* occur after Kalifius had left.

Those who attended this second series of séances—they included Shaw Desmond, the novelist, T.H. Pierson, of the American S.P.R., Lord Charles Hope and Dr. C.M. Joad—all thought Rudi's powers genuine. And Price gave him an enthusiastic testimonial in the name of his Council:

"It is with very great pleasure," he wrote in January 1930, "that I hereby certify that during the experiments which we have conducted with a view to ascertaining the present status of your mediumship, we have arrived at the considered conviction that we have witnessed absolutely genuine phenomena at these séances under conditions of control which defy criticism. You have submitted to every form of control which we imposed upon you and have never questioned our methods or reasons for any experiment. You have cheerfully placed yourself in our hands in order that we might arrive at the truth concerning your powers."

The Schneiders were delighted with this praise—and so was Rudi.

*   *   *

Rudi returned to Braunau in the third week of January, 1930. In April, accompanied by his parents, he gave a series of sittings in Prague which produced good results. In October he put himself at the disposal of the Institut Métapsychique in Paris and remained fifteen months in the French capital. A detailed report—"*Les Pouvoirs Inconnus de l'Esprit sur la Matière*" was published in 1932 by Eugene and Marcel Osty about these experiments. Most of them concerned the study of telekinetic phenomena. Tactual control was used instead of the Price-Schrenck-Notzing electrical system and the experimenters utilized the well-known apparatus of directing rays from the infra-red end of the spectrum through a filter on to a photo-electric cell—the method of measuring the amount of energy in a beam of light. When the beam is obstructed (and the amount of interference can be measured by instruments) a relay comes into operation, an electrical circuit is closed, and the current can be utilized in different ways—firing a magnesium flash for taking photographs or ringing a bell.

The chief drawback of the elaborate and costly infra-red installations —as Harry Price and others pointed out—was the fact that the beam was open and unprotected; it guarded the object to be operated upon, but did *not* guard the medium or the sitters. If the medium was able surreptitiously to release a hand or foot and intercept the rays in any way (or if any sitter did the same thing) it would have the same effect on the beam and on the instruments as if a "psychic body" had obstructed it.

Dr. Osty and his colleagues claimed that they had discovered the existence of an invisible "something"—a psychic "force", "energy" or "power" externalized by the medium which affected the infra-red rays. Price and others expressed their regret that Dr. Osty had not adopted the electrical system which they had used, tested and believed in. This led later to an angry and prolonged dispute. Price was much upset by a letter Dr. Osty sent him about the latter part of the Paris séances (the fifteen months were interrrupted by Rudi's various holidays) in which the French scientist hinted at the possibility of an accomplice who was aiding Rudi's apparently fading mediumship. This mysterious "X" was a young and charming Austrian girl, Mitzi, with whom Rudi had fallen in love and to whom he was now engaged to be married. Strangely enough (or perhaps not so strangely for this was happening often enough in psychical research) Dr. Osty did not mention the girl at all in his report and maintained that Rudi's phenomena were both more impressive and more genuine than the good doctor himself believed. Price kept his own counsel about Osty's private warning. Late in July he went to Braunau accompanied by Miss May C. Walker, Mrs. K.M. Goldney and Miss Ethel Beenham, his secretary. They had one séance at the Schneider house and signed a statement which was also signed by Dr. Gerda Walther who had travelled from Munich to join them.

"For the first time at any Braunau sitting," the statement said, "an attempt was made to secure an absolutely fraud-proof séance as regards the Schneider family. Every door and window was sealed by means of brass staples, string and knots sealed with a signet-ring. Father Schneider was locked a prisoner in his bedroom and the keyhole covered with adhesive plaster. The undersigned, Gerda Walther and Frau Bauer then individually controlled the three members of the Schneider family. Phenomena of a most brilliant character were obtained under our very noses and as far away as ten feet from the medium. A large 'snow man' phantom was observed by several present, water was splashed out of a basin, a handkerchief was knotted and another was taken out of Miss Walker's hand by a pseudopod, curtains were knotted, a dish was several times removed from the table, etc. We, the undersigned, are convinced that the phenomena were of supernormal origin."

Price, however, found it very difficult to persuade Rudi to come to London again. The young man wanted to settle down, get married and work at his trade. And if he was to visit London, he wanted to have Mitzi with him. There were long negotiations—Rudi demanded more money than he had received during his first two visits. In two of the angriest letters he ever wrote, Harry Price protested violently to Herr Schneider: "Years ago you used to pride yourself on the fact that both Willi's and Rudi's mediumship were not exhibited for money—but for science. Now, apparently, Rudi is selling himself to the highest bidder. If Rudi is so anxious to make money out of his mediumship, why does he not go on the music halls?"

Finally, after Rudi had spent another period at the Institut Métapsychique and had come under attack by Professor Nils von Hofsten of Upsala University (who had had two sittings with him in 1930), the young medium wrote a humble letter of apology to Price. Price replied in a friendly, forgiving manner and at last new terms were arranged for his third London visit. Mitzi was to accompany him; both were to be guests of the National Laboratory for Psychical Research and he was to receive £10 weekly in addition. He undertook to stay no less than three months in England and, if it was so desired, to remain another nine. There were to be at least two séances per week. Fifteen days before Rudi's arrival, Price received Dr. Osty's confidential warning about the medium's "confederate". In his reply he called it "very disturbing" but he was confident that he and his associates could keep an eye on the young lady and prevent her interference. Dr. Osty emphasised that Rudi himself had never done anything suspicious, and though the phenomena had been feeble, the Paris researchers had not regretted the time and money spent on the long investigation.

Rudi and Mitzi reached London on February 29, 1932. They stayed until May 6 and Rudi gave twenty-seven séances. It became evident that his powers were beginning to fail—that, like so many physical mediums he had exhausted that reservoir of occult power which he possessed and which seemed to be of a definite limited amount. This time the electrical control was discarded because Price wished to use the automatic photographing apparatus which he had devised and a new form of infra-red detector. Instead of the metal overshoes and gloves, the medium was controlled by hand—two people holding his hands and his legs being gripped between the legs of the first controller.

Although the results were less brilliant than before, "apparently good phenomena" were witnessed and some remarkable pictures were secured by the automatic electric camera. But at the twenty-fifth séance, held on April 28, 1932, a distressing incident occurred. This is Price's account of it:

"Three cameras were in position, and when, on the day following the séance, I developed the plates automatically exposed the previous evening, I received something of a shock. One of the cameras in the electrical circuit failed to make instantaneous contact with *one* of its *two* Vaku-Blitz bulbs, so that the bulbs fired one after the other, thus taking two superimposed and consecutive photographs on the same plate. The plate in the overhead stereoscopic camera was fogged by the light of the flash striking the lenses. The stereoscopic camera at the side of the counterpoise table revealed the fact that Rudi had managed to free his left arm and put it behind his back. The photograph shows it sticking straight out behind him. The handkerchief had been snatched off the counterpoise and dropped to the right of it. . .Before Rudi could get his arm back into control again the flash—or rather flashes—ignited and recorded the incident. . ."

This was one of the incidents fairly common in psychical research where two sides contended bitterly over the elusive truth. Price believed that Rudi had cheated or tried to cheat. Others, who had attended the séance maintained that, as one would expect, Rudi had been startled and jerked violently at the vivid photographic flash. Price, also jerking, had loosened his hold on Rudi and Rudi's arm had flown outwards as the second photograph showed it. It seemed that he had not used his arm to remove the handkerchief, since it would have been difficult if not impossible for him to do this with the arm farthest away from the counterpoise table.

When Price confronted the young man with the evidence, having developed the three plates in his presence, Rudi could offer no explanation. He first said that it must have been a "spirit" arm—but as it was wearing a pyjama jacket identical with the one Rudi usually wore at the séances, this was hardly likely. In the end he was silent under the charge of having cheated.

The situation was complicated by the fact that Lord Charles Hope and some other members of the research council had decided to form a separate group to investigate Rudi after Harry Price had finished with him. This made Price angry. But after Rudi left London, they still continued to correspond and there was considerable discussion about another series of séances. Then, more than a year after the ill-fated April 28th séance, Price published his report. This led to a violent argument with the usual charges and counter-charges, resignations and bitterness. Rudi came once more to London and gave fifty-five sittings for the committee of the Society for Psychical Research in 1933-34. These, at least according to Price, did not produce a single phenomenon. Price's side of the argument was strengthened by Professor K. Przibram of the Vienna *Institut für Radiumforschung* who provided a lengthy account about having caught Rudi cheating as early as 1923-24. Others spoke of a "mixed mediumship"—common enough—and this was Price's own view. "As far as physical phenomena are concerned, the Schneider boys are the sheet-anchor of psychical research," he wrote in 1939, long after the dispute had died down.

As for Rudi, he married his pretty Mitzi, became a prosperous garage-proprietor and gave up all thought of occultism. According to recent reports he still lives in Braunau. He must feel happy to be all but forgotten because his life—and his brother's—proves what an uncomfortable situation it must be to become a producer of psychical phenomena, whether real or faked.

★　　★　　★

CHAPTER FOUR

Stella: The Gentle Maiden

ONE DAY early in 1923, Harry Price, the British psychical researcher was travelling from London back to his home in Pulborough and found himself sharing the compartment with a young, slim, pretty girl. Price had a pile of newspapers and magazines at his side. The young lady had apparently exhausted her reading matter. He offered her his evening paper which she refused—but asked whether she could look at the copy of *Light*, the spiritualist paper, which he had also bought.

This led to a conversation during which Price asked his travelling companion whether she was interested in psychical matters. The girl replied that it was a purely academic interest. Her only experience of anything occult was an occasion when she attended a spiritualist circle in her home town. She was eleven—and she had to be removed because she was seized by an irresistible fit of giggling.

But, she added—and this made Price sit up—there had been certain things that had puzzled her. What kinds of things? asked Price. Well, two or three times a year there were sudden strong breezes in the room she happened to be in—even though the weather was quite calm or the windows closed. Small objects moved by themselves—as if someone or something shifted them about. There were raps and occasional flashes of light. She added that the "breezes" nearly always occurred when there were flowers near her. She was passionately fond of flowers. Sometimes as she sat writing or reading at a table bearing a vase of flowers, a strong but gentle breeze would sweep across the room, fanning her cheek and bending the blooms.

This had happened on a hot, still night, when there was not the slightest ripple in the atmosphere—or in the depth of winter with every door and window tightly closed.

There were strange, telekinetic phenomena as well. Sometimes, when Stella was about to touch a box of matches, the box would suddenly jerk itself away from her as if it had been flicked by the finger. Raps occurred on her bedstead and in various parts of her room. The rarest of the phenomena were the "lights". On two or three occasions she had been mildly startled by slight, percussive sounds, accompanied by blue sparks. As she described them, Price thought that they were strangely like the sparks produced by the electrical discharge across the points of a Ruhmkorff coil.

All this seemed to have little or no effect on Stella. She thought them strange but felt little concern about them. She was perfectly happy in her chosen career—a hospital nurse and dispenser—and had never before talked about her unusual experiences.

Harry Price listened to her story with deep interest and mounting excitement. He was convinced almost at once that he had made a real discovery—that Stella was a great potential medium. It had always been his ambition to find a "psychic subject" before the full development of his or her psychical faculties, to watch the growth of the phenomena and direct the "emanations into predetermined channels for experimental purposes."

He explained to the girl his work and his purpose and he did not find it difficult to persuade her to co-operate.

The first series of sittings began shortly afterwards, on March 22, 1923 and consisted of thirteen séances ending in October of the same year. Price made careful preparations for registering any temperature changes, checking the medium's pulse rate and temperature, arranging for the proper lighting (mostly red illumination), for careful recording of the phenomena. The sitters included members of the London Spiritualist Alliance and of the Society for Psychical Research, barristers, authors, journalists—all of them, including Price, complete strangers to the medium before the experiments started. Dr. E. J. Dingwall, the Research Officer of the S.P.R. attended three séances; Dr. V. J. Woolley, the Honorary Research Officer, two. Among the sitters were Miss Nellie Tom Gallon, the novelist and Mrs. E. J. Garrett, herself a remarkable medium—both of these ladies were present throughout the series. Price was attacked for using incense at the sittings but he defended this by saying that its use was "probably advantageous not only as a harmonizing element (like music) but because Stella was particularly fond of its perfume and used to burn it in her own home." Price did not suggest that this was helpful in the production of phenomena; but it pleased the young girl which was his constant aim. Also, the burn-

Stella C

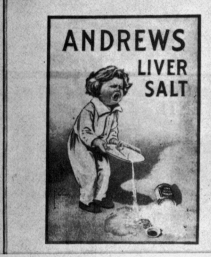

Copy of *Daily Mail* May 19th 1923 which Stella "read" five weeks before it was published

The inner gauze cage of the "double cage" table showing the musical toys that were "activated" by Stella

ing incense might have had the same effect upon Stella as the scent from the flowers which seemed to have provoked the spontaneous telekinetic and other manifestations.

At the very first séance, attended by seven people, they obtained a remarkable set of phenomena. They discovered that Stella, like most mediums, had a control. It was called "Palma"—and apparently it was an "intelligent entity". It followed requests and moved a heavy oak table, weighing $43\frac{1}{2}$ lb, in accordance with the directions given to it. Several sitters felt distinct vibrations through the woodwork; the table became violently agitated, it reared on two legs and rapidly moved across the room. All the time the medium's hand and feet were tightly controlled. Another remarkable feature of the séance was a rapid drop in the temperature.

Similar phenomena occurred at the second séance, held a week later with six sitters. The vibrations were present during the whole of this sitting "alternating with a peculiar pulsating or tremulous effect, as if the table were imbued with life." The table was in a state of almost continuous motion; it was completely levitated at least six times.

Another curious phenomena, noticed by all sitters, was the dimming of Mrs. Garrett's left hand—"as if a heavy shadow had fallen across it." All the sitters' hands were lightly placed flat on the table, all were visible, all received the same amount of illumination. Yet Mrs. Garrett's left hand became gradually obscured by some substance (some suggested it was teleplasm) and just as gradually the shadow or "substance" passed away. Raps were heard which were later used to obtain intelligent answers to various questions; the so-called psychic breezes were experienced by all the sitters; it became noticeably cooler during part of the sitting—something which the thermometer also recorded, showing a fall of 11.5 degrees below the normal temperature.

The third séance was also attended by seven people; the table levitated three times, the temperature dropped again. The heavy table was changed for a lighter one—and this showed even more remarkable movements, once rising completely above the heads of the sitters. The manifestations then became really violent:

"The lower platform of the table," Price's record reads, "struck the chin of Mr. Price (who had remained seated, and had lost contact), and came to rest on his chest. The sitters then removed their hands from the table, only the finger-tips of the medium remaining upon it. Movements of the table still continued. The sitters again placed their fingers on the table top, when still further power was developed with increasing violence, two of the legs breaking away from the table with a percussion-like noise as the fracture occurred. At this juncture Mr. Pugh (one of the sitters) excused himself and the séance continued without him. Colonel Hardwick, Mrs. Pratt, and Mr. Price still retained their fingers upon the top of the table, which was resting on the remaining leg. Suddenly, without warning, and with a violent snap, the table top broke into two pieces; at the same time the remaining leg and other supports of the table crumpled up, *the whole being reduced to what is little more than matchwood*. The sitting then concluded."

No wonder that at the end of the sitting the participants all complained of exhaustion. A psychic force that could reduce a hexagonal deal-table to matchwood was much to contend with! "It was an extraordinary sensation," Price wrote, "to feel a strong wooden structure crumpling up beneath one's hands; the table appeared to melt away."

Perhaps the most successful sitting of all was that of April 12, 1923, (with seven sitters). Curious movements of the table (the shattered three-legged one had been replaced by the earlier heavy one) were observed, and answers were obtained by raps to questions. About half-way through the séance, Stella became very sleepy. At the questions of one of the sitters, Miss Phillimore, she suddenly proceeded to describe a newspaper—the front page of the *Daily Mail* with the date "*May* 19 1923" clearly visible. She could also see in large letters the name "Andrew Salt." In addition she had a "sensation" of seeing a boy falling, and a man who appeared to be a doctor bending over him and pouring a white powder from a bottle or tin which he was giving the boy. The details, like all the particulars of every séance, were duly recorded but nothing was done about this "vision". Then, thirty-seven days *after* the sitting, the *Daily Mail* appeared, carrying on the top half of its front page a large advertisement for *Andrews Liver Salts*, a patent medicine.

There were ten definite points in which Stella's remarkable prediction was correct: (1) The Daily Mail, (2) the date, (3) the name of the company—at the séance it was thought that it referred to a man named "Andrew Salt," whom nobody knew among the sitters, (4) the name of the article, (5) the "large letters," (6) the boy, (7) the "falling" or "letting fall"—the illustration accompanying the advertisement showing a small boy spilling some liver salt, (8) the "tin", (9) the "white powder," (10) the "being poured out." Price added an eleventh: the suggestion of a "doctor" standing behind the boy looked very much like a *symbolic* visualisation of the medical nature of the article advertised.

Of course, immediate steps were taken to investigate the circumstances of this strange event. The Andrews people declared that they had prepared the advertisement *after* the date of the séance. As a matter of fact, it was substituted fairly late for another layout they had intended to use. Their advertising department was in the North. Stella never had any contact with them and knew nothing of Andrews Liver Salts or individual newspapers. The affair created very considerable interest in the *Daily Mail* office, too. There was an immediate editorial conference to decide what action to take. The editor finally wrote to Harry Price that he was "quite convinced by the evidence submitted," but that if he were to have the case written up, ninety per cent of his readers would put it down as an "advertising dodge."

It was one of those peculiar, inconclusive, mysterious incidents that crop up now and then in psychical research—tantalising and baffling because it seems to be without purpose. The sceptics might well ask, why, of all things, a medium should "see" seven weeks in advance a patent medicine advertisement—and if she did, why couldn't she "see" the result of a race or the outcome of some important event in world politics? But mediumship just does not work that way. It is as if the veil of Isis may be lifted only haphazardly and then show but a tiny, chance fragment of the future—a pin-hole view through an opaque curtain stretching into infinity.

This was but one incident in the long series of sittings. The fifth sitting was remarkable for the renewed violence of telekinetic action and an extraordinary drop in the temperature; the table (heavy and awkward) was hammering at Colonel Hardwick's knees with quite painful blows until he removed them. "I consequently. . .expected the table to crash to the floor. My knees were still red from the blows when I got home some two hours after. . .To my surprise, the table did not go beyond the position where my knees would have been, but it made one or two smart blows as if to ensure that they had been removed. . ."

Quite an aggressive force at work and a somewhat mischievous one! By this time it was established that Stella's control, "Palma" was a child—so perhaps this may explain her playful attitude but not the violence of the movement.

At the sixth séance, with nine sitters, the first "apport" was recorded—a large sprig of lilac, in full bloom, with leaves and flowers quite fresh, fell upon the table, striking two of the sitters. "The nearest lilac," Price recorded, "was in a vase in the library, on the floor beneath. The door of the séance room was locked and no one brought any lilac into the room. But about an hour previous, a vase of lilac had been removed from the séance room, and placed in the library, and it is possible that a piece of the blossom had been left in the room. If this be so, no explanation is forthcoming as to how it apparently fell from the ceiling on to the table top. The hands of all the sitters were visible all the time..." There were the usual movements of the table, followed by raps and a "bright blue electric flash", repeated six times, above and near the medium. A new control named "Hendras" manifested itself, explaining that "it" was helping "Palma."

The seventh séance had eight participants. On this occasion it was decided to ask the "control" or entity at work to manifest upon a number of musical instruments, writing pad and other objects. A handbell was moved, a mouth-organ was played repeatedly, there were again blue and yellow flashes. For the first time at any sitting, the medium became completely entranced. And as she did so, the phenomena also became more diversified.

For the next séance, with nine sitters, a new table was devised by Mr. H. W. Pugh and control of the medium and the sitters considerably tightened. The "Pugh" table was

"actually two tables—an inner and an outer, the inner table being quite incapable of being levitated except by some force applied beneath it. It is physically impossible for any of the sitters to raise this inner table from its upper surface; and to stop any manipulation from the underside, the inner table is surrounded by four trellis gates which prevent the medium or sitters from approaching it in any way. These four trellis gates form a cage in which various articles are placed previous to the commencement of a sitting. The inner table has a trapdoor (in its top), eight inches square, the hinged flap of which is flush with the surface of the table, and is incapable of being opened except by an upward pressure from within the cage..."

On the first occasion when the new table was used the first phenomena were cold breezes, followed by the mouth-organ being blown in the cage, an autoharp's strings were struck twice, the mouth-organ and the trumpet were blown, the hinged flap in the centre table was opened and closed several times, the rattle was thrown out of the cage, a rubber dog was handed out of the trapdoor by the invisible "force" at work. Price noted that the use of the "Pugh" table seemed to stimulate the "force" responsible for the phenomena; the trap-door proved very effective and a decided attempt at materializing hands or "pseudopods" was made.

At the ninth séance—with nine participants—Price used for the first time an instrument of his own invention which he called the "telekinetoscope". This was a brass cup, mounted on a metal tripod with levelling screws and had a turned-in flange. Around the periphery of the cup, stamped in the flange, were twelve small holes. Placed loosely inside the cup was a contact-maker made of thin sheet fibre, connected with two brass strips to which the leads (composed of best rubber and silk insulated flex) were fastened. The whole was mounted on a thick rubber base.

The contact-maker was made of fibre in order to minimise the area of metallic surfaces which were thought to inhibit the psychic "force". A narrow strip of thin metal was fastened round the contact-maker connecting, by a piece of pure tin fuse-wire, to the brass screw holding the fibre slip. When the contact-maker was placed in the brass cup, a soap bubble (composed of distilled water, glycerine and Castile soap) was drawn across the top of the cup, effectively sealing it. In this condition it was normally impossible to depress the contact-maker (thus completing circuit) without destroying the bubble. As a further precaution—and to prevent the bubble drying too rapidly or bursting spontaneously—a glass shade was put over the whole of the instrument. Under favourable conditions it was found that the bubbles lasted some hours. The small apertures around the periphery were the only means by which the psychic force or power could enter the cup and, if possible, depress the contact-maker the spring of which could be adjusted to any degree of sensitivity. The whole instrument was put inside a cage in order to register, if possible, the presence of psychic power. The recording part of the apparatus—a small red four-volt pea lamp, enclosed with its battery under a small glass shade, securely sealed to a wooden base taking the flex leads—was connected with the cup by wires and placed on the table in full view of the sitters. It was absolutely impossible to make an electrical circuit and thus light the red lamp, unless the contact-maker in the cup was depressed. To do this normally meant the removal of the covering shade and the breaking of the sealing soap film—two safeguards that were impossible to overcome by fraudulent means without at once telling the investigators that the apparatus had been tampered with.

And yet twice during the séance the small red bulb was lit up. Cover and bubble were examined immediately and found to be intact.

"I have no explanation to offer as to how the psychic power found its way into the bubble." Price wrote, "and became powerful enough to depress the fibre contact-maker. Normally, it takes a two-ounce pressure to do this. Certainly, no solid body could have penetrated the instrument and worked the indicator. . ."

At the tenth séance—with a dozen people participating—several new pieces of apparatus were tried. This time the "entity" did not make use of the impressively named telekinetoscope but there were raps, the mouth-organ was blown, the handbell rung inside the cage, various objects were moved; there were flashes and "Palma" spelled out Dr. Dingwall's Christian name (it was the first time he had attended these séances). Dingwall, the Research Officer of the S.P.R., a noted sceptic, issued a separate report, describing the "pseudopods" he saw under the medium's chair and séance table.

"When the red light was switched on under the table," he wrote, "I lay down on the floor and looked through the passage towards the luminous screen. From near the medium's foot, which was invisible, I saw an egg-shaped body beginning to crawl towards the centre of the floor under the table. It was white, and where the light was reflected it appeared opal. To the end nearest the medium was attached a thin white neck like a piece of macaroni. It advanced towards the centre and then rapidly withdrew to the shadow..."

The Shadow Apparatus, used first at this sitting, was designed to see, if possible, shadows of the psychic structures or telekinetic forces responsible for the movement of objects placed in the cage under the séance table. It consisted of a projector, a light filter and a special screen upon which the shadows were thrown. During the séance it was found that the objects, which had been focussed upon the screen, had been moved right out of the pencil of light. A little later a shadow of a short structure, like a lead-pencil, was seen upon the screen. A so-called pressure flap was also constructed and used to measure the finer air pressures caused by the entity or psychic force when it blew a mouth-organ or trumpet. This, too, was very successful.

At the next sitting Stella was unwell yet several phenomena were observed. This was the last of the first series of séances; Price's contract with Stella had come to an end. She was exhausted by the weekly sittings—again and again in the record there is mention of her tiredness, her excessive pulse-rate, her shivering fits—and she was a little frightened by her own powers. "I felt so very queer last evening," she wrote to Price in June 1923, "that I paid another visit to the doctor. He has advised me to rest for a day or two." In July 1923, there was some discussion of her going to America under the auspices of the *Scientific American* and Price tried to find her a suitable companion as he could not go himself. He also approached a number of hospitals to get Stella a position as a nurse as she had lost her former job. The American trip came to nothing. Price was abroad a good deal during the summer and lost touch with his "discovery". It was then that Dr. V.J. Woolley, the Honorary Research Officer and a member of the Council of the British S.P.R. approached him with a view to continuing the experiments at the rooms of the S.P.R. Woolley and Price agreed to collaborate.

Having returned from Warsaw where he had attended a congress of psychical researchers, Price had a difficult time persuading Stella to give more sittings. While he had been abroad, she had found a secretarial post with a firm of manufacturers (she had received only a token payment for the séances); but after a while, she agreed to another series.

This consisted of two séances. At the first (the twelfth Price had with the young girl) there were seven people present; the "Pugh" table was used with a powerful red light, much brighter than at previous sittings and closer to the séance table; all sitters were plainly visible. The Shadow Apparatus was placed in position, showing clearly the shadow of a trumpet on the luminous screen.

"Palma" produced many raps and creakings in various parts of the table. A message was then obtained by Price spelling out the alphabet and "Palma" giving a rap at the appropriate letter. It said: "*Stella knows Munn she will leave.*" It was then asked whether the word "*Munn*" was intended for the name of the proprietors (Munn & Co.) of the

Scientific American. "Yes" was spelled out. This was accepted as another clairvoyant manifestation—for Stella, though she knew of the American negotiations (they had not yet been abandoned at this stage) had never heard the name of "Munn". "Palma" also imitated various raps given by Price and other sitters and even the "sawing" noise Dr. Dingwall produced. "She" obviously had a sense of humour, too, for when Price asked whether she could name the thief who had on the previous day stolen some of his collection of gold coins, she rapped out: *"Dingwall knows hide I don't."* Needless to say, this was not taken seriously by those present. Nor was "Palma", of course, right about Stella's American trip which never materialized.

The thirteenth sitting had only six participants apart from the medium. Raps and creaks in the table were frequent; then, without warning, the shelf or upper platform of the inner table gave way with a rending sound. Two notes upon a wind instrument were given—coming from the "G" tube of the pitch-pipes placed beneath the table. There were bright blue-white flashes and the Shadow Apparatus showed the shadow of the trumpet moving from its noted position on the luminous screen. Again, "Palma" imitated the various raps of sitters. At nearly the end of the sitting, a rubber dog was removed from the floor under the table where it had been placed and was somewhat violently flung across the séance room, striking Dr. Woolley and Dr. Dingwall in its path. The medium's hands became extremely cold during her trance and when she awoke, she complained of being very cold and sleepy.

Perhaps the séances were too much for her; perhaps she did not like the new surroundings—in any case, shortly after this séance Stella wrote to Price and told him that, however much she regretted it, she could not go on. Her employment fully occupied her time and she felt that the séances were too much of a drain on her energy.

Price summed up his first series of experiments cautiously but positively:

"If Professor Richet, after thirty years of incessant application to the subject, is unable to find satisfactory answers to the series of riddles evolved by psychical research, I have no inclination to theorize concerning the phenomena we saw. The spirit hypothesis is as good as any, and may prove the correct explanation when the laws governing phenomena are known. . .At least these Stella experiments have absolutely proved, beyond cavil or contradiction, that the temperature of the séance room falls during the psychic exudations of some mediums; also, that the power of 'force' in an attenuated state, is able to permeate a soap film and exert its strength to a pressure of at least two ounces. These two facts we have proved by instrumental means."

Modest conclusions indeed, and, if we except the vision of the *Daily Mail* advertisement, there was little "sensational" about Stella's mediumship. I have described the first thirteen séances in some detail just because it seems to me that in spite of the lack of "shattering manifestations", hers was a remarkable mediumship. Control was as perfect as possible and though the vexed question of "*I* haven't been there, why should *I* believe it?" could be raised (as with any supernatural or extrasensory phenomena), this is, indeed, the only objection that can be made.

★ ★ ★

In his "Stella C.", Price wrote: "Though I do not, like Stella, possess the power of prevision, I feel certain that some day she will come back to us. She will receive a warm welcome. There is a vast amount of work still to be done, and many experiments left unfinished. I am positive that with a sympathetic environment, and with suitable sitters, Stella could produce the whole *gamut* of psychic phenomena."

In December 1925 Price met her again. Stella had become engaged in the meantime but continued working for a Clerkenwell firm of manufacturing silversmiths. By late January 1926 she had accepted his suggestion to start another sieries of séances. Just before they began in February, she wrote to him:

"I thought I would like to write to you and thank you for taking an interest in me again. You know that by starting the sittings it will help me a great deal. I am sorry I was so ungrateful to you the last time but you have given me the opportunity to make up for it now. I thought at first you only asked me to come back because everyone else was keen and you thought it might look queer if you did not and candidly I was surprised to find you meant it. I have come to the conclusion that I badly misjudged you. . ."

She was a very sensitive girl and perhaps she did feel that she had let her "discoverer" down when she ended their connection rather abruptly. The first of the new series of séances was held on February 10 1926. I have studied the original reports in the *Harry Price Library;* they have been drawn up on forms beautifully printed in two colours and apart from the number of the séance, Stella's name in large red letters, the date, place and time, contain entries for temperature at start and finish, the health and pulse of the medium, the nature of the experiment, the weather, the period during which the medium was entranced, the sort of illumination, the list of the sitters and finally ample space for a detailed description. Price was eager to establish a general pattern for séance reports rather than use the haphazard recording of less professional organisations.

The description of the first séance of the new series might show how systematically and thoroughly this was done:

SITTERS

Position in Circle, commencing clock-wise from left of Medium: Harry Price, Lord Sands, Dr. Fielding-Ould, Dr. Urquhart, Mr. E.W. Janson, Major Peters, Mrs. Mallus, Stella, Miss Lucy Kay taking notes

DESCRIPTION OF SITTING

This sitting was the first of a new series given by Stella, after a lapse of nearly three years. The above list of sitters does not represent the permanent Circle, but was hastily called together in order that the medium could get used to the new surroundings and the unfamiliar séance room. The ordinary table of the séance room was used (weight about 60 pounds) in order that any power available could manifest by movements of this article of furniture. It is not intended that table shall form part of the apparatus to be experimented with.

The medium seemed very bright and cheerful at this sitting, and she appeared to be much more interested in the proceedings than when the séances were abruptly broken off in October 1923, the 13th sitting having been held on the 14th of that month. Only one sitter (Harry Price) of the present Circle had previously sat with Stella. This fact alone did not help to produce conditions conducive to the production of phenomena.

Stella was not entranced at any period of the séance; on the contrary, she seemed particularly interested in the proceedings. She afterwards stated that she felt very sleepy.

No alteration from normal was apparent in the temperature of the séance room. The telekinetic movements of the tambourine and table were interesting, occuring as they did in a ·fair light (a 60 watt bulb). No other experiments were tried.

What happened at this first séance, was by no means sensational. The table slid away from one sitter towards another; the tambourine rocked and fell, the table "moved incessantly" for two minutes, cymbals clinked, the tambourine moved and fell again and there was violent motion of the table. The control throughout was strict and the medium had no possible access to any of the objects.

At the second sitting, a week later, there were some good but weak phenomena and the raps recommenced. This time Stella was entranced for about fifty minutes. A cage table was used again into which various articles—a luminous bell, a mouth-organ, a celluloid trumpet, rattle-bells, a rubber squeaker and an auto-harp—were placed. The trapdoor of the cage was sealed with paper strips and sealing-wax. The luminous objects within the cage were on a level with the eyes of the sitters. During this second séance the bell moved several times, there was the usual "psychic breeze" and numerous raps answering questions, posed by Susan, Countess of Malmesbury who identified one of the "entities" present as an old spirit-friend named Erica. The third séance of the new series was remarkable for brilliant blue flashes—about four feet from Stella—and incessant raps. The fourth also produced some "very fine flashes of a blue-white nature" but the raps were very infrequent and weak. It was discovered that Stella gave a convulsive shiver just before the occurrence of each flash and Price thought that this was "compatible with the theory that the flashes are the sudden release of energy taken from the sitters and stored up by the medium." The outstanding features of the next séance were the playing of the zither harp and mouth organ inside a new isolation chamber which was carefully locked and sealed, the large brilliant blue flashes both inside and outside the cabinet close to which the chamber was placed. The mouth organ was played in different chords; one sitter had her comb violently removed from her hair and it was flung across the circle. The next sitting was attended by Professer Dr. Hans Driesch, President of the Society for Psychical Research and his wife. The control was as usual and once again there were telekinetic movements within the isolation chamber, the sealed mouth-organ was blown several times and brilliant blue flashes were produced—once at request. Harry Price did not attend the seventh séance, being away in Paris; during it the mouth-organ was almost incessantly blown; for a while it kept time with Weber's *Oberon Overture* which was played on a gramophone record; rhythmic raps also "joined in" the performance. The flashes and the telekinetic movements of various objects were repeated at the next two séances.

It seemed that the phenomena could be controlled and developed to a certain extent—that if the psychic "force" was given directions —definite tasks to perform or objects to work on—it would do its best to please the sitters. Price made a point of varying the control of the medium lest anyone could charge him with collusion. Yet at the tenth séance of the new series brilliant blue flashes occurred *inside* the cage into which the usual musical toys had been put; repeated attempts were made to levitate the *inner* table and the luminous bell was ringing continuously inside the cage table. During the next séance the isolation chamber was rocked from side to side, knocking the floor loudly; the flashes of light were excellent though less frequent. The twelfth sitting was almost entirely negative, only producing some faint raps. After it there was a gap of about a month because of the medium's illness and the next sitting, held late in May 1926, an extremely hot day, brought the phenomenon of a clearly discernible drop in the temperature as soon as Stella became entranced. Raps, musical notes, movements of bell and table, the shadow of a large hand passing in front of the red light were some of the manifestations. On the next occasion a scarf was repeatedly moved and so was a zither inside the cage; several of the sitters felt cold breezes.

In June two séances were held which were attended by Dr. R.J. Tillyard, F.R.S., the chief entomologist to the Australian Government, who had co-operated with Harry Price in various investigations. He also conducted a special test séance at which only he, his wife and Stella were present. Raps and telekinetic movements were observed and a distinct lowering of the temperature was noted. Dr. Tillyard was greatly impressed, and in a long article published in *Nature* expressed the opinion that Stella's powers were genuine and deserved the most careful scientific investigation. After the first June séance, Miss Mercy Phillimore, the secretary of the London Spiritualist Alliance, wrote to Price: "There seemed to me to be a tremendous lot of power about. I felt far more than I have ever felt before. In the earlier sittings I remember recognising the presence of power, but yesterday there was a personal sensing that was new to me." A staunch Spiritualist—the Alliance's President was Sir Arthur Conan Doyle—Miss Phillimore nevertheless approved of Price's stringent control measures. "Stella is indeed unique," she wrote in the same letter, "in being so free of fads and perfectly quiet and willing to do all that is required of her. . ."

In August Stella again refused to act as medium but she gave some séances in the next year—1927—chiefly to help with the thermal experiments which Price wanted to conduct in order to discover whether the "cold breezes" experienced during séances with some mediums were a physical and not merely a physiological effect. By installing a delicate recording thermometer, he established that any sudden changes in temperature "appeared to synchronize with violent telekinetic displacements." He claimed that some psycho-mechanical power must have been responsible; some small portion of the kinetic power dissipated itself in displacing the metal index in the tube of the thermometer, independent of the cooling of the séance room. Later experiments confirmed this view.

In March 1928, just before her marriage, Stella agreed to a final series of séances. Nine sittings were held between March and July and a panel of scientists (including Professor Julian Huxley, F.R.S., Professor E.N.da C. Andrade, F.R.S. and Dr. R.J. Tillyard, F.R.S.) was formed to take part in the experiments. Dr. C.E.M. Joad, Lord Charles Hope (who financed this series of sittings), Dr. E.B. Strauss also took part in some of them. Many manifestations were again witnessed under excellent conditions of control—though it was evident that Stella's powers (as with most mediums) were after these many sittings growing weaker or her interest in psychical research was getting less.

But even so, the phenomena, if weak, were good. Lord Charles Hope, in his report published in the *British Journal of Psychical Research*, stated clearly:

"Thus at three out of the last four sittings considerable phenomena were obtained, clearly denoting a supernormal origin. . .These phenomena, although not appearing to indicate the direction of any profound intelligence, yet did not give the impression of an uncontrolled force at work. The table was moved at times in a suggested direction, and raps denoting an affirmative or negative answer were repeatedly made either in or on the surface of the table. . .On no occasion were the musical instruments inside the cage played, with the possible exception of the squeaker (a rubber bulb with reed which, when pressed, emitted a musical note) which on two occasions was thought by Professor Huxley to have been sounded. . ."

The first séance of this last series (on March 24 1928) was marked by a curious incident. Many raps were heard. Dr. E.B. Srauss heard —or felt—two raps under his hands and the table jerked slightly. Again more raps and a "curious movement of the table was felt by Professor Huxley, Dr. Strauss and Mr. C.C.L. Gregory. Dr. Strauss and Professor Huxley felt a strange feeling up their arms." The official report went on: "At 4.41 Professor Huxley deliberately relaxed and nearly went into the trance state." The future Secretary General of UNESCO was probably himself a potential medium though unaware of it. The "strange feeling up their arms," reported by Huxley and Strauss was of an unfamiliar character and apparently not in response to any ordinary sensory stimulus such as parasthesia connected with cramp.

*   *   *

René Sudre, the eminent French writer and educator, described Stella as "a most gifted medium, who produced truly remarkable phenomena of telekinesis and even clairvoyance under conditions which Harry Price imposed and which were completely scientific." And Stella's mediumship was remarkable for many things quite apart from the phenomena she produced. She never wanted to become a professional medium— though she was paid a modest fee for her services —and had little interest in occult things. She had never been accused of cheating. She was one of the very few mediums in whose genuineness all the people who sat with her believed without reservations. She was never "temperamental", she did not demand any special ritual and made no stipulations. She gave Harry Price the first experience of mediumship tested under conditions *he* chose and evolved. The book he wrote about her in 1925 covered only the first series of sittings but he reported on the later experiments in various papers and devoted chapters to her in his various books. His detailed report was published in America, France and Germany almost simultaneously. When his book appeared, it was reviewed widely and appreciatively. Stella C. brought him the first serious success in psychical research and he remained grateful to her for the rest of his life.

Following the example of Dr. Gelcy and Baron Schrenck-Notzing, Price and his colleagues always referred to the "gentle maiden" as Stella C. Today, with Stella happily married and out of psychical research, there is no reason for this reticence. Her real name was Stella Cranshawe and she married a man named Leslie Deacon. Now in her early sixties, she may sometimes think back with nostalgia, though perhaps without regret, to the five years during which she worked in the séance room, in the strangely assorted company of convinced spiritualists and hard-headed, sceptical men of science.

★   ★   ★

CHAPTER FIVE

Laszlo: Goose Fat and Cotton Wool

NUMBER 3, Visegradi Street in Budapest, was a bleak, shabby tenement house. Several of its apartments were used as miniature *hotels garni* where couples could rent rooms by the day or even the hour.

The landlady of one of these transient "love-nests" rented one of her rooms to a young, pretty blonde and a man with dark, piercing eyes, a small moustache and thick, greasy hair, brushed back from a low forehead. He was in his early twenties and, like all customers, he paid in advance—for a tenancy of twelve hours, beginning at seven o'clock in the evening.

Shortly after the twelve hours had passed, the landlady was startled by the sound of two revolver shots inside the room. The door was locked but she summoned help and it was broken down. Inside they found the girl lying dead and the young man unconscious with a chest wound. The couple had been lying on the sofa with the girl on the outside; it was she who had fired the two shots. The second had pierced her heart while the first had gone straight through her left shoulder and had seriously (though not fatally) wounded the young man.

The young man was taken to hospital. The bullet was lodged in his lung and caused interior bleeding; for several days he could not be questioned. But the police found letters in the shabby room and established the identity of the couple. The dead girl's name was Emmy Knis, a secretary aged nineteen; the boy was called Laszlo Laszlo, a bizarre enough name (the Hungarian equivalent of Leslie Leslie). He was about twenty-two and had a long police record.

The suicide pact caused a great sensation in Budapest; most of the papers published long articles about the dead girl and her Laszlo. He had recovered consciousness only to say that he was a playwright whose latest work had been accepted by the Hungarian National Theatre. This, like so many of Laszlo's statements, turned out to be untrue. Several startling facts were established. Emmy Knis and Laszlo had

This photograph of Laszlo Laszlo is reproduced from a Hungarian Newspaper (1926) printed throughout in Sepia. It is one of the few available photographs.

not been lovers; the girl was engaged to another man. It seemed that they were chance aquaintances who had met and decided to die together. Laszlo was said to have organized a spiritualist society; its members were university students, young artisans and a number of girls. Including Laszlo, seven members of the society had attempted suicide—and six of them had succeeded.

The years after the first world war were chaotic and hectic in Central Europe. Spiritualism and the various occult sciences degenerated into fads and crazes. Suicide had become an epidemic. Hypnotists and clairvoyants, fake mediums and religious fanatics flourished like luxuriant weeds. Laszlo Laszlo was one of the most characteristic representatives of a pathologically excitable, feverish and unbalanced generation.

★   ★   ★

Laszlo Laszlo was born of a working class family on 23 September 1898, in Budapest. His father was a locksmith. The boy grew up without much parental supervision; his schooling was haphazard and he spent much time reading cheap, fantastic adventure stories. He quit school when he was thirteen and was apprenticed to an electrician. His master treated him harshly and he ran away several times but his father had the police return him on every occasion. He was beaten regularly and learned little of his trade as he was mostly employed in household chores. When he finished his apprenticeship after three and a half years, he took his revenge—he beat up his master so brutally that the man was bed-ridden for two weeks.

He ran away again and for a couple of years worked steadily and honestly at his craft. He was sixteen and a fervent patriot when the first world war erupted. He volunteered for the army but was refused because of his age. Whereupon he recruited several of his friends; they bought uniforms from a theatrical costumier, altering them suitably, even acquired a flag and boarded a train from Budapest to the northeastern frontier of Hungary which the Russians were menacing from the Carpathians. At Maramarossziget, the capital of Ruthenia, they reported for duty to the C.O. of a front-line regiment. But instead of being enrolled in the army, they were handed over to the gendarmes who escorted them back to Budapest and delivered them to their respective parents. The escapade brought nothing but a good beating.

Laszlo went back to his work but his patriotic fervour remained unabated. In February 1915 he heard that a Polish Legion had been formed in Vienna to fight on the Austro-German side against the Russians. Once again he left his job and home and set off for the Austrian capital. This time he was accepted, went through a rather cursory and brief training period and within a few weeks entrained for Kolomea, in Poland. This was the headquarters of the Polish Legion and a further training period of eight weeks began. But Laszlo felt that he knew all about fighting and loathed the discipline of the base. He discovered that a regiment was being sent up to the front-line. He met a corporal with whom he became friendly and persuaded him to smuggle him on to the train. No one seemed to have noticed the extra recruit; Laszlo and the corporal were the only Hungarians in the unit and they became close friends.

In March 1915 they arrived at the frontier of Bukovina and Bessarabia (Poland and Rumania), marching through knee-deep snow to reach the front line. The first night Laszlo was sent on patrol and received his baptism of fire; his squad lost four men and several were wounded. But the young boy took it calmly; he seemed to have no fear of death. He was soon promoted to corporal and then twice decorated. He spent eleven months in the front line—his parents still had no idea where he was—until in February 1916 he was severely wounded and shell-shocked. He spent the next four months in hospital. Recovered, he was immediately returned to his regiment. He thought this unfair as he had hoped for leave and when he was detailed for a front-line company in Warsaw, he deserted. Hitchhiking, walking and hiding from the military police, he managed to get to Budapest. His parents who had believed him to be dead received him with more affection than they had ever shown before; but after two weeks he was picked up by the police and sent back to Ivangorod to the Polish Legion—and court-martialled. He demanded that he should be transferred to a Hungarian regiment and though he was threatened with being shot, he persisted. After a month in prison he was returned to Budapest, escorted by a Czech military policeman. But on the train he enlisted the help of several Hungarian soldiers (Czechs and Hungarians were at loggerheads in the Austro-Hungarian army) and together they overcame the M.P., Laszlo put his own shackles on his escort and then took him to the Budapest garrison command where he made a formal complaint about the "inhuman treatment" he had received at the hands of the Polish Legion. Though his story was not taken seriously, he was transferred to an Alpine unit and sent, in June 1916, to the Italian front.

For seven months he was in the Dolomites; promoted to sergeant, he was again twice decorated for conspicuous bravery. In January 1917 he was badly wounded by shrapnel and spent five months in hospital. He recovered completely and, in July 1917, he was given convalescent leave, returning to his parents in Budapest.

During his leave Laszlo met a girl of eighteen, an orphan named Katalin. He fell in love with her; she seemed to return his feelings and they became unofficially engaged. After his two months' leave was up, he was sent back to the Italian front. Another two months went by—but Katalin did not answer his letters and he was getting more and more uneasy and restless. Finally he deserted a second time and reached Budapest in November 1917. Katalin had given up her job as a secretary but the young man tracked her down and found that she had become a prostitute. He pleaded with her to give up her "life of sin" but she told him that this was the only way she could make a living. Laszlo, still in love with her, offered to support her until they could get married. But being a deserter he could not take an ordinary job. His parents helped him financially—but this was insufficient to provide for two people. So he joined a gang of burglars. The war was going badly for the Central Powers, the police were under strength, the capital was swarming with deserters and for a few months Laszlo and his friends had a rich harvest. Most of his share in the burglaries went to Katalin until Laszlo discovered that while she was constantly demanding money from him, she still continued as a street-walker, kept pimps on his earnings and deceived him regularly. Deeply disillusioned, he broke with her and started to drink heavily. The members of his gang were caught by the police and Laszlo himself was on the run. Katalin, furious because he had left her, denounced him and, after a violent struggle in a cheap restaurant, he was also arrested. He tried to commit suicide but was prevented by the detectives who beat him up and threw him into a cell. Once again he faced a court martial and escaped execution only because of his youth and record of bravery. He was reduced to the ranks, his decorations were taken away and he was sent to prison.

He spent eight months in a cell, in close contact with burglars and thieves. At first he refused to talk to them but gradually they wore down his resistance and even involved him in an escape attempt which failed. For two months he was in solitary confinement, heavily shackled until, late in October 1918, the liberal revolution in Hungary brought a general amnesty and he was freed.

He decided to go straight but this resolution did not last long. He joined another gang of burglars and crooks. His parents disowned him. In the troubled, chaotic months the gang's work was easy. Their loot was considerable and Laszlo led a life of luxury until April 1919 when he and another man were caught breaking into an apartment in broad daylight. His accomplice was caught—but Laszlo jumped from the second storey and had a miraculous escape. He was tenaciously pursued but managed to get away through an apartment house with two entrances.

For a few days he remained in hiding, then took a train to southeastern Hungary and joined a company which was fighting the Rumanians on the frontier. In the meantime Bela Kun's Communist *coup* had swept over Hungary. Laszlo became involved in an anti-Communist plot, was arrested by the Communists and sentenced to be shot together with forty other officers and N.C.O.s. Their execution was to take place early one morning but during the night before two White regiments stormed the town and freed the prisoners. Laszlo returned to the front and continued fighting the Rumanians until his unit was overwhelmed by superior forces. Most of them were taken prisoner and transported to the death-camp of Jassy where hunger and typhoid decimated them. Laszlo must have been very tough indeed for he survived three months' hard labour, beatings and starvation. At the end of this period he escaped with four others. Two of them died on the way but the remaining three managed to reach Szeged, the second largest city in Hungary, where it took several weeks of hospital treatment before they recovered from the ordeal.

After the collapse of the short lived Communist regime, Laszlo returned to Budapest. He hoped that his criminal record had been lost or forgotten (many of the archives had been burned) and he decided to make another attempt at an honest living. According to his autobiography, which he wrote in January 1924 (and which remained unpublished), he was actor, variety artist, film extra, author, playwright, electrotechnician, painter, book-keeper and general clerk in turn—a somewhat unlikely variety of occupations, some of which must have existed only in his disordered imagination. In any event, he kept out of trouble for almost a year.

One day he attended the performance of a music hall hypnotist and this led to his growing interest in occultism. He bought a number of books—most of which he barely understood—and decided to imitate the charlatans and fakers who were exploiting the rising tide of psychic fads and fashions. He organized séances—often in the homes of wealthy and distinguished people—and delivered lectures, rather ill-digested outpourings of mysticism and half-baked philosophy. He became a passionate believer in spiritualism.

★   ★   ★

After the death of Emmy Knis, the police and newspaper reporters probed into Laszlo's past. One journalist discovered that a young engineering student, Ferenc Horvath, had committed suicide about nine months before the shots were fired in Visegradi Street; he shot himself in a small restaurant and died at once. He left a letter addressed to his parents:

"Forgive me for causing you sorrow. I long for the Great Beyond; I am dying but I shall live on as a spirit. Dear father, I shall often appear to you—expect me on May 1 and June 1."

It was a characteristic document—the farewell letter of a confused, neurotic young man who really had no motive for suicide. Horvath's father accused Laszlo bluntly; "My son," he told the reporter, "was a decent, intelligent young man until he met Laszlo. But since then he talked of nothing but spirits; once his friends came to our home and wanted to hypnotise several people, including myself. Ferenc was a quiet, sensible boy but if we dared to argue with him about his beliefs, he became angry and rude. . .In the last few weeks he was in a terrible state of nerves, all he could talk about was the 'spirit world.' So I forbade Laszlo the house and told my son quite firmly to break with him —but they continued to meet secretly. . .until one day my poor boy shot himself. . ."

Another place where Laszlo organized séances and hypnotic experiments was a small resturant. Here he found an excellent medium in a girl called Kamilla Ferenczy who came from Transylvania. However, she refused to join him as a regular "séance partner" and later returned to her parents.

A few weeks after Horvath's suicide Laszlo shot *himself*—in a telephone booth. Apparently this had nothing to do with the spirit world but was the result of an unhappy love affair. In June 1920 Laszlo tried to board a fast-moving tram, slipped and suffered serious injuries. He spent two weeks in hospital where he met a pretty girl who was recovering from an appendix operation. Laszlo fell deeply in love with her but the girl paid little attention to his passionate declarations. One day he called her from a public telephone booth, demanded that she should agree to their engagement—and when she laughed at this, he shot himself. His aim was not good for instead of his heart he hit his shoulder. Once again he landed in hospital and it was here that he was visited by Emmy Knis. The girl had been a schoolmate of Laszlo's younger sister but there had never been any close aquaintance or sexual relationship between them. However, both had a highly emotional and morbid disposition; and as they exchanged their various experiences, they discovered a mutual inclination to suicide.

For the time being, however, Laszlo's affair seemed to prosper. After his suicide attempt, the girl he courted seemed to relent; she took him down to the small village near Lake Balaton where her parents lived and they became formally engaged. But after their return to Budapest, Laszlo received a summons—his attempted suicide had revived police interest in his past. He told his fiancée about his criminal record and she apparently believed that he was a reformed character —but the summons (which he ignored) preyed on his mind and he began to play again with thoughts of suicide. The girl he loved was very much upset and pleaded with him to give himself up. Once he got as far as the steps of Police Headquarters but lost his courage at the last moment and began to tramp the streets aimlessly.

It was then that he met Emmy Knis once again and they formed the idea of the double suicide. Characteristically, the girl wanted to wait until her dressmaker had finished a new dress—for she wished to die clothed in the latest fashion—and so they postponed it for a couple of days. Then, they took the room in Visegradi Street. For half-a-day they argued about how to commit the suicide, which of them should press the trigger, in what position they should die; in between they wrote half-a-dozen farewell letters, drank a bottle or two of sweet liqueurs and discussed "the problems of life and death." Once or twice Laszlo's resolution faltered and he began to plead with the girl to give up the whole idea; but she persisted—and finally, a few seconds after their time in the room was up, Emmy fired twice. She died from the second shot which entered the heart and Laszlo lost consciousness.

★ ★ ★

The thin, wiry Laszlo had a tenacious hold on life—for his condition improved rapidly. He was visited by his mother, his fiancée and the dead girl's mother all of whom made bitter reproaches. Laszlo, however, felt that he was not to blame—after all, he had tried to stop Emmy and she was the one who had been so grimly determined to die. Unfortunately she was dead and could not bear out his contention. On the fourth day he was arrested, charged with manslaughter—the indictment was having caused Emmy Knis's death by driving her to suicide through hypnosis. Laszlo was transferred to prison hospital. He felt so bitter about this that he tore off his bandages and reopened his wound. But his new attempt at self-destruction was discovered and he was placed under strict supervision. In two weeks he had sufficiently recovered to be transferred to police headquarters for questioning. The police established that apart from Ferenc Horvath and Emmy Knis three others, young men named Laszlo Kemeny, Sandor Markus and Ferenc Pal, had committed suicide—and all of them had belonged to Laszlo's spiritualist group.

It was characteristic of the post-war years that the police took the spiritualist elements of the case quite seriously. One detective, while questioning Laszlo, suddenly faltered, started to perspire heavily and told his colleagues:

"I can't stand his eyes. . .I don't know what's wrong with me. . . I can't go on—you'd better take over. . ."

Probably Laszlo had some rudimentary hypnotic powers and was quite ready to use them. The detective, an experienced, level-headed man, must have been a sensitive hypnotic subject without being aware of it.

Even stranger was the spiritualist séance *held at police headquarters* during the investigation. A spiritualist group led by Dr. Odon Nerai, a retired, high-ranking civil servant, offered its services to the police —and the police accepted. In the presence of two superintendents and the spiritualist group a séance was organized with Laszlo as the medium. Afterwards Dr. Nerai issued a statement which was distributed to the press by the P.R.O. of the Budapest police—one of the most extraordinary police releases ever made:

"Laszlo Laszlo has become the victim of a malevolent spirit who used to live in the thirteenth century and called himself Ramuntan. As the spirit told us, he suffered some great indignity while in the flesh and this he wished to revenge by driving a number of people to suicide. He attached himself to persons who could be influenced easily and persuaded them to end their lives. This was the case in the present instance where he used psychic force and all kinds of tricks both on Laszlo and Emmy Knis to destroy their will to live. Laszlo was being 'possessed' by Ramuntan and therefore cannot be held legally responsible."

This statement was taken quite seriously both by the police and the magistrate's court. Laszlo was kept for three weeks in custody; the charge of manslaughter was reduced to "participation in attempted suicide" and he was released without bail.

(In his autobiography Laszlo described the extraordinary séance in plain language: "A spiritualist séance was held and I acted the medium — or rather, the fake medium. I fooled them with a fantastic story by pretending that a so-called spirit was speaking through me. The main thing was that they believed me.")

After his release he broke off his engagement — he found his fiancée "unworthy of the love of a man who twice tried to die for her." This so unbalanced the young lady that she staged a *fake* suicide, leaving a letter in which she said that Laszlo had hypnotised her and suggested killing herself. Laszlo was arrested again but cleared of the charge. They never met again.

One of the Budapest dailies gave him a nominal job as a reporter and he published a few articles about occultism and spiritualism; half-illiterate, confused pieces. It was one of the editors of the paper who introduced him to the Hungarian Metapsychical Society and its president, William Torday.

William Torday, like Dr. Nerai, was a retired, high-ranking civil servant who became interested in the occult in the early years of the century. With a number of physicians, psychologists, scientists and interested laymen, he founded the Hungarian Metapsychical Society, modelled on the British Society for Psychical Research and other European organizations — though the Hungarian society had only modest financial resources and never more than a hundred members. It published monographs, investigated reported hauntings and other phenomena;

it had almost everything such an organization needed—except a medium.

This might be the explanation why the elderly, slightly deaf former civil servant became so deeply interested in Laszlo Laszlo—a young man with a long criminal record, an obviously unstable character with strong suicidal tendencies. He believed that Laszlo was a reformed man—and in any case, his "brilliant occult talents" seemed to be more important than any moral deficiencies. Torday and his colleagues gave Laszlo regular financial support; he signed a contract that he would not give séances to any other group or society. The experiments began a few weeks after Laszlo was discharged from prison hospital and continued for about a year. They were interrupted in 1922 when Laszlo was again arrested because of his earlier criminal activities, spent eight months in prison and finally received a retrospective sentence of seven months for attempted burglary so that he was immediately released. Between January and December 1923 he continued working with Torday's group—until the inevitable unmasking of a bare-faced, cynical fraud.

The "phenomena" which Laszlo produced were certainly impressive and of a considerable variety. Spirit heads and hands appeared, a so-called "rigid ray" moved various objects, there were acoustic and light phenomena, *apports* and other telekinetic manifestations. All were carefully recorded, sometimes photographed and solemnly discussed at the meetings of the Society. Public lectures were delivered about the "unique medium", elaborate theories built on his "powers". The final accolade came with the Budapest visit of Baron Schrenck-Notzing, the distinguished German psychical researcher who attended two of Laszlo's séances. Apart from the famous Baron, several university professors, the director of the leading Budapest mental asylum, a well-known medical hypnotist and other noted men of science and learning participated in the sittings. "Their names alone are guarantees," wrote one of the Budapest papers enthusiastically, "that there could be no trickery nor a case of superstitious hallucinations. The medium was completely undressed and was then clad in a one-piece bathing-suit. Control was so strict that on one occasion even a stomach pump was used on him. His hands, feet and head were held by the university professors; another distinguished scientist sat on the floor at his feet and watched every movement. . .In spite of this the most striking phenomena were produced. . .and everybody was completely convinced of Laszlo Laszlo's genuine powers."

Everybody? It is certain that until December 1923 when the scandal exploded, neither Professor Schrenck-Notzing nor anyone else made a public statement questioning the medium's *bona fides*. Yet Laszlo was cheating all the time—brazenly, audaciously and successfully. It is perhaps best to quote his own detailed confession as to how he did it:

"For the last five years I have been deeply interested in occult problems. I decided that by hook or crook I must learn all there is to know about these matters. I bought scores of books and spent day and night studying them.

Gradually I acquired sufficient information which enabled me to imitate things I had seen, reproduce the so-called phenomena. I familiarized myself with the proper behaviour of mediums and the activities of the spirit world. In those days I was a fanatical believer myself. Hardly a day passed without my attending a séance. I was invited to many circles but I was not yet myself a medium. Or rather —I was never really a medium. Later I was invited to a family séance where a young girl went into a trance. I knew very well what a genuine trance should be and I soon discovered that she was shamming —but I pretended to believe her. However, I was disillusioned by spiritualism. This became complete when I happened to find a slip of paper with the 'spirit message' which the medium had learned by heart and repeated like a parrot. I began to study the behaviour of mediums and discovered that they were mostly hysterical, fanatical creatures, suffering from self-deception and various psychological disorders. . ."

All this, however, did not prevent the "student of occultism" from accepting Dr. Torday's offer to train him as a medium and engage him for a series of experiments. In his confession he explained quite cynically how this happened:

"Several experts had declared that I was a medium. I liked to play this part and considered it as a sort of game. While the so-called 'experiments' began, I was given to read Professor Schrenck-Notzing's book which was full of photographs of innumerable 'materialisations'. This gave me the idea to imitate the phenomena. To be frank I never believed that such things could ever be genuine.

Dr. Torday told me that light phenomena were frequent during séances. I wondered how I could produce them and hit upon the solution by accident. I was working at the time as an electrician. Once I stood on a ladder repairing a faulty overhead cable which had to be freshly insulated. It was late in the evening and when I pulled at the insulating tape, I noticed that it gave a phosphorescent light in the dark. I compressed the tape to the size of a bean and hid it in my collar. My pockets were searched but that was all. During the séance I pulled at the tape and the phosphorescent light appeared. In order to provide some variety, I stood on my chair and repeated the trick with outstretched arms. The sitters were so impressed and frightened that they declared, the flashes of light had descended from the ceiling. When control became stricter and I had to undress before the séance, I hid the insulating tape in the armchair I was sitting on and afterwards when I dressed, I put it again into my pocket.

Let me explain why they never found anything on me. As soon as I arrived, before I was undressed and searched, I hid my bits and pieces either in the armchair or—which was hardly more difficult —in the pockets of my controllers. I used Dr. Torday, Professor Schrenck-Notzing and all the others as my living 'cloakrooms'. They were kind enough to act as depositories for all I needed and of course they never thought of searching *each other*. They were all so excited and expectant. And when I needed anything from their pockets, it was not hard to divert their attention while I retrieved it. I followed the same method during the séances. After exhausting them by long periods of waiting, it was child's play to distract them. . .''

The Metapsychical Society was especially proud of Laszlo's "versatility". In their report they called his "telekinetic phenomena exceptionally brilliant." Laszlo gave a full description of how he performed these "marvels":

"Once I lifted a vase from the top of a chest of drawers and threw it on the carpet. It caused great terror and amazement; though there were ten people in the room, no one noticed that it was a trick; they all called it a splendid example of telekinesis. On another occasion they all formed a 'magnetic circle' but I was left out of it. I asked them to count up to a hundred. I slipped under their linked arms, crawled to the far side of the room, took some flowers from a vase and carried them back to my place. When I threw the flowers into the middle of the circle, I was given full marks for another instance of 'miraculous telekinesis. . .'

One afternoon I walked along the Danube and happened to pick up a fair-sized pebble which had an unusual shape. I thought it would be a good prop for the next séance—as I had promised them something 'extraordinary'. Before the sitting I hid it in the armchair. They examined and undressed me, then made me change into a bathing suit. Naturally they found nothing. They also searched the armchair but rather superficially and did not discover the pebble. Then the armchair was pushed into the dark alcove, the lights were switched off with only a red bulb remaining. The curtain was drawn, I fell into a pseudo-trance, produced a convincing rattle, dug the pebble from its hiding-place, put it on my head and then stretched out my hands so that my controls on both sides could hold them. Then suddenly I swung my head and torso forward—naturally, the pebble flew into the middle of the room. At the clatter they put on the light and found the 'apport'. Immediately they declared that it must be of extra-terrestrial origin—that it probably came from Mars. Dr. Torday put it away under lock and key, hoping that it would not 'dematerialise'."

As the séances continued and Laszlo found that he was getting away with even the crudest trickery, he became more and more audacious.

"The door of my bed-sitter was squeaking and I had to oil it. This gave me a new, brilliant idea! I cut off the finger of a rubber glove, filled it with oil and fastened it with cotton thread, producing a small, air-tight container. As I was a passionate chain-smoker, I found it difficult to be without cigarettes during the long séances. I cut off the mouthpieces of two corktipped cigarettes and put them, with the striking side of a matchbox and four matches, into the same miniature parcel with the oil-filled rubber finger. I hid it in the bottom of Dr. Torday's armchair because I was given a cane-bottomed chair and could put nothing there. I had announced in advance that I would produce a 'liquid telekinetic phenomenon' and asked for a glass to be put into the alcove. During the séance I simply reached out and collected my parcel; I opened it and poured the oil into the glass. Then I lit a cigarette and set the paper cover of the parcel alight. It provided a wonderful flash of spirit-light! I managed to get rid of the ash and handed the second cigarette to Torday who put it away as further evidence of telekinesis. The oil was analysed and they found some mysterious 'extra-territorial' element in it. It must have been a little dust from the armchair. . ."

Another Laszlo "speciality" was the so-called "rigid ray". Again it was a crude trick he played on the "metapsychicians":

"One Sunday afternoon I went to an amusement park and noticed several young men playing with little paper balls fastened to rubber bands—I think they were called yo-yos. I bought one myself but lost the ball. While I was playing with the rubber band, I suddenly remembered the so-called 'rigid ray' of which Schrenck-Notzing had written at some length. At the next séance I presented this 'shattering manifestation'. I wound the end of the rubber band around a match and took it between my teeth. Holding the middle of the rubber band with two fingers, I also kept a hold of the far end. I had previously asked that a matchbox with a bent pin to serve as a hook at one corner should be placed on the table in front of me. In the darkness I managed to slip the rubber band around this hook and then lifted the matchbox in the dim red light. One of the men present tried to touch the rubber band but I released it and it recoiled to the match I held between my teeth. Naturally, the matchbox fell back on the table. The participants in the séance declared that the 'rigid ray' had returned, had become absorbed by my hand. . ."

One of the strangest parts in Laszlo's trickery was played by Attila Sassy, a talented but highly eccentric Hungarian painter. He seemed to find a sardonic pleasure in helping the fraudulent medium while at the same time pretending to Dr. Torday and his friends that he believed in Laszlo's powers. He drafted a number of mystifying letters, which he smuggled into the séance-room. In one of his letters he wrote: "You must be convinced by now that I can see and hear everything from my studio—that I know of all that happens in the sittings. Thus if I see from here that the spirit manifestations are to continue without a pause, even with increased intensity. I cannot allow any of the participants to think that I have a share in them. . ."

Sassy's pose was that of a "master seer"; actually he was playing a rather childish and unscrupulous game. In another "magic letter" he pontificated: "Laszlo Laszlo's mediumship is mysterious. It is propelled by the same dynamic force which imbued the medium of Schrenck-

Notzing and especially that of Prof.Crawford. We are faced with phenomena which we must register. The observations of several outstanding spiritualists were beyond doubt free of fraud." Sassy foretold that two hands would materialize at one of the séances and he described the "telekinetic pebble" without having been present. The members of the Metapsychical Society were duly impressed by all this "occult" knowledge until they discovered that the eccentric painter—whose works included a series about drug-addicts and one about "denizens of the spirit-world"—had a "spy" at the séances who immediately afterwards gave him a detailed report; Sassy wrote his letters the same night and managed to catch the last post at Budapest Central Post Office so that the letters were delivered next morning giving the impression that they had "passed through the fourth dimension."

All this was childish enough; but Sassy enjoyed playing the role of the puppeteer, pulling the strings of both the trickster and his victims. Laszlo himself made it quite clear in his long confession:

"In Schrenck-Notzing's book I also saw some 'materialized heads'. I went to Attila Sassy's studio and studied the technique of his portraits, especially the eyes. I asked him for some pastel chalk which he readily gave me. At home, on a thin, fine piece of linen I drew a portrait of Emmy Knis—I had a photograph of her so it wasn't difficult. I cut out the head and fastened a long piece of gauze to the bottom edge. I hid it in the usual armchair and when the red light came on, pinned it to the dark curtain behind me. The end of the gauze I slipped between my neck and my collar.

I gave the signal, a flash was used and they took a photograph of the 'ghost head'. Then I put back the whole thing into the armchair and retrieved it after I had dressed. . ."

After this séance one of Attila Sassy's friends, Dr. Eugene Stark, who had attended most of the séances, sent for Laszlo and told him that he knew all about his trickery; unless he stopped the fraud, he would denounce him. But Sassy who was also present, defended Laszlo and told him to continue with his "psychological experiments". When Dr.Stark protested, Sassy silenced him, saying that as Dr.Stark had acted as his, Sassy's "agent", he was an accomplice and he would be in a most difficult position himself if it came to a scandal. The painter was still playing the role of the "puppet-master". The séances continued and Laszlo now began to produce almost exclusively "ecto-plasmic materialisations."

"At first I used gauze which I soaked in water and then immersed in oil for several days. Later I ran out of oil and started to use goose-fat instead. I thought this would make it really *kosher*—even though I was a Roman Catholic. . ."

(Orthodox Jews in Hungary invariably use goose-fat for cooking as pork-fat is forbidden by their religion and mutton-fat is unpopular. It evidently appealed to Laszlo's warped sense of humour to follow this ritual custom.)

"This proved to be perfect and I never had any trouble—nor would they have ever found out what I was doing if I had not decided to 'unmask' myself. I used to take the piece of gauze or cotton-wool from my accustomed hiding place and put it into my mouth. Then the curtain was drawn apart and they could all see the 'mysterious ectoplasm' hanging from my lips. No one ever dared to touch it because Schrenck-Notzing had warned about this in his book, saying that it might cause the death of a medium. In any case, I accompanied it with such horrible noises that the sitters all shook in terror. Some-times, as a magnanimous gesture, I would permit a light touch—but the 'ectoplasm' could not be grasped or torn; I screamed and moaned whenever I felt anybody was getting too inquisitive.

Through my 'spirit control' I asked for music at the séances—partly because I loved good music and partly because I was terribly bored. I also noticed that music provided inspiration for new and more original tricks. Once a famous violinist played in an adjoining room for a whole hour. I was delighted.

After each séance I hid the greasy cotton-wool in my pocket and then threw it into the river on my way home.

My fame as a medium grew apace and I made hands and various strange shapes to appear. But as control became more and more strict, I had to invent new tricks. I used both cotton wool and gauze; I hid my props in the pockets of the sitters. I even used Professor Schrenck-Notzing for a 'cloak-room' when he attended a séance (he had come to Hungary for this purpose alone); he was just as easily duped as the others though at first I was somewhat intimidated by him.

Whenever I needed my material I had hidden in the pockets of my dupes, I simply used my 'spirit voice' to call them into the alcove where in the darkness nothing was easier than to pick their pockets.

When Professor Schrenck-Notzing was present at the séances, he sat very close to me. I took the 'spirit heads' from his pocket. By that time I had learned most of his book by heart and was an accomplished medium. After he left Budapest, I began to get very bored with the whole comedy. I knew how other mediums worked, I knew that almost all of them were fakes and I wanted to put an end to the whole silly business. But at the same time I was afraid that the Metapsychical Society would be furious with me—I could not see any way out of my dilemma. It was about this time that Eugene Schenk, the well-known 'professor of telepathy and master-hypnotist' called on me and offered to go into partnership with me. He said that by joining forces we could make millions. I decided to make use of him. He actually helped me at one of the séances; but he was so envious of my success, that he went to the newspapers and told them about my cheating. Strangely enough, they did not believe him and his article 'unmasking' me was never published. . ."

Eugene Schenck, who made a good living as a music-hall hypnotist and clairvoyant, was furious. He denounced not only Laszlo to the police but also the journalists and psychical researchers who, according to him, had turned "shameless fraud into big business." In his letter to the police he wrote: "These gentlemen (the people who took part in the séances) were all decent, honest people, physicians, university professors, high-ranking civil servants—and it was just because they were gentlemen, well-meaning and somewhat fanatical about the occult, that Laszlo was able to mislead them. When I unmasked him, their blind belief was still so strong that they attacked *me*—instead of thanking me for having opened their eyes. . ."

Whatever Schenck's motives, after the first attempt he kept silent. And so Laszlo decided to "unmask" himself—at least that is how he put it in his long confession. He deliberately acted so clumsily that he was caught cheating.

In his confession, part of which he made publicly during a large-scale lecture arranged at the biggest concert hall of Budapest, he said: "It is no intention of mine to make the spiritualists laughing stocks or to harm them in any way. I'm sorry for any disappointment or unpleasantness I caused. I hope that Dr. Torday and the others will forgive me. . ."

★   ★   ★

They never forgave him. As soon as he was unmasked—or unmasked himself (for no two people agreed about the exact events) a storm of vituperation burst upon his head; and all the learned men who had for long months taken part in the séances without saying a word, came forward with detailed explanations of *why* they knew that Laszlo had been cheating. Dr. Torday wrote:

"It is difficult for me to deal with this painful matter at all as it brought such shattering and discouraging lessons for me. I would have never believed that a man could exist who asked for and accepted my support and help, my well-meaning trust with the greatest complacency —and at the same time, taking God's name in vain, deceived me with satanic cold-bloodedness and deliberation, dragging me into the morass of a terrible scandal. And I would have never believed either that another, highly intelligent gentleman who pretended to be my friend, would back this scoundrel out of hurt vanity and help him to play his despicable part—and even, when I once became suspicious of him, give his word of honour that he had no share in the other man's fraud! I am really nauseated when I think of all this —and I'm surprised that in spite of such sad experiences I am still optimistic about the future of mankind!"

The friend was Attila Sassy; but Dr. Torday had somewhat lost his sense of proportion when he practically despaired of humanity because of the trickery of an ex-criminal.

Professor Schrenck-Notzing published a pamphlet about Laszlo Laszlo a few months after the fake medium's unmasking.

"This fraudulent medium," the German psychical researcher wrote, "used various methods and as a practiced magician he loved to surprise. He was skilful in adjusting himself to any given situation and his audacity often involved him in the danger of exposure. . .While in the alcove, Laszlo could only cheat if his hand was somehow free. I immediately noticed the faulty control—whenever the curtain was closed which always happened at his request, his hand was from time to time released so that he had a chance to get out the objects he had prepared or to hide them again. If he had been seated outside the alcove or if his hands and feet would have been held from the beginning of the séance, no frauds of such magnitude could have occurred. He could never have worked them with his mouth and tongue alone. At the end of the sitting he often threw the tiny parcel under the desk or some other piece of furniture only to collect it later. This was possible because the séance-room was overcrowded with furniture.

The motives for the systematic frauds carried on for more than a year can be largely found in Laszlo's psychology. His psyche was not such an obedient, blind instrument as it was believed at first. Laszlo is a born psychopath, with a certain moral apathy, unreliable, egotistic, vain, mendacious, always in financial difficulties, easily yielding to bad influences, ready to rob others of any credit he could claim for himself, scribbling pathetic letters in a fantastic style, crammed with multi-syllabic words to his numerous 'fiancées.' Passionate in dreaming about wealth, unscrupulous in his ways and means. Now he glories in the role of a hero unmasking the spiritualists, explaining the materialisations phenomena, running to newspapers and making largely lying and contradictory confessions."

This was a classic case of hindsight; though Schrenck-Notzing had warned Torday before Laszlo's exposure about his doubts in a letter which the President of the Hungarian Metapsychical Society ignored. "As for the Laszlo-experiments," Schrenck-Notzing wrote, "I must accept unreservedly your methodical procedure, your scientific earnestness and unselfishness. But I definitely advise you against publication in the near future—the results are not sufficiently mature for this and certain details are obscure...The experiments are not convincing enough and show definite contradictions to other experiences..."

But of course Dr. Torday did not heed this warning; there are comparatively few psychical researchers who can keep quiet about a medium they discovered. Nor did he listen to Professor Edmund Németh, a well-known forensic expert who made a statement after the scandal exploded publicly:

"I warned William Torday already in October 1922 that the Laszlo-experiments were based on fraud. I even pointed out the methods which he used. Strangely enough I was never invited to a séance, though I had examined Laszlo as a medical expert when he was in prison. When Schrenck-Notzing came to Budapest, Professor Moravcsik was asked to be present and when he suggested that I should also be there, Torday refused—saying that I was not a *believer*. But is it not the sceptics who must be converted? I never heard of missionaries being sent to the Vatican! On the contrary, their work is always done among the pagans and idolaters. . .

I firmly believe that the mysterious substance called 'plasma' can be touched, torn off and put in your pocket. This cannot cause the medium's death. The effect can be fatal only in a single circumstance —if the medium suffers a stroke because he has been exposed as a fraud. I never heard of any medium having died because the plasma was forcibly removed. . .

I found especially interesting the trances of Laszlo—or rather the way he imitated them. Even a layman can establish from the trembling of a medium's eyelids that he is not in a trance. If Torday had invited me to a séance, I would have certainly seized the plasma. . ."

Professor Németh spoke as a thorough sceptic, denouncing even the experiments of Schrenck-Notzing and Richet, declaring roundly: "no supernatural matter can ever materialize—because no such substance exists and can only become tangible in the minds of sick, psychopathic people. . ."

Another professor of forensic medicine, Dr. Charles Minich, was equally scathing about Laszlo's mediumship. But not one of these experts had bothered to make a public statement until the medium had been exposed—or exposed himself.

The funny-bone of the public was tickled by one detail in the confused and sorry tale: the goose-fat in which Laszlo soaked his gauze or cotton-wool. Frederick Karinthy, the brilliant Hungarian satirist, wrote a long piece about it in one of the Budapest dailies. And while he made fun of the whole business, he also had some highly sensible things to say about mediums and séances in general:

"A spirit which insists on red Bengal light lit in its honour, must be suspected at once of turning out to be in sunlight cotton-wool soaked in goose-fat. It is probable that a true spirit would not occupy itself so pettishly and pompously with its own 'presentation'—but would rather try to prove by its actions and effects that it possesses extraordinary abilities; it would not exhaust all its efforts in proclaiming that he *is* a spirit and that the sceptics must accept him. To be frank, I believe—it is my feeling though I wouldn't like to swear to it—that a true spirit in certain moments (perhaps in the very moment of manifestation) forgets completely that he is a spirit; perhaps it imagines itself an ordinary living being and whistles gaily because it is happy that it can manifest itself. I didn't like this ectoplasmic spirit, its visage was very grim and solemn. It made a comic impression upon me. I had to laugh at it—because I never saw it laugh.

And I also had to laugh at the deadly serious awe of the believers; under its spell they did not notice this comic element; the unconscious comedy hidden in the *style*. To the expert eyes and ears this points far more convincingly than any objective proof to the source from which such 'phenomena' spring.

I wish that the explorers of the mysterious and supernatural powers would at long last believe me: the training, the education of sight and hearing leads us—if not as directly but far more certainly— to the centre of the labyrinth where the solution of the Riddle awaits us. Far more so than the so-called seventh sense which recognizes the spectre but is deaf and blind to the trickery of goose-fat and cotton wool. . ."

After the articles, the lectures, the interviews, the recriminations and "sensational disclosures" had their usual run of a nine-days' wonder, Laszlo Laszlo sank into obscurity.

It was almost ten years later that he made his last public appearance —in the dock. Together with a locksmith, a mechanic and a chauffeur, he was charged with burglary and house-breaking. The gang chose a large variety of places to loot—the famous mineral baths of St. Margaret's Island, the National Institute of Chemistry, a publisher's home, the home of the Swiss Consul General, the club house of the Harness Racing Society among several others. Laszlo's counsel asked that his mental condition should be examined. The hearing was adjourned for a medical report. Before it could be completed, Laszlo died of a lung haemorrhage.

The last time I heard Laszlo's name mentioned was during the London *Blitz* when, after a night spent chasing "incidents", a group of journalists gathered at the Press Club for a much-needed breakfast. One of our colleagues was in a farcical mood and discussed the effect of the Luftwaffe's attacks on the ghosts of London. He seemed to possess an unlimited fund of spirit-lore and soon we started to swap experiences, weird and ribald, mysterious or fraudulent. Suddenly he said:

"You're Hungarian, aren't you? I remember one of your mediums —must've been a marvellous fellow. He had a queer name—or rather, same first and last name—and I was told he could materialize not only human beings but the spirits of animals, too. A goose was the most successful, I believe. Isn't it a gruesome thought that every living thing has its spirit counterpart—insects and reptiles included! A bed-bug is bad enough 'in the flesh'—but just imagine a dozen or so ghostly fleas and ants torturing you!"

I did not disillusion him—I found something enchanting in the process that had turned Leslie Leslie's 'spirits', well-lubricated with goose-fat, into spirit geese. . .And if there *is* a spirit world, this sorry cheat, small-time burglar and fake mystic probably has a fine time of it, giving séances and "materializing" flesh-and-blood creatures for the delight and instruction of ghostly metapsychicians.

★　　★　　★

CHAPTER SIX

Eusapia: Watch Out or I'll Cheat!

IN 1893 THE *Bulletin of the Psychological Section of the Medico-Legal Society, New York*, published a detailed report on a series of séances (seventeen in total) which were held in Milan, at the home of Dr. Giorgio Finzi, the physicist. The participants included some of the most famous men of science of the late nineteenth century: Giovanni Schiaparelli, director of the Milan Astronomical Observatory who had discovered the "canals" of Mars; Carl du Prel, the German philosopher, author of four or five basic works on spiritualism, mysticism and the secret sciences; Angelo Brofferio, Professor of Physics at the Royal School of Agriculture, Portici; Dr. G.B. Ermacora and the host, Dr. Finzi; some of the sittings were also attended by Professor Charles Richet, the great French philosopher, historian of science and physiologist, winner of the Noble Prize in 1913, and by Cesare Lombroso, professor of medicine whose theories of crime and heredity were the most original if not the most enduring of his age.

The medium was a fat Neapolitan woman, just under forty years of age, called Eusapia Palladino. At the end of the sittings the distinguished panel issued a report with the following conclusions:

"In making public this brief and incomplete account of our experiences we must again express our convictions, namely:

1. That, in circumstances given, none of the manifestations obtained in a more or less intense light could have been produced by any artifice whatever.

2. That the same conviction can be affirmed in regard to the greater number of the phenomena taking place in darkness.

For the rest, we recognize that from a strictly scientific point of view our experiments still leave much to be desired. They were undertaken without the possibility of our knowing what we should need, and the instruments and different appliances which we were obliged to use had to be improvised. Nevertheless, that which we have seen and verified is sufficient in our eyes to prove that these phenomena are most worthy of scientific attention. We consider it our duty to express publicly our esteem for and gratitude to Signor Ercole Chiaia for having pursued for so many years with such zeal and so much patience, in spite of opposition and protest, the development of the mediumistic faculties of this remarkable subject, calling the attention of the studious to her having but one object in view, the triumph of an unpopular truth."

The statement was signed by Schiaparelli, Du Prel, Brofferio, Ermacora and Finzi. And the woman to whom this testimonial was given had aroused equal enthusiasm in scores of other scientists and occultists—since Professor Ercole Chiaia began to work with her in the eighteen-eighties.

There are a number of contradictory versions of her origins and early life. Eusapia herself told Dr. Hereward Carrington (who had a series of séances with her in Naples in November and December 1908) that she had been "an outcast since quite a little child", had been adopted by a family of friends and had discovered her mediumship accidentally at the age of fourteen. She denied indignantly that her first husband had been a conjurer—though she admitted that he was "connected with theatricals", familiar with stage mechanism and various trick devices.

Camille Flammarion, in his *Mysterious Psychic Forces*, says that Eusapia was born on January 21, 1854, in a village of La Pouille; her mother died in childbed and her father was assassinated by brigands in 1862. She married a Neapolitan shopkeeper named Raphael Delgaiz.

"She manages the petty business of the shop," Flammarion added, "is illiterate, does not know how to either read or write, understands only a little French. I conversed with her, and soon perceived that she has no theories, and does not burden herself by trying to explain the phenomena produced by her. . ."

Signora Paola Carrara, the daughter of Professor Lombroso, gave a striking character sketch of Eusapia whom she met at her father's house for the first time in 1907, when she spent two months in Turin.

"I always thought that her real personality is as interesting as her personality as a medium," wrote Signora Carrara, "and that it is the result of the strangest product which the human race can supply. . .

Eusapia is a mixture of many contrasts. She is a mixture of silliness and maliciousness, of intelligence and ignorance, of strange conditions of existence. Think of a saleswoman of Naples, transplanted without any preparation into the most elegant drawing-rooms of the aristocracy of Europe. She has gained a smattering of cosmopolitan intellectuality but she has also ingeniously remained a woman of the lower class. . .She has been carried on the wing of universal renown and yet she has never cast off the swaddling clothes of illiteracy. No doubt this. . .saves her from vanity, for she knows nothing of all the rivers of ink which have been spent upon her. . .

Her appearance and words seem to be quite genuine and sincere. She has not the manner of one who either poses or tricks or deceives others. She has had the perversity, a rare occurrence, to remain as nature made her: outspoken, sincere, instinctive, to such a degree that however wonderful may be the tales she tells, they are true. . . Her physiognomy is not ugly. . .Her face is large, marked by some suffering, and bears traces rather of the spiritistic séances, of the effort and the fatigue which they involve, than of the fifty-three years she has lived. . .She cherishes her appearance, or, at least, she shows some coquetry about it. She has magnificent black eyes, mobile and even diabolical in expression. . .She displays coquettishly her famous white lock among her dark hairs. . ."

(This "famous white lock" was something of a trade-mark. Eusapia claimed that when she was about a year old she was dropped by her foster-mother and a hole was made in her head. This was the cranial opening from which, in moments of trance, a cold breeze was supposed to issue. On the scar a tress of hair grew that, the medium maintained, had always been white, since her infancy.)

"Her hands are pretty, her feet small," Signora Carrara added in her sketch. "She always keeps them visible outside her dress to show that they are closely shod in polished shoes."

Though she had given occasional private séances for many years and had systematically been tested by Professor Chiaia, Eusapia did not become known to the wider public until in August 1888, Chiaia published an open letter in a Rome newspaper, addressed to Professor Lombroso. Lombroso had been highly sceptical of all occult phenomena and considered all mediums cheats, without a single exception. Chiaia now challenged him to have some séances with Eusapia Palladino

—claiming that the great expert on physiognomy would soon become convinced of her genuine supernormal powers. It took almost two and a half years before Lombroso agreed to have these sittings. Apart from him, Professor Tamburini, Signori Gigli, Vizioli, Ascensi and Ciolfi also took part in two séances which were held in Naples in February 1891. These were still the early days of psychical research; methods and controls had not yet been developed. But though the séances were held in complete darkness, Signor Ascensi (who had received a signal from Professor Tamburini) managed to get close to the medium and strike a match unexpectedly. Its brief blaze showed a small bell vibrating in the air, then falling upon a bed about six feet behind the medium.

Harry Price or Professor Schrenck-Notzing would not have been satisfied with the lack of illumination and the very brief glimpse of what was going on. But Lombroso, four months after the séance, apologised for his past doubts; he wrote in a letter: "I am filled with confusion and regret that I combated with so much persistence the possibility of the facts called Spiritualistic. I say facts, because I am still opposed to the theory. . ."

In other words, he was convinced that at least some of the phenomena Eusapia had produced were genuine—but he could not swallow the explanation or the theory that would account for the phenomena. And indeed, this is a very hard decision to make for any scientist. At the second Naples séance Eusapia was bound with ropes but in spite of this there were various telekinetic phenomena, together with raps and "spirit" touches.

Lombroso's "conversion"—for Eusapia's followers and the spiritualists hailed it as nothing less—awakened the interest of other European scientists and the committee, headed by Professor Schiaparelli, met in Milan for a long series of sittings. Apart from those already mentioned, Professor Buffern and D.D. Home's friend and kinsman-by-marriage, Nicholas Aksakoff, also took part in some of the séances. The most striking phenomena (in full light) were levitations of a table and the alteration of the medium's weight in the balance. The levitations were partly photographed and the committee tried to duplicate them under the same conditions as imposed upon Eusapia—but without success. During the experiments in varying her weight, Signora Palladino "diminished her weight by at least 8 kilograms-$17\frac{1}{2}$ lbs. . .We are certain that she threw nothing away. . .and equally certain that she derived no support from any neighbouring object. . ."

These results were not considered completely convincing; but the "spirit" touches and raps were. Charles Richet who did not sign the committee's report, declared cautiously:

"Absurd and unsatisfactory though they were, it seems to me very difficult to attribute the phenomena produced to deception—conscious or unconscious—or to a series of deceptions. Nevertheless, conclusive and indisputable proof that there was no fraud upon Eusapia's part, or illusion on our part, is wanting,—we must therefore renew our efforts to obtain such proof."

When the Schiaparelli report was published (and it was translated into many languages) Eusapia was invited to various capitals and centres for séances. The first of these were held at Naples in 1893 under the direction of Professor Wagner, of the University of St. Petersburg. The Russian zoologist seemed to have been completely convinced of Eusapia's genuine powers; but his critics pointed out, a little unkindly, that he was extremely short-sighted and also hard of hearing—not the ideal observer of psychic phenomena. However, it was Professor Wagner who arranged Eusapia's visit to Russia some time later.

In 1893-94 another series of sittings was held in Rome directed by the two Polish investigators, Dr. Julien Ochorowicz and M. Siemiradski. Movements of objects without contact, touches by invisible hands, luminous apparitions and auditory phenomena were "vouched for" by the investigators; the later séances in Rome were attended by Professor Richet, Baron von Schrenck-Notzing, Professor Lombroso, Professor Danilewski (University of St. Petersburg) and Dr. Dobrzycki, director of the Warsaw *Medical Gazette*. Dr. Ochorowicz invited Eusapia to Warsaw—which has always been one of the centres of psychical research—where forty séances were held. Here, again, the numerous participants, recorded as "genuine" partial and complete levitations of the séance table, movements of objects without contact (witnessed by more than a hundred people), touches and visible hands, levitations of the medium onto the table, luminous phenomena, abnormal marks upon paper, "exteriorization of sensibility" and instances of clairvoyance.

By now Eusapia's "control" had become familiar. "He" was a person named John King. When Signora Carrara asked her about this spirit "guide", Eusapia told her:

"That is the strangest part of my story, which many persons will not believe. At the time when I began to hold spiritistic séances in Naples, an English lady came there who had married a Neapolitan, a certain Damiani, a brother of the deputy, who still lives. This lady was devoted to spiritism. One day when she was at the table, a message came to her informing her that there was in Naples a person who had lately arrived, who lived at such a number, in such a street, and was called Eusapia, that she was a powerful medium, and that the spirit who sent this message, John King, was disposed to incarnate himself in her and to manifest by marvellous phenomena. The spirit did not speak in vain, for the lady at once sought to verify the message. She went directly to the street and the number indicated, mounted to the third floor, knocked at the door and inquired if a certain Eusapia did not live there. She found me, though I had never imagined that any such John had lived either in this world or another. But almost as soon as I sat at the table John King manifested and has never left me since. . ."

Certainly, John King was accepted by all who sat with Eusapia— as a polite convention (as the "controls" or "guides" of Stella C., the Schneider brothers or of other mediums were accepted). Dr. Ochoro-wicz considered "him" a "subliminal creation of the medium"—a sort of reflex of her unconscious thought "which has the capacity of ex-ternalizing itself in space, and producing real, objective effects in the physical world."

The Warsaw experiments were hailed as highly satisfactory by their organizers. Somewhat naively, the Polish researchers referred to the several improvised or "unofficial" séances which "strangely enough, restore the forces"—while the official séances, under strict scientific conditions, only "irritated and exhausted the medium." Yet Ochoro-wicz thought that "the objective character of the facts was proved beyond all reasonable doubt."

Four séances were held in the same year in Professor Richet's house on the Ile Roubaud: the participants were Sir Oliver Lodge, F.W. H. Myers (both later to be Presidents of the British S.P.R.) and Dr. Ochorowicz. The island was owned by Professor Richet and the possibility of any confederates was excluded by locking doors and windows and holding the séances when all the servants had retired. There were, indeed, few mediums who could boast of such distinguished "clients", of attracting such a galaxy of scientists and psychologists. Sir Oliver, in his report, faced up squarely to the problem of mixed mediumship in general and Eusapia's special attitude in particular:

"I happen to have had only good sittings with Eusapia," he wrote, "and my own experience of what was likely to happen in the others was based upon what happened when she was not entranced at all. Judging from that experience, I thought it not unlikely that she may sometimes somnambulicly attempt to achieve effects which she thinks desired, in what may readily appear a fraudulent manner. Later experience with sittings of a less uniformly successful character, though it has not so far verified that conjecture, leads me to supplement it with further opinions—(1) that it must be possible, by sufficient precautions, to check such attempts, even if made; and (2) that if undue latitude were given, it would be reasonable to expect some such attempt sooner or later. . .All danger of unfair accusation will be avoided if sitters will only have the common sense to treat her not as a scientific person engaged in a demonstration, but as a delicate piece of apparatus, wherewith they themselves are making an investigation. She is an *instrument*, whose ways and idiosyncrasies must be learned, and to a certain extent humored, just as one studies and humours the ways of some much less delicate piece of physical apparatus turned out by a skilled instrument maker. . ."

For the experiments in his island home, Richet had constructed a table, measuring 39 inches square, and 39 inches high. It weighed 44 pounds. At the first séance it was levitated completely. "As soon as Eusapia touched this heavy table," Richet wrote in his *Thirty Years of Psychical Research*, "with the tips of her fingers, it tilted, swaying about, and without the legs being touched at all, it rose up completely with all four feet off the ground. All hypotheses that attempt to explain this by normal mechanics are absurd." And Lodge, seeking an explanation of all he had witnessed, added: "Instead of action in a distance in the physical sense, what I have observed may be said to be more like vitality at a distance—the action of a living organism exerted in unusual directions and over a range greater than the ordinary. . .The effect on an observer is usually more as if the connecting link, if any, were invisible and intangible, or as if a portion of vital or directing energy had been detached, and were producing distant movements without apparent connection with the medium. . .The result of my experience is to convince me that certain phenomena usually considered abnormal

Eusapia Palladino

do belong to the order of nature, and, as a corollary to this, that these phenomena ought to be investigated and recorded by persons and societies interested in natural knowledge. . ."

Eusapia often gave warning that a phenomenon was about to occur and on these occasions the observers redoubled their vigilance in controlling her. The ringing of a bell at a distance from the medium, movements of articles some feet away from her, the flight of objects, knocks, raps were among the phenomena witnessed by the eminent scientists. A peculiar feature of Eusapia's mediumship was that the telekinetic movement of objects often synchronized with violent muscular movements on her part. She groaned, she threw herself about, she trembled and shook—so that her control was far from easy and often needed considerable strength.

Sir Oliver made his report to the Society for Psychical Research in London; corroborative testimony was offered by Myers, by Professor Sidgwick and his wife who had attended some of the séances. Sir William Crookes pointed out the similarities between Eusapia's phenomena and many of those *he* had witnessed with D.D. Home. Certainly, Myers and the others were considerably impressed by the sittings at Roubaud. Myers arranged a further series of experiments at his own home in Cambridge. These were to be held in August and September 1895. In the meantime the Lodge report and the record of the Roubaud sittings had come under fire from Dr. Richard Hodgson, then Secretary of the American S.P.R. Though he had not been present at the Richet home, he had developed his theory as to the different ways Eusapia *could* have cheated and he harshly criticized the inadequate control methods. He thought that the medium could have leviated the table by a hook inserted under its edge and attached to a strap passing over her shoulders. All four of the participants in the Roubaud séances replied to Dr. Hodgson, declaring unanimously that his theories did not explain the larger part of the phenomena and that the manual control of Eusapia's hands was more or less complete and perfect.

Dr. Hodgson was invited to the Cambridge sittings. And these certainly provided ample argument for *his* view. There were few and uninteresting phenomena—and the lady from Naples was found again and again cheating quite brazenly. During the twenty séances the observers included Sir Oliver Lodge, John Nevil Maskelyne (the magician) and Mr. and Mrs. Myers. Dr. Hodgson purposely allowed the medium to free her hand—in order to see if she would cheat. And of course, she did! For Eusapia, with commendable though disconcerting frankness, had already told Lombroso: "Watch me! You must watch me all the time—or I'll cheat. John King makes me do it!"

This was plain enough even though "John King" was not a very satisfactory alibi. Professor Sidgwick declared: "Inasmuch as Eusapia Palladino has systematically practised trickery for years. . .I propose to ignore her performance in the future as those of other persons engaged in the same mischievous trade are to be ignored. . ."

The publication of the joint report in the Journal of the British S.P.R. (October–November 1895) caused a tremendous outcry in the world of psychical research. For weeks the columns of the London and provincial newspapers, the spiritualist and scientific journals were filled with letters and arguments. Myers still thought that the Roubaud sittings were quite genuine and free from fraud; others blamed the Cambridge experimenters for *not* practising rigid enough control—and thereby "encouraging" Eusapia to cheat.

Dr. J. Maxwell, in his *Metapsychical Phenomena*, attacked Dr. Hodgson by declaring: "As far as his (Hodgson's) experiments with Eusapia Palladino are concerned, I will reply to him that in a great measure he and his friends were responsible for her frauds, and almost wholly responsible for the failure of the experiments. They appear to have neglected the psychological side of a medium's role, and forgot that a medium is not a mechanical instrument...." Describing his own experiences with the lady from Naples, Dr. Maxwell ended: "My judgment will convince no one. In such matters we must see for ourselves in order to be convinced. Dr. Hodgson himself knows this to-day. My testimony contradicts formally and explicitly the conclusions of the Cambridge investigators. Eusapia does not always defraud. With us she rarely defrauded. . ."

Certainly the Cambridge fiasco did not put an end to the Palladino mediumship. In the same month when the damning report was published in England, Colonel De Rochas formed a committee at his house at l'Agnelas which consisted of Dr. Maxwell, Professor Sabatier, the Count De Grammont, the Baron de Watteville and Dr. Darieux. Later De Rochas published a detailed account under the title "The Exteriorization of Motivity". Control was much more severe than at Cambridge—though Dr. Carrington and others pointed out that it was still far from being perfect—and yet a number of phenomena were observed, among them various movements of the table and the curtains; there were loud raps, a toy piano was lifted from the cabinet on to the séance table, a large armchair was levitated, invisible hands touched the sitters, pulling their hair and pinching them. Eusapia, perhaps a little remorseful over the Cambridge business, invariably announced in advance the character of the next phenomenon and asked that control should be thoroughly checked, (this, of course, reminds one a little of the conjurer's pattern — largely designed to direct the attention of the audience to the *wrong* place while the trick is being performed.)

The l'Agnelas sittings more or less balanced the Cambridge fiasco — or at least established Eusapia's "mixed" mediumship: she would cheat when given the chance; but she could produce phenomena under strict control that could not be explained by fraudulent or mechanical sources.

There was another series of experiments in 1895 at Naples where four séances were held under the direction of Dr. Paolo Visani-Scozzi, Professor of Nervous Diseases at Florence, and attended by Dr. Visani, Countess Helena Mainardi, Professor Chiaia and others. There were the usual, varied phenomena — among them, the most important "an imprint of a hand and of a face, obtained in clay, which in no way resembled those of the medium." But though these séances were striking, Eusapia's biographers did not attribute much evidential value to them — mainly because the methods of control were not properly recorded.

In the following year the medium gave séances at Tremezzo — where "various interesting phenomena were observed, when both hands of Eusapia were distinctly *seen*, resting upon the table" — and a series of seven sittings at Auteuil, directed by Dr. Darieux. These were attended by Sully-Prudhomme, the poet and Nobel Prize laureate, and several other French writers. The result was "again, to convince the sitters of Eusapia's undoubted supernormal powers." A third series of sittings, held at Choisy-Yvrac, was organized by Colonel de Rochas with the Count de Grammont, the Count de Watteville and Dr. J. Maxwell among the participants. At these sittings various experiments were tried — for instance, the effects of electricity upon the medium and the phenomena — and magnetizing and hypnotizing her. Electricity, in some way, increased her "powers" — but nothing conclusive was established about its role in mediumship.

1897 was another busy year for Eusapia. In April there were séances in Naples (held by Ernest Mayer and Jean Boulloche); in June there was one in Rome organized by de Siemiradski and in July a whole series in Paris and at Montfort l'Amaury. Though this last series consisted only of three séances, Guilleaume de Fontenay published a book of almost three hundred pages, with copious notes, bibliography and illustrations about it—probably the most detailed record to appear of any psychical investigation.

The séances were held at the home of M. Charles and Mme Emmy Blech—the hosts, their daughter Aimèe and de Fontenay formed the original circle and were later joined by M. Camille Flammarion and others. Fontenay's book devotes almost forty pages to each of the three sittings, prints the testimonials of the Blech family, of A. de Rochas, M. Boissoux, Charles Blech jr., A Gourbine and M. and Mme R. Koechlin. Flammarion himself wrote a vivid account in his book *Mysterious Psychic Forces*—which gives a good general idea of what these Eusapia séances were like:

"Five raps in the table indicate, according to a convention arranged by the medium, that the unknown cause seeks for less light. This is always annoying; I have already said what I think of this. The candles are blown out, the lamp turned down, but the light is strong enough for us to see very distinctly everything that takes place in the salon. The round table, which I had lifted and set aside, approaches the table and tries several times to climb up on it. I lean upon it, in order to keep it down, but I experience an elastic resistance and am unable to do so. The free edge of the round table places itself on the edge of the rectangular table, but hindered by its triangular foot, it does not succeed in clearing itself sufficiently to climb upon it. Since I am holding the medium I ascertain that she makes no effort of the kind that would be needed for this style of performance.

The curtain swells out and approaches my face. It is at this moment that the medium falls into a trance. She utters sighs and lamentations and only speaks now in the third person, saying that she is John King, a psychic personality, who claims to have been her father in another existence, and who calls her, 'My daughter.'

Five new taps ask for still *less light* and the lamp is almost completely turned down, but not extinguished. The eyes, growing accustomed to the clare-obscure, still distinguish pretty well what is taking place.

The curtain swells out again and I feel that I am touched on the shoulder, through the stuff of the curtain, as if by a closed fist. The chair in the cabinet, upon which are placed the music box and the bell, is violently shaken, and the objects fall to the floor. The medium again asks for less light and a red photographic lantern is placed upon the piano, the light of the lamp being extinguished. The control is rigorously kept up, the medium agreeing to it with the greatest docility.

For about a minute the music box plays intermittent airs behind the curtain, as if it was turned by some hand.

The curtain moves forward again toward me, and a rather strong hand seizes my arm. I immediately reach forward to seize the hand, but I grasp only the empty air. I then press the two legs of the medium between mine, and I take her left hand in my right. On the other side, the right hand is firmly held in the left hand of M. de Fontenay. Then Eusapia brings the hand of the last named toward my cheek, and imitates upon the cheek, with the finger of M. de Fontenay, the movement of a little revolving crank or handle. The music box, which has one of these handles, plays at the same time behind the curtain in perfect synchronism. The instant that Eusapia's hand stops, the music stops; all the movements correspond, just as in the Morse telegraph system. . .

I feel several touches on the back and on the side. M. de Fontenay receives a sharp slap on the back that everybody hears. A hand passes through my hair. The chair of M. de Fontenay is violently pulled, and a few moments afterwards he cries, 'I see the silhouette of a man passing between M. Flammarion and me, above the table, shutting out the red light!'

This thing is repeated several times. I do not myself succeed in seeing this silhouette. I then propose to M. de Fontenay that I take his place, for, in that case, I should be likely to see it also. I soon distinctly perceive a dim silhouette passing before the red lantern, but I do not recognize any precise form. It is only an opaque shadow (the profile of a man) which advances as far as the light and retires.

In a moment Eusapia says there is someone behind the curtain. After a slight pause she adds:

'There is a man by your side, on the right; he has a great soft forked beard.' I ask if I may touch this beard. In fact, while lifting my hand, I feel rather a soft beard brushing against it.

A block of paper is put on the table with a lead pencil, with the hope of getting writing. The pencil is flipped clear across the room.

I then take the block of paper and hold it in the air: it is snatched violently from me, in spite of all my efforts to retain it. At this moment, M. de Fontenay, with his back turned to the light, sees a hand (a white hand and not a shadow), the arm showing as far as the elbow holding the block of paper; but all the others declare that they only see the paper shaking in the air.

I did not see the hand snatch the packet of paper from me; but only a hand could have been able to seize it with such violence, and this did not appear to be the hand of the medium, for I held her right hand in my left, and the paper with arm extended in my right hand and M. de Fontenay declared that he did not let go her left hand.

I was struck several times in the side, touched on the head, and my ear was smartly pinched. I declare that after several repetitions had enough of his ear-pinching; but during the whole séance, in spite of my protestations, somebody kept hitting me.

The little round table, placed outside the cabinet, at the left of the medium, approaches the table, climbs clear up on it and lie across it. The guitar in the cabinet is heard moving about and giving out sounds. The curtain is puffed out, and the guitar is brought upon the table, resting upon the shoulder of M. de Fontenay. It is then laid upon the table, the large end toward the medium. Then it rise and moves over the heads of the company without touching them. It gives forth several sounds. The phenomenon lasts about fifteen seconds. It can readily be seen that the guitar is floating in the air and the reflection of the red lamp glides over its shining surface. A rather bright gleam, pear-shaped, is seen on the ceiling of the other corner of the room.

The medium, who is tired, asks for rest. The candles are lighted. Mme Blech returns the objects to their places, ascertains that the cakes of putty are intact, places the smallest upon a little round table and the large one upon the chair in the cabinet, behind the medium. The sitting is resumed by the feeble glimmer of the red lantern.

The medium, whose hands and feet are carefully controlled by M. de Fontenay and myself, breathes heavily. Above her head the snapping of fingers is heard. She still pants, groans, and sinks her fingers into my hand. Three raps are heard. She cries, 'It is done!' M. de Fontenay brings the little dish beneath the light of the red lantern and discovers the impression of four fingers in the putty in the position which they had taken when she had gripped my hand.

Seats are taken, the medium asks for rest, and a little light is turned on.

The sitting is soon resumed as before, by the extremely feeble light of the red lantern. John is spoken of as if he existed, as if it was he whose head we perceived in silhouette; he is asked to continue his manifestations, and to show the impression of his head in the putty, as he has already several times done. Eusapia replies that it is a difficult thing and asks us not to think of it for a moment, but to go on speaking. These suggestions of hers are always disquieting, and we redouble our attention, though without speaking much. The medium pants, groans, writhes. The chair in the cabinet comes forward and places itself by the side of the medium, then it is lifted and placed upon the head of Mme Z. Blech, while the tray is lightly placed in the hands of M. Blech, at the other end of the table. Eusapia cries that she sees before her a head and a bust, and says '*E fatto*' (It is done.) We do not believe her, because M. Blech has not felt any pressure on the dish. Three violent blows as of a mallet are struck upon the table. The light is turned on, and a human profile is found imprinted in the putty. Mme Z. Blech kisses Eusapia on both cheeks, for the purpose of finding out whether her face has not some odour (glazier's putty having a very strong odour of linseed oil, which remains for sometime upon one's fingers). She discovers nothing abnormal. . .''

The great astronomer's record is singularly matter-of-fact, tinged with a little exasperation about Eusapia's insistence on feeble light —not to mention the persistent pinching. But for all that, he does not express the slightest doubt about the genuineness of the phenomna—however childish and inconclusive they are—obviously confident that the control was strict and effective enough. M. de Fontenay's compte rendu' devoted more than 160 pages to the various theories that might possibly explain Eusapia's mediumship—always on the premise that it was a genuine psychic power she exercised and if not ignoring her previous "unmaskings", at least not ascribing too much importance to the earlier proven frauds. The theories de Fontenay offered included the "animistic-spiritual", the "dynamic" and the "mysterious constitution of all matter." The book also examined the possibility of photographing materialisations "nascent and as yet invisible" (that is, to the human eye, if not to the camera) which de

Fontenay called "transcendental" photography—and the dangers and usefulness of psychical research. "No hypothesis is definite," he ended. "Theories are nothing but halting places of the human spirit on the road to truth. Therefore only stick with moderation to your theories. Endure patiently their discussion—or even if they are despised—and above all, hope for their improvement and perfectioning. . .Do not venture upon this dangerous and treacherous territory unless you have considered the problems at length and have vowed to apply Lord Chesterfield's famous and most wise recommendation: 'No heat!' "

★   ★   ★

In November 1898 Eusapia was invited to Paris by a scientific committee which included some of the most illustrious scientists, philosophers and writers of France—among them Flammarion, Richet, de Rochas, Sardou, Claretie, Adolphe Brisson, Gustave Le Bon, Jules Bois, André Bloch and several others. The séances were held in Flammarion's drawing room; before each Eusapia was undressed and dressed in the presence of two ladies and control was carefully organized.

Professor Flammarion's "Mysterious Psychic Forces" contains a full account of these sittings, and M. Arthur Levy recorded what must have been one of the most extraordinary séances in all psychical history. It began with minor phenomena and continued with a struggle between M. Levy and two invisible hands over the possession of a tambourine—in which the invisible hands apparently won. But more marvels were yet to come:

> "Eusapia utters repeated cries," M. Levy wrote, "a kind of rattling in the throat. She writhes nervously, and, as if she were calling for help, she cries, 'The chain, the chain!' We thereupon form the chain by taking hold of hands. Then, just as if she were defying some monster, she turns, with inflamed looks, towards an enormous divan, which thereupon *marches up to us.* She looks at it with a satanic smile. Finally, she blows upon the divan, which goes immediately back to its place. . .
>
> Eusapia was evidently very tired; her burning hands seemed to contract or shrivel; she gasped aloud with heaving breast, her feet quitting mine every moment, scraping the floor and tediously rubbing along it back and forth. She uttered hoarse, panting cries, shrugging up her shoulder and sneering. The sofa came forward when she

looked at it, then recoiled before her breath; all the instruments were thrown pellmell upon the table; the tambourine rose almost to the height of the ceiling; the cushions took part in the sport, overturning everything on the table; M. M. was thrown from his chair. This chair—a heavy diningroom chair of black walnut, with stuffed seat—rose into the air, came up on the table with a great clatter, then was pushed off. . ."

Such violence was not unusual at the Palladino séances and made control sometimes difficult if not impossible. Yet Dr. Le Bon, another participant in the 1898 Paris series, thought that Eusapia was "undoubtedly a marvellous subject. It struck me as something wonderful that, while I was holding her hand, she was playing an imaginary tambourine, to which the sounds of the tambourine that was behind the curtain accurately corresponded. I do not see how any trick is possible in such a case. . ."

After the Paris séances there was a break in the Palladino mediumship as far as scientific examination and observation were concerned. But in 1901 Eusapia gave a series of remarkable séances at the Minerva Club in Genoa, attended by the Italian *savants* Lombroso, Bozzano, Morselli, Porro, Vassalo, Venzano and others. Professor Porro's conclusions were accepted by the whole group. He said:

"The phenomena are real. They cannot be explained either by fraud or by hallucination. . .While admitting it as the most probable hypothesis that the intelligent beings to whom we owe these psychical phenomena are pre-existing, independent entities, and that they only derive from us the conditions necessary for their manifestation in a physical plane accessible to our senses, ought we to admit also that they are really the spirits of the dead?

To this question I will reply that I do not feel that I am as yet capable of giving a decisive answer. . .

Still, I should be inclined to admit it, if I did not see the possibility that these phenomena might form part of a scheme of things still more vast. In fact, nothing hinders us from believing in the existence of forms of life wholly different from those which we know, and of which the life of human beings before birth and after death forms only a special case—just as the organic life of man is a special case of animal life in general. . ."

The next series of experiments was held in July and August 1902 at Palermo, under Dr. Carmelo Samona, and in 1905 at Rome and at Paris. The former were organized by Dr. H. Carreras, the latter by the Count de Grammont—but neither added much to Eusapia's record. In 1906-07 Professor Morselli renewed his investigations of the Neapolitan medium at Genoa; these, according to Hereward Carrington, completely converted him—so that he decided to publish his lengthy work which he had held in proof-form for five years because of his scientific scruples. The professor enumerated thirty-nine distinctive types of phenomena, ranging from "oscillations and movements of the table without significance" to "movements and swelling out of the medium's clothes"; from "spontaneous changes of weight on a scale" to "raising of the medium's body in the air" and "appearance of forms having determinate and personal characters."

During this series of sittings a very typical incident occurred at the third séance—something Professor Morselli called "a classic example of mixed mediumship." While the experimenters were forming a chain around the table at which the medium was also seated, with her back turned to the cabinet, Morselli called out: "E.T.V. !" This was a pre-arranged signal, meaning that the medium had withdrawn one of her hands or feet from the control of her two neighbours (the "E.T.V." stood for "Eugene Torelli-Viollier", one of the experimenters who had observed such a trick.) Eusapia, in fact, had freed her left hand from that of Professor Morselli and stretched it out toward a trumpet which was on the table. But she had no time to do it—the Professor, as he pronounced the warning, "possessed himself again of the fugitive hand and the experimenters increased their vigilance. Eusapia understood, and said, in a saddened tone: 'Don't say that!' "

But at this moment, as the report continues,

"while the control was certainly more vigorous than ever, the trumpet was raised from the table, and disappeared into the cabinet, passing between the medium and Dr. Morselli. Evidently the medium had attempted to do with her hand what she subsequently did mediumistically; such a futile and foolish attempt at fraud is inexplicable. There is no doubt about the matter; this time the medium did not touch, and could not touch, the trumpet; and even if she could have touched it she could not have conveyed it into the cabinet, which was behind her back."

The six séances all brought something new and remarkable—and apart from the single attempt at fraud (a very childish and obvious one) the investigators were completely satisfied with the medium's behaviour. Not long afterwards, Professor Lombroso, with his two assistants, Dr. Imoda and Dr. Audenino, organized another series in the clinical chamber of psychiatry at Turin University. These were attended by a number of eminent scientists and control was especially vigorous. A report was first published in *La Stampa* and later in *The Annals of Psychical Science* of the four séances. "Even the cleverest trickery could not begin to explain the majority of the phenomena observed," was the unanimous opinion of the participants.

At the end of the first séance, one of the doctors "placed his hand on the deep scar which the medium has on the left side of her head and felt a cold, strong, continuous breeze issuing from it, like a human breath. He subsequently felt the same cold breeze issuing, though less strongly, from the tips of her fingers." At the second séance in order to eliminate all doubt as to any confederates among the sitters who might help to produce the phenomena, a double chain was formed: the first six sat round the table, the other eight behind, joining hands in a second row connected at each end with the inner chain—so that every movement was under the observation of the next sitter. Eusapia herself was closely controlled; yet there were again a number of phenomena "clearly visible, complete in all its phases, distinct, incontestible and convincing." A toy piano was repeatedly played, lights appeared around the medium's head and a tambourine responded "to an invisible hand." The third and the fourth séances were equally successful and at the final one the complete levitation of the table was photographed by a magnesium light. Lombroso and his associates gave Eusapia an enthusiastic testimonial. Soon after this series, Dr. Herlitzka, Dr. Charles Foa and Dr. Aggazzotti arranged still another group of experiments in Turin, held in the house of Count Verdun. Control was "incessant and reciprocal control was exercised by all those present." The phenomena were varied and extremely violent—"John King" apparently took a strong dislike to one of the sitters, Dr. Arullani and pounded him over the head, pushed and hit him. A table was broken into small fragments (rather like at the famous Stella C. séance) and altogether, a tremendous amount of "psychic energy" was expended. Indeed, this particular year of 1907 marked a peak in Eusapia's powers. There were a number of séances at Naples during which Professor Bottazzi, Professor Galeotti,

Dr. DeAmicis, Dr. Oscar Scarpa, Dr. Luigi Lombardi and Dr. Sergio Pansini made determined attempts to obtain *graphic* records of the phenomena, by means of mechanical instruments. The sittings took place in the laboratories of the University of Naples; the medium was safely prevented from tampering with the instruments—not by any control of the sitters but by the construction and placing of the instruments themselves. The first séance was not very productive and at the second Eusapia "protested for a long time, saying that she did not know their meaning" (that is, the purpose of the instruments), "that she could not find them, that she did not know how to do it, that they were too far off." Yet in the ensuing sittings, in spite of her protests, the various recording instruments *were* moved—buttons were pressed, the rod of a metronome was set swinging. Dr. Bottazzi's conclusion was that the hands operative (the "spirit" hands) had to become "familiar" with the instruments—just like human hands—before they were able to use them. At the end of the series Bottazzi summed up:

> "It would be necessary to have Mme Palladino's fingers in the palm of one's hand, as I had that evening, in order to be convinced that the levitations, the twanging of the strings, etc. all synchronized with the very delicate movements of her fingers, and with the dragging and pushing movements of the medium's hand, as if she were directed in the execution of these movements by a will which knew the effect to be produced. These were not irregular, impulsive, disordered movements—they were precise and coordinated. Whether they were movements of one finger, or of several fingers, and were identical with those which we should make if we tried to seize or to vibrate the strings with precision and delicacy. . .The medium does not only move objects, but also feels with her invisible limbs, and while the movement was performed on the left, phenomena occurred to the right of Mme Palladino... The phenomena are undoubted—whatever their interpretation. Fraud has never been even attempted. . .Eusapia never used any expedients to deceive me— on the contrary, she invariably warned us every time she moved a table or a curtain with her own hands. To those who deny without having seen, affirming *a priori* the impossibility of these phenomena, one must reply: 'First see; then you may argue.' "

The British Society for Psychical Research, much impressed by the French and the Italian reports, decided in 1908 to send a commission to Naples—to determine "once and for all" whether Eusapia was genuine or not. The investigators were Dr. Hereward Carrington, W.W. Baggally and the Hon. Everard Feilding. Carrington and Baggally were both expert amateur conjurers. The sittings were held in their own rooms at the Hotel Victoria, Naples, in November and December 1908—and of course, every precaution was taken to exclude fraud, the introduction of any confederates or suspect apparatus. The usual varied telekinetic phenomena and materializations were witnessed, under perfect conditions of control. The illumination they used enabled them to see the medium at all times and her limbs were controlled separately by the observers—during some of the séances she was actually tied to their hands. Notes were taken by a stenographer in a far corner of the room.

This inquiry finally set the seal on Eusapia's genuineness so far as British psychical research was concerned. Everard Feilding, then Honorary Secretary of the S.P.R., who had been a life-long sceptic was at last convinced that physical phenomena were possible. On one occasion, as Mr. Feilding told Harry Price, while he held Eusapia's two hands (which were in full view) a *third hand*, from behind the cabinet curtain, grasped his fingers so tightly that he could feel the nails pressing into his flesh. The paranormality of Eusapia's phenomena was scientifically demonstrated. Dr. Carrington's "Eusapia Palladino and Her Phenomena", published in 1909, devoted over 300 pages to the detailed description of these and other séances and to Eusapia's psychic history; a full account of the Commission's findings appeared in the Proceedings of the S.P.R. It seemed that her place in the history of occultism would be not only assured but outstanding.

And so it is—even though less than two years after the triumphantly successful Naples séances the American correspondent of the London *Sunday Chronicle* reported: EUSAPIA EXPOSED: UNMASKING A FAMOUS MEDIUM. 'TECS UNDER THE TABLE.

"Eusapia Palladino is the most talked of spirit medium in the world today," the article began. "Great professors have believed in her and she has been hailed in Europe and America as the greatest spiritualistic phenomenon of the last decade. But she has refused the challenge of some American University professors who suggest that she shall be placed in a canvas sack with an opening at the neck only. The opening shall be laced up the back, they say, and the lacing done in such a way that it can be opened only by cutting. They further suggest that the sack shall be fastened to the floor, and at the close of the séance shall show no signs of having been tampered with. Another condition is that she shall submit to an examination by women, to prove that she has no apparatus concealed. Signor (sic!) Eusapia does not, however, like the idea and has refused to submit to a trial in this form. She says she tried it once in Venice, and nearly died. She offers to perform her spiritualist feats with her feet and hands tied..."

The article went on describing Eusapia as a "coarse-looking woman of the Latin type" who, when anyone doubts her genuineness, "shrieks and gets very excited."

The "unmasking" came at a séance held at Columbia University attended by "four professors and several scientific women". Two detectives, dressed in "tight-fitting black suits and black stockings" were secretly introduced into the darkened séance-room and wriggled their way along the floor till they had reached their assigned positions on either side of the séance table, under the chairs of the sitters. There they were in a position to observe Eusapia closely—while she evidently hadn't noticed their entry at all. They saw her for a few minutes tapping the feet of the controls with her own feet.

"Then she placed her right foot cross-wise, so that the heel rested on the foot of one control and the toe on the foot of the other. To these men it would seem that she had both feet on theirs. Presently a foot came from beneath her dress, and it was placed under the leg of the table which was gently chucked into the air. Then the foot withdrew and the table descended to the floor. It was repeatedly lifted after this and every time, whether in a partial or complete levitation, the medium's foot was used as the compelling force. At different times throughout the séance the medium caused rappings upon the table by striking the free foot on the left leg of the table about three inches from the floor. . ."

The "psychic breeze", one of the detectives said, was produced by "blowing upwards with the bottom lip protruding, just as a woman does when she desires to blow a stray hair from her eyes. . ."

Other details of trickery were given; and the article ended by the proud boast that "it has remained for a party of American investigators to expose the trickery which had impressed learned men of many countries. . .to believe in the genuineness of her mediumistic phenomena. . ."

Carrington, himself an American, came to a different conclusion in his long book. ". . .it is to be hoped," he wrote, "that Eusapia Palladino will be ranked, not as a vulgar impostor, but as a rarely gifted individual, possessing powers worthy of the deepest study and respect; as a delicate and sensitive piece of organic machinery, which should be guarded and cared for with the utmost kindness and consideration."

Eusapia died in 1918. Her reputation has grown rather than dimmed since her death. Many of her séances were held under rigorous control; many of her phenomena had never been duplicated. But she was, as one Italian professor put it, "half-angel, half-cheat—and are not most women the same?"

★   ★   ★

CHAPTER SEVEN

Eleonore: The Devil Girl

ELEONORE Zugun was born on May 24, 1913 in the Rumanian village of Talpa. Her parents were peasants, working a few acres of land, raising a few pigs and earning a little cash by seasonal work in the forests. She was about twelve when she went to live with her grandparents at Buhai, a village a few miles from Talpa. It was here that Eleonore's strange psychic life-story began.

A few days after she arrived at her grandparents' cottage, a shower of stones hit it, smashing several windows. This happened at night; but next day, in broad sunlight, a big stone, a piece of china and half a brick were hurled at the cottage, breaking more windows. No one was ever seen to throw these missiles—which always landed at the little girl's feet. An iron ring fell from a stove, close to Eleonore's leg; a small mug fell off a dresser. Her grandparents were frightened by these "evil things" and convinced that she was either bewitched or even possessed by the Devil, they hurriedly sent her back to Talpa.

A day or so after her arrival home the family were sitting at dinner in their kitchen when a stone came crashing through the window. It was wet and round—like those found in the river Seret which ran a few yards from their cottage. This time Eleonore's father hurriedly fetched a priest. The priest marked the stone with a cross—and threw it back into the river. Then he returned to the house to watch and pray over the girl. A little later the *same* stone—identified by the *popa's*, (the village priest) mark—was flung through the broken window again.

Satan, the Zugun family reasoned, was so powerful that he could even defy the mark of the Cross; the only thing to be done was to get rid of Eleonore—at least temporarily. So they sent her to a neighbour whom they bribed with gifts of food and clothes to take her in. But the people of Talpa became more and more convinced that the Evil One, *Dracu*, was at the root of all trouble—strange and frightening things followed the girl from place to place, and were not confined to any particular place. Eleonore was beaten and they threatened to send her to a lunatic asylum. Terrified, the child ran home to her parents. Hardly had she stepped over the threshold when huge potatoes seemed to leap into the air from under the bed and rain down upon her father's shoulders.

This time her father resolved to have Satan put to flight. Next morning he and fourteen other peasants took Eleonore to the famous *Popa* of Zamostea, the bedridden Father Macarescu who was over eighty but still a mighty exorcist. But *Dracu* evidently mocked at the most powerful saintliness. Soon after Eleanore was pushed into the popa's bedroom, an iron pot burst into many pieces and a few seconds later an earthenware vessel, standing on the hearth, also burst, its splinters flying through the window into the courtyard. The people who had escorted the girl retreated in terror—only to be showered with glass as the inner windows of the room (as usual, the bedroom had double windows) shattered into splinters. The outside windows, however, remained intact.

Though he hadn't walked for weeks, the old priest jumped from bed and hobbled into the courtyard; he was followed by his son and by the village school teacher named Teodorescu. Stopping outside, the teacher glanced through the window and saw a big chest which stood against the wall, dance backwards and forwards, then slide from side to side, moved by the "devil's power." Only one young man named Juon Ostafi had remained in the room. When he saw the chest moving, he put his hands on its side and said: "Wait, devil, I see you cannot do it alone—I will help you!"

Dracu obviously resented this offer of aid—a plank, hidden in a corner, hurtled forward and hit Juon across the back, injuring him. His cries of pain brought back the others. One of the Talpa men proposed a pilgrimage to St. Johannes at the Convent of Suczava—the saint might help where the saintliest mortal had failed. This appeared to infuriate *Dracu* again—a stone was thrown against a picture of the saint on the wall, smashing it and the stone remained lodged in the wall as a reminder of the Evil One's resentment. After this only Teodorescu, the teacher, dared to stay indoors. He sat opposite a bench on which a can of water had been placed. Suddenly this can levitated eighteen inches, described a half circle and came down on the other end of the bench without spilling a single drop of water. The peasants begged Father Macarescu to hold a Mass and cast out the devil—but this, too, was of no avail. Nor did the pilgrimage to Suczava help; on the contrary, the manifestations became more and more frequent and violent.

Eleonore was sent to the Convent of Gorovei near her native village of Talpa. And here the "most amazing phenomena happened", as Countess Zoe Wassilko-Serecki tells us in her book "Der Spuk von Talpa" (The Spook of Talpa). A heavy refectory table, seating twenty-four, levitated; the habits of the monks were wafted from one cell to another through locked doors and the thickest walls. Masses were said for Eleonore's salvation; she was repeatedly exorcised, she was examined by psychiatrists; she was hypnotized. But if she *was* possessed, it must have been by the most powerful of all evil spirits for nothing made the slightest difference. The phenomena still continued in an almost unbroken sequence. The university of Czernowitz became interested in the little peasant girl but nothing practical came out of that. Eleonore, inevitably, was taken up by the newspapers. There were long articles about her in the *Czernowitzer Morgenblatt* and the *Allgemeine Zeitung*. These reports reached Fritz Grunewald, the distinguished German psychical researcher (who was an engineer by profession). Grunewald was fascinated by the controversy that was raging with extraordinary fury in the Rumanian and Central European press. Some of the papers wrote that the whole "sorry business is a swindle"; others were convinced that the little girl was a certifiable lunatic; while some who had actually sent reporters to investigate the matter, maintained that the phenomena were genuine. But the argument was settled, at least for the time being and to the satisfaction of *some* disputants when the child *was* certified insane and committed to the local asylum. There she was kept in almost total darkness, in solitary confinement—treated much as the "recalcitrant" patients of Bedlam were treated in seventeenth-century England.

Grunewald travelled to Rumania and visited every place where Eleonore had stayed, he talked to scores of people either directly or through interpreters; he persuaded Eleonore's father to take the child from the asylum and was able to witness many of the phenomena himself. All this convinced him that a thorough scientific investigation was both necessary and worthwhile. He took the girl to the Convent of Gorovei and kept her for three weeks under close observation. All the phenomena were confirmed under as close control as he could establish outside a psychical laboratory. Then, early in July 1925, Grunewald went back to Berlin to make arrangements with friends to provide Eleonore with a home. He could not do this himself as he was a bachelor and lived alone.

But before he could make a definite arrangement, Grunewald suffered a heart attack and died. Strangely enough, Harry Price, the British psychical researcher, had an appointment with him to discuss the preface Grunewald was to write for a German edition of one of Price's books. Price called at the flat in the Spandauerstrasse and hammered on the door when no one answered his ring. There was no answer and Price left—with no thought that his colleague and friend was sprawled dead only a few feet away. It was twelve days before Grunewald's body was discovered.

His death was a terrible blow for Eleonore who was waiting for her benefactor to return and take her to a new home in Berlin. It seemed that she would be sent back to the convent again if not to the asylum. Unexpectedly, the Countess Zoe Wassilko-Serecki, a Rumanian lady living in Vienna, long interested in psychical research, came to the little girl's rescue. She travelled to Talpa and, not without a great deal of difficulty with the Rumanian authorities, arranged to adopt Eleonore. She brought the child back to Vienna in September 1925. She didn't quite know what she was letting herself in for—especially during the first few months. Three years later when defending herself against an attack of trickery, the Countess wrote in the Leipzig "*Zeitschrift für Parapsychologie*":

"...After recognizing Eleonore's mediumistic talents in their extraordinary power, I made great financial sacrifices to save her for science. In the East such affairs are settled in a different way from the West's. I took a filthy little peasant girl who was like an animal, dominated by all the usual whims and fancies of a medium—a creature that was unable to stand or walk properly, did not know how to speak or eat, how to wash or dress herself—I took her into my home and, because of the housing shortage, into my own room. I have educated and trained her, fed and clothed her and made her into a normal, healthy human being. For two years I have lived with her day and night, making all the minor but constant sacrifices in time and effort which only a mother is expected to make—being solely responsible, without any help, even in conflict with my friends and relatives. I have given up practically everything myself in order to fulfil the duty I have undertaken—and I am having Eleonore trained in a craft so that she can later earn her living. I nursed her through an infantile disease and was myself infected; for two years I spent innumerable nights instead of sleep in fighting with the poltergeist phenomena (almost all smaller objects were shattered in my home repeatedly), had to get up to clean the floor and the bedclothes from the fragments of broken inkwells and similar 'projectiles'; I sat for hours at the child's bedside when she was tormented by the scratches and bites of whatever or whoever persecuted her. . .I never worried about 'wasting my time' or missing some chance. . .No one can really imagine how much patience, what nervous energy such a task demands. . ."

Certainly the Countess succeeded in turning an ignorant, suspicious and superstitious peasant child into a well-behaved, charming and responsive young lady. But a young lady around whom strange things were still happening. After her arrival in Vienna, Eleonore's phenomena grew stronger and more spectacular. Naturally Austrian scientists were intrigued by her. Professor Hans Thirring, the distinguished physicist of Vienna University was one of the first to examine Eleonore and to have a series of sittings with her at the Countess's apartment. In July 1925 Fritz Grunewald's report about his Rumanian experiences with Eleonore had been published in the Munich *Psychische Studien* (just a day or two after his tragic death) and this was being widely discussed among psychical researchers. Professor Thirring called the attention of Harry Price, the British expert (who was then Foreign Research Officer of the American S.P.R.) to the case and in April 1926 Price travelled to Vienna, partly to deliver a talk on psychical research at the University and partly to investigate Eleonore.

This first series of tests Price had with the girl impressed him greatly. He gave detailed accounts not only in the *Proceedings* of his National Laboratory of Psychical Research but also in three different books— "*Leaves from a Psychist's Case-Book*", "*Poltergeist over England*" and "*Fifty Years of Psychical Research*".

"I found Eleonore." Price's most detailed record begins, "installed in the Countess's charming flat in the Josefstädterstrasse and I at once set about arranging a test. I decided to utilise the Countess's bedroom-study for my experiments. This room was divided longitudinally by a matchboard partition, about six feet high, with an opening at one end for communication between the two divisions. A pair of French windows, leading to a balcony overlooking a quiet wooded garden, provided ample illumination for both study and bedroom. . ."

Price carefully fastened both doors and windows and minutely examined the study and bedroom areas of the apartment. In the bedroom there was a bed, toilet table, chairs and cupboards; in the study a low bookcase, filled with books, a couch, a writing table, chairs, etc. were placed in convenient positions. Eleonore and the Countess watched him silently (but not without amusement) while he completed his check. He had known the Countess for some time, having met her during a previous visit to Vienna.

"I found Eleonore," Price reported, "to be an intelligent, well-developed, bright girl with a sunny disposition. She was then nearly thirteen years old. Though physically strong and healthy, she was 'young' mentally. In many ways, she was more like a girl of eight; her shyness, her extreme fondness for simple toys, her simple games and childish ways. But she could read and write well and was even something of an artist. She was five feet tall and weighed 123 pounds. The Countess and I seated ourselves on the couch and watched Eleonore playing with a toy that fascinated her: a spring gun that projected a celluloid ping-pong ball, which was caught in a sort of conical wire basket that was attached to the gun. Suddenly, as we watched, the ball came to pieces, its component halves falling at our feet. The girl ran to the Countess and asked her to mend it. She jumped up, and so did I. As I watched my hostess examining the join, a steel stiletto with handle, used for opening letters, the whole about ten inches long, shot across the room from *behind* me and fell against the closed door. I instantly turned round and a minute investigation revealed nothing—and no one—that could have projected the stiletto, which was normally kept on the writing table behind us, against the wall farthest from where we stood. . ."

Price was convinced that no one in that room—certainly not the girl—could have thrown the paper-knife. They were at least ten feet from the table and he had both Eleonore and the Countess in full view. Eleonore held one half of the ball in her right hand and the gun in her left; the Countess had the other half of the ball in *her* hand and

Price was actually watching both his hostess and the child; the stiletto came from behind and to the right of them, with Price between it and the door.

"It was a brilliant introductory phenomenon," Price continued. There were many others, including "the precipitation of a small mirror over the partition *from the bedroom side*, while we three were in the study portion. Then a metal cap followed the mirror. A large black cloth dog, that Eleonore used to cuddle, shot from the study side of the room, over the partition, and fell on to the coal-scuttle near the bed. No one was nearer to the dog (which was lying on a chair near the French windows) than ten feet, and Eleonore, at the moment of the flight, was pushing a table against a wall, using both her hands. Then I saw a cushion on one of the chairs *begin* to move. As I watched, it slid *slowly* off the chair, and fell to the floor. No one was near it. After each of the phenomena, and many others, I examined the room, the furniture, etc. but everything was normal. I reiterate that there were no wires, threads, spring releases, rubber bands, compressed air tubes, springs released by the gradual expansion of a viscous substance or similar contrivances: things difficult to hide and easy to find in this sunlit room."

Price, not an easy man to convince, was much impressed by what he had seen. He decided to invite Eleonore and the Countess to London and test the phenomena in his own laboratory. His invitation was gladly accepted; the "Poltergeist girl" and her benefactress arrived in England on the last day of September, 1926. The first "phenomenon", though not under controlled circumstances, was the disappearance of a silver finger ring from Eleonore's dressing table on the first night —and its reappearance "from nowhere" as she was playing with a Cairn terrier that used to visit Price's Kensington laboratory.

But this was only the "overture".

"Soon after the ring incident," Price's report went on, "two or three Press representatives came to see me. One of them, Mr. E. Clepham Palmer, had brought Eleonore a large package of toys, including a wonderful clockwork black cat, with eyes that spat fire if not brimstone; a fit plaything for *Dracu*. It was a pleasure to watch the child's face as she undid the parcel. When she came to the clockwork toy her eyes sparkled almost as much as the cat's.

She at once wound up the cat and placed it on the floor. We were all watching with amusement the glee with which she was handling the toy and were interested to see how the thing would work. Eleonore wound it up, stooped down, and placed the cat on the floor—at the same instant as something fell upon her head and dropped to the floor. I immediately picked up the object and saw that it was an L-shaped piece of metal (size 14 × 11.5 mm, weight 24 grains) enamelled white. I at once thought it was a part of one of the toys which Mr. Palmer had brought for the girl, but upon closer inspection it was quite obvious that the object was a small metallic sign such as is used for affixing to notice-boards. I then remembered that I had seen a notice-board in the hall on the ground floor on which were a number of similar letters which are magnetic, thus easily attaching themselves to the metal surface of the board. We naturally thought that the L had come from the board and that its absence would at once be noticed. We accordingly rang through by means of the house 'phone in order to confirm our assumption. To our astonishment, the young lady typist informed us from the library that every letter on the noticeboard was in its allotted position and none was missing. We then descended the four flights separating the laboratory from the library in order to investigate. We found every letter in its place on the notice-board and asked to see the remaining stock, if any. It appears that six specimens of each letter were supplied with the set sold with the notice-board, which had arrived only the previous day. Upon checking the unused letters, we found that one was missing—the letter L. Only three persons in existence knew where the unused letters were kept. One of these was out, and the other two—the typist and a youth employed in the library—were actually in the room (the library), when the letter appeared in the laboratory. The unused letters were in the box secured by two fasteners, and kept in a closed cupboard. It was proved absolutely that no one in the Laboratory suite had entered the library for days—the Countess and Eleonore have never been in to this day—and the notice-board and sets of letters had not been in the building twenty-four hours. The Countess was not in the building at the time. Mr. Palmer in his report (*Daily News*, Oct. 2., 1926) stated that he saw the letter drop from the ceiling, falling upon my shoulder, and then to the ground. I distinctly saw the letter strike the girl's head and then fall upon the floor. Not being under stringent test conditions, we are not hailing the L incident as a phenomenon. On the other hand, there is not the slightest evidence that anyone was cheating; nor have we yet discovered how it was possible for a person to abstract the letter from the fastened box and closed cupboard in view of the fact that three persons only knew where the letters were kept. None of these was connected with the Laboratory. It has been suggested that because the letter is magnetic it might have had some affinity for the girl, but I think this theory is fantastic. The fact remains, though, that these magnetic letters played a major role in the manifestations which occurred during the girl's visit. But how the L found its way from the library to the laboratory—a distance of forty-eight feet—is still a mystery. . ."

Next day Price was able to observe the "spontaneous movements" of some coins when he was alone with Eleonore in the Laboratory —at least one of them was "an exceptionally brilliant phenomenon" in his opinion. It was a one franc piece, falling from the wide lintel of a door; it fell right in front of Price's eyes with Eleonore nowhere near it. "The fall of the franc," Price reported, "was the first telekinetic phenomenon of Eleonore's witnessed at the Laboratory, concerning which I was absolutely satisfied. The falling of the coin off a ledge may be a simple movement, but for this movement to take place automatically, by mechanical means, would require fairly elaborate apparatus which could not be rendered invisible. . ."

There were many other, striking manifestations. A group of eminent scientists attended many of the observational periods, including Dr. R.J. Tillyard, W.R. Bousfield, Edward Heron-Allen, Professor William McDougall, Prof. Hans Thirring (who made a special trip from Vienna), the Hon. Everard Feilding, Prof. A.O. Rankine, Dr. Theodore B. Hyslop.

However interesting the telekinetic poltergeist phenomena were, the scientists—especially the psychologists—were more fascinated by the stigmata which regularly appeared and disappeared on the young girl's skin. Eleonore had a fixed idea that *Dracu*, the Devil—whom she seemed to treat as a rather rough but by no means sinister, invisible playmate—used to bite and scratch her. This was an obsession which Price and his associates tried hard to uproot—but without any success. The painful weals, teethmarks and scratches which Eleonore experienced constantly were stronger than any logic or analytical treatment.

★   ★   ★

"I have not yet been able to make up my mind which of the two classes of Eleonore's phenomena, the telekinetic or stigmatic, were the more convincing. The stigmatic marks and abrasions which spontaneously appeared on various portions of Eleonore's body were. . .the most interesting of the phenomena said to occur with this medium," Harry Price wrote. "I saw several of them during the periods I kept the girl under observation. The marks were of several varieties, including teeth-marks, long scratches, oval, annular, elliptical, and other marks of varying shapes. The teethmarks, it must be admitted, were similar to those made by Eleonore's own teeth; and tests carried out proved that if Eleonore bit her own arm, identical impressions to those alleged to be abnormal were found, except that the number of teeth indentations varied. But no one saw Eleonore play tricks of this description, although she was kept under observation for days by different investigators. Teeth-marks were never found on any part of her body not accessible to the medium's mouth; they invariably appeared on her arms or hands. This applied also to the scratches and other markings which appeared on her chest, arms, wrists and hands. But she was never caught making these marks, some of which must have been exceedingly painful. The marks were always sore afterwards. And pins and needles in her proximity would suddenly appear in her flesh. . ."

The weals emerged with startling rapidity, their ridges being particularly white and thick. Price and several others witnessed this again and again—Eleonore playing with a ball or a toy, giving a sharp cry of pain, hurrying over to the observers and letting them roll up her sleeve or uncover her chest to witness the progress of the phenomenon. The teeth-marks always appeared first as red indentations on a white ground. The white surround gradually turned red at the same time as the indentations became white, rising in a thick ridge above the level of the flesh. Within a few minutes the ridge turned quite white and disappeared. Indentations and teeth-marks made in the fleshy part of the girl's hand in a normal manner showed exactly the same process.

Scratches and other marks of supposedly abnormal origin produced within a few minutes thick white weals and then disappeared rapidly.

"During my investigation of the girl in Vienna," Price wrote, "and later in London. . .these stigmatic markings occurred very frequently. At Vienna during the first few minutes of my preliminary observational period, Eleonore gave a short, sharp cry of pain, and Countess Wassilko at once pulled up the left sleeve of the child's bodice, and on the fleshy part of the forearm, some distance above the wrist, were the deep indentations of teeth-marks, six above and five below, forming together an elliptical figure. If the reader will bite the fleshy part of his own arm, he will get an exact representation of what we saw. . .Though the markings *could* have been made by the girl herself, I did not see any suspicious move on the part of Eleonore. In London we proved that at least some of the stigmata could not have been produced normally. . .During the first stigmatic phenomenon I watched the indentations on her arm gradually 'fill up', turn red, then white and finally rise above the surface of the flesh in the form of weals. I examined the sleeve of her bodice for marks of saliva, because if the girl had bitten her own arm, she must have done it through her sleeve. But there was no sign of moisture. The weals became gradually less distinct. Eleonore was convinced that '*Dracu*', her 'devil', had *bitten* her. . ."

This faith was so firm that the girl regularly tried to propitiate the over-boisterous, invisible "playmate". She would leave him bits of cake, an extra large nut or some other tit-bit around the room—believing that these would save her from more serious injury. *Dracu* obviously had a sweet tooth; his favourite was chocolate. During Price's Vienna experiments, Eleonore put one on the bookcase in full view of both observers. A moment later she cried out again; this time they found an annular marking on her left arm, about the size and shape of a chocolate. It was deeply indented in the fleshy portion, superimposed on the still faintly visible, earlier teethmarks. During his stay in Vienna, Price saw scores of these stigmatic markings. He believed that they must be associated with some mental process, as after each, Eleonore's pulse-rate increased—though otherwise she appeared perfectly normal.

A couple of days after the "Poltergeist girl's" arrival in London, the *Morning Post* published an article by one of its reporters:

"An example of the stigmatic manifestation occurred yesterday morning in my presence," he wrote. "Soon after I entered the room a mark was noticed rapidly growing on the girl's arm. As I watched it it grew into a number of cruel-looking weals which might have been inflicted by a whip or a thin cane. I am satisfied that neither the girl nor anyone else could have inflicted any such blow. Within a few minutes the marks had disappeared. Some minutes later, while I was helping Eleonore to wind up a clockwork cat, of which she is inordinately fond, I myself saw similar weals beginning to appear on her other arm and at the back of her neck. Nobody but myself was near her at the time and both her own hands were fully occupied with the toy. . ."

E. Clepham Palmer, the correspondent of the *Daily News* (who had once accompanied Price to Braunau to have sittings with the Schneider brothers) attended several observational periods—after his gift of the clockwork cat spitting fire had proved such a success.

His reports, published in his paper, were equally positive.

"It may be only coincidence," he wrote on October 5, 1926; "but, at any rate, it happened yesterday that these phenomena came thick and fast only when I turned up with another offering in the form of a toy. We were having tea in the laboratory and Eleonore was in the act of raising her cup to her lips when she suddenly gave a little cry of pain, put down her cup and rolled up her sleeve. On her forearm I then saw what appeared to be the marks of teeth indented deeply in the flesh, as if she or someone else had fiercely bitten her arm. The marks turned from red to white and finally took the form of white raised weals. They gradually faded, but were still noticeable after an hour or so.

While Eleonore was sitting in her chair under full observation similar markings appeared every few minutes. Once she jumped in her chair and pointed to the side of her face as if she had felt an acute pain there. On immediately examining her face I found two long parallel marks, like superficial scratches, extending from the top of her forehead down to her chin. As I watched they developed into prominent raised white weals and were quite a nasty disfigurement. For about twenty minutes the markings continued to appear more or less severely in various places. The whole time the girl appeared very uncomfortable and resentful of what she considers the attentions of '*Dracu*' or the Devil. Although I kept a close eye on her I failed to detect any self-infliction of the marks. The laboratory was brilliantly lit and I was at liberty to go as near Eleonore as I liked."

Next day the observers included Captain H.W. Seton-Karr, the big-game hunter, Colonel W.W. Hardwick, Mr. Robert Blair and others. Again there were the usual, 'devilish' manifestations of bites, scratches and other marks. "The girl was under close observation," Colonel Hardwick said in his report, "and could not have produced these herself by any normal means. . ." Captain Seton-Karr wrote to Price: "I was present on October 5 when the so-called 'stigmatic' markings appeared on the face, arms and forehead of Eleonore Zugun under conditions which absolutely precluded the possibility of Eleonore producing them by scratching or other normal means. The marks were photographed in my presence."

Price enlisted the help of Professor McDougall to try and hypnotise Eleonore. This had been done frequently by Countess Wassilko and she was even able to suggest to the girl that certain letters or marks should appear on her skin. The London experiments were not very successful—perhaps because of the presence of too many strangers. Professor McDougall thought that Eleonore was a very difficult subject and that it would need a considerable number of experiments to make her react quickly to post-hypnotic suggestions.

"Various theories have been formulated to account for Eleonore's spontaneous stigmata," Price wrote later. "Though many saints and ecstatics have been subject to stigmata, I believe that Eleonore is the only *medium* who has produced such phenomena. There can be little doubt that the infliction is a psychological one and must not be confused with urticaria, a disease of the skin characterised by evanescent rounded elevations resembling weals raised by a whip, attended by intense itching when the skin is knocked or rubbed. Eleonore's stigmata did not itch. And in urticarial subjects, the weals do not appear spontaneously, as in the case of Eleonore's markings. There is a curious belief that those who suffer from urticaria have a layer of skin too few!"

G.E. Browne, the scientist and psychical researcher, pointed out that in most poltergeist and in *all* stigmatisation cases there was hysteria at the base—not advanced or pathological but a "decided thinning

of the crust or division between the thinking mind and the under
dreaming mind." Mr. Browne quoted Janet's saying: "All mediumship is dislocation" and continued:

"Students of the mental side have been struck by the repeated emergence of a habitual control showing the intelligence of a child—
usually a girl, undeveloped, whimsical, tricky, full of mischief and
energy; in large measure uncontrollable and reckless of consequences. . .Saints dream of God and His wounds and the dream mind in
ecstasy (self-induced hypnosis) produces the wounds. Another type
of secondary adopts the child's conception of a devil and uses it to
spite the primary by marking its face with scratches, and its arms
with bites. Naturally there is no biting on the back or face; *it can't
imagine it*, but you suggest it under hypnosis and it is most probable
that it would be done. It bites when it is particularly displeased
with its primary, waiting until in a moment of distraction it can get
command of the body and its functioning (vascular). It bites *when
it is bored*. I will engage that when Eleonore Zugun is kept amused there
is no biting, no scratching; for then the secondary is also amused,
which it loves most of all. Similarly, when the secondary enjoys
the play of the primary, *especially motion of any kind*, ball-playing,
running about, motion games—then you may look for objects
being thrown about and perhaps even more elaborate telekinesis. . ."

Browne's theory was that of a split personality—and the subconscious being strong enough to cause the weals, teethmarks, etc. to
materialize. He was certainly right when he said that the telekinetic
phenomena were more frequent when Eleonore was in motion (he
had *not* met the girl during her visit to London) and that the "stigmata"
usually appeared when she was quiet.

The psychologists who examined and observed the girl traced back
the stigmata to her subconscious. Because of the poltergeist phenomena,
she was threatened with "Dracu" in her early childhood—the peasants
of Talpa foretold the dire things that the devil would do to her if she
"persisted in evil". Thus the idea of whippings, bitings, scratches
became connected in her subconscious with "*Dracu*". During the
London experiments some attempts were made to eliminate this complex but without success. The stigmata were the outward and visible
signs of influences that were the reflex responses of the higher nervous
centres to external stimuli. No one ever discovered, though, what

these stimuli were. The experiments were too short to bring definite results. Yet it was proved that the stigmata were genuine, spontaneous and not self-inflicted. This was the generally agreed view of all who had a chance to observe the "Devil Girl". The *Daily News*, in a leading article, committed itself fully to this opinion:

> "The temptation to believe that these phenomena are produced by trickery is obvious. Yet it must be remembered that these 'stigmata' have appeared not in a darkened room before the credulous but in a laboratory of psychical research in South Kenington, before men expert in tracing every form of conscious deception or complex hysteria. The genuine character both of the markings on her flesh and the movements of the articles in her room have survived the most searching tests...Altogether the eccentricities of the Poltergeist girl have provided one of the most bewildering problems, both psychical and psychological, of this generation..."

The leader writer of the *Morning Post*, speaking of the telekinetic phenomena, was equally puzzled as to explaining the cause of the manifestations:

> "The same difficulty occurs in the attempt to discover by what means the coins were moved in the recent experiments. . .Was the force drawn from the medium? or was it external to her? Or was it an external force acting upon the medium? No one knows. Nor does anyone know the nature of the force we call electricity. . ."

★　　★　　★

One of the most startling telekinetic phenomena connected with Eleonore's London visit was also connected with another of the magnetic letters used on the notice-board of the building in which Harry Price's National Laboratory was housed.

Ten days after the letter "L" fell from nowhere on to the laboratory floor, Price asked for the stock of letters to be checked again, suggesting that after the report the remainder should be locked up. This was done—and it was discovered that one each of the letters "C" and "W" was missing. The "W" never turned up again, but the "C" made its reappearance in a dramatic fashion.

Price said goodbye to Eleonore and the Countess on Thursday, October 21 as he was leaving London and they were to return to Vienna on Sunday, October 24. But Dr. R.J. Tillyard, F.R.S., chief entomologist to the Australian Government (who was killed in a motor accident in January, 1937) visited the Laboratory on Friday, October 22nd, for a few minutes; he saw Eleonore and the Countess and said goodbye to them—but neither came nearer to him than an arm's length. Except for Harry Price's secretary there was no one else present in the Laboratory; nor did Dr. Tillyard see or speak to anyone in the building.

Dr. Tillyard gave his own account of what happened:

"Having a very busy day, I had no intention of going to the Laboratory at all. Mr. Price was away and I had not heard of any arrangements for a séance. . .Eleonore's engagement was due to end the following day.

While going to the Underground train in the morning, I felt in my left overcoat pocket for some coppers for my fare. I pulled out what I thought was sixpence, and was just going to present it to the booking office when I noticed that it was a bronze 50-centime French piece. Thinking Eleonore might have put it there somehow, I decided to examine it carefully. Having found some other coppers and got my fare, I settled down in the train and examined the coin, which I discovered was not one of my thirteen marked ones. I therefore placed it carefully away in the left pocket of my coat where I always keep my knife and scissors, and I distinctly remember feeling carefully in the pocket to see if there were any other coins in it and extracting an odd halfpenny, which I transferred to my greatcoat pocket for use on the railway. I also quite clearly felt my knife and scissors, and if anything else had been in the pocket, I am sure I should have noticed it.

I had arranged to lunch with Professor Julian Huxley. We met at King's College at 1 p.m. and went to the Common Room for luncheon. After lunch we returned to his rooms, where we met Dr. Church, and had a long talk. This man left later, and talk turned to psychic matters. Huxley asked me to demonstrate to him the method of tying thumbs by which I had secured Harold Evans, the physical medium, in a séance held in June last. I consented, and Huxley went to look for some white cotton for which I had asked him. He returned and stated that he could not find any cotton, and asked whether a piece of thin string would do. I said it would, but that it was too long and must be cut (it was too strong to break). I then felt

179

in my left-hand coat pocket for my knife and scissors. These I produced in my left hand, the scissors in a cloth case, the knife in a leather case. While I momentarily debated as to whether I should cut the string with knife or scissors, Huxley had got his own knife out, and we agreed to cut the string together with his knife. I replaced my knife and scissors both in my left hand pocket, and held the string while he cut it in the place indicated by me. I then showed him how I tied the thumb-knots and left special lengths hanging on each side, so as to catch Evans, and he thanked me. At 2.45 p.m. I took my leave, but, just before I went, Huxley presented me with an autographed copy of his book, *Essays of a Biologist*, for which I thanked him and then walked down the stairs.

That afternoon I went to the Natural History Museum and later attended a meeting of the Association of Economic Biologists at the Botany School of the Imperial College of Science. Having lost my way, I arrived late, but stayed for afternoon tea and a talk with Dr. Pethebridge and Dr. Imms of Rothamsted.

Leaving shortly after five, I took farewell of my Rothamsted friends and began to think what I should do next. I had arranged to go down to my wife's people at Rochester for the week-end, but had told them I should catch the 8.20 train from Victoria Station. As I had about three hours still to fill in, it suddenly occurred to me that I had not said goodbye to the Countess and Eleonore, so I decided to walk to the Laboratory to do so. Arriving somewhat warm after a brisk walk, I went to the men's room on the third floor and took my greatcoat off and washed my hands. I then walked upstairs into the Laboratory, where I saw Countess Wassilko sitting at the table writing in a small book of accounts. I stood and talked to her for about two minutes, passing compliments on the success of her visit and finally saying goodbye and shaking hands. I then asked where Eleonore was, and was told that she was probably in the next room. As I thought I heard her playing in the baffle-chamber (a narrow room separating the laboratory and the séance-room which trapped the light when a person passed from one room to the other), I went to the door of it, but she disappeared quickly and ran round to the outside of the door of the Laboratory, where she stood smiling at me with a diabolo set in one hand and holding out the other to me. I took her hand and said goodbye, then went out and downstairs, put on my overcoat and walked to the Underground Station

Eleonore Zugun: the photograph shows stigmata appearing on the medium's face.

"Dracu's" teeth marks appearing on Eleonore's hand.

at South Kensington. From there I travelled to Charing Cross, picked up my baggage at the cloak-room, returned by the Underground to Victoria, walked up to the restaurant there, and sat down to a quiet dinner at a table all by myself. About 8 p.m. I got up and paid my bill, took a ticket for Rochester and found a seat in the train. Before it started (8.20 p.m.) one other man came in and sat, immersed in his newspaper, opposite me. I had an evening paper which occupied me about as far as Bromley. Then I took out Huxley's book from my greatcoat pocket and began to read it. By the time we reached Swanley, I had read eight pages and was then interested enough to be considerably annoyed when I found that the next few pages had not been cut. So I opened my greatcoat, put my hand down into the left pocket of my coat, and felt for my knife to cut the pages with. Then a curious feeling came over me. The knife did not feel like my knife at all. I drew it out and found firmly attached to the metal half-ring of the leather case enclosing it a white metallic 'C' which effectively closed the case. I realised at once that it was the 'C' which had been lost eleven days before from the notice board of the ground floor of 16, Queensberry Place, and the loss of which had been generally attributed to '*Dracu*'."

I must confess that I have quoted this long, elaborate account by he late chief entomologist of the Australian Government with deliberate njoyment. It is full of homely detail, piling it on and on—up to the limax. And to the layman it is more of an anti-climax at that! A small metal letter getting itself somehow wound around the leather case of pen-knife! Is this all the supernatural forces, the spooks and devils re capable of? In the Arabian Nights the *ifrits and djinns* build palaces nd move cities overnight; but modern poltergeists and 'Dracus' vork modest, cut-rate miracles!

Yet to the investigator the white "C" twined around Dr. Tillyard's nife was a major event, almost a landmark in psychical research. It as its very modesty and homeliness that made it convincing. And certainly marked the end of Eleonore's London stay "with a great ourish of trumpets, psychically speaking. . ."

*   *   *

A few months after the London visit, in January 1927, the responsible nd widely-read *Vossische Zeitung* published a special supplement

devoted to Eleonore—an unprecedented step for such a staid and old
established newspaper. A physician discussed Eleonore's psyche. Coun
tess Wassilko-Serecki gave the story of her discovery and past achieve
ments. Alfred Döblin, the famous German novelist who was also
doctor, thought that she was "possessed" and Professor C. Zimme
declared that her phenomena were certainly genuine.

However, only a few weeks later came some disconcerting reports
The Countess and Eleonore were in Munich to make a film witl
the Eku Company of Bavaria about the young girl's mediumship. On
February 20, 1927, the *Berliner Tageblatt* published an article by Dr
Hans Rosenbusch, a Munich doctor, in which he accused the Countes
of helping to produce the strange weals and scratches on the girl'
super-sensitive skin and Eleonore herself was charged of "helping th
phenomena". Count Carl von Klinckowstroem, one of the leadin
German psychical researchers, supported the charges of Dr. Rosen
busch.

"The Unmasking of the Rumanian Devil". . . "Eleonore Zugun an
the Dragon Dracu. . ." "The Film Shows It Up". . . These were som
of the headings of Rosenbusch's attack. The Munich physician de
clared that *all* phenomena were fraudulent and that the Countess ha
deliberately and regularly aided and abetted Eleonore in her deceptio
by presenting her to scientists and psychical investigators. Dr. Rosen
busch ended by saying: it was not his task to accuse the Counte
—she should be given a chance to "disappear in silence".

The patroness of Eleonore Zugun was certainly not willing to d
that. A month after the publication of the article she sued Dr. Rosen
busch for slander. The main defence of Dr. Rosenbusch was that h
article was simply a "critical judgment of a scientific effort" by th
Countess; that it was "privileged comment" and that he "had take
into consideration justified interests" in order to prove that his attitud
towards occult phenomena was the right one. There was a good de
of legal argument; the Countess's lawyer, Dr. G. von Scanzoni pointe
out that Dr. Rosenbusch spoke of "unmasking" in his article rathe
than of scientific criticism—it was an attempt to denounce her, to ex
pose her to shame and ridicule. No one could call it "critical judgment
if someone reviewed a literary work and accused the author of stealin
the manuscript from another writer's desk-drawer.

However, the Munich Criminal Court found for Dr. Rosenbuscl
Countess Wassilko-Serecki's accusations of slander were rejected c

the basis that the *form* of the article by Dr. Rosenbusch did not show any *intention* of libel. Shortly after the Countess entered her suit, Dr. Schrenck-Notzing came to her support in an article published in the 'Zeitschrift für Parapsychologie"; he, at least, was convinced of Eleonore's genuine powers. Harry Price also declared: "There is not the slightest doubt that our careful experiments made under ideal scientific conditions, have proved that stigmatic markings appeared spontaneously on various parts of Eleonore's body; that she was not consciously responsible for the production of the marks; and that under test conditions movements of small objects without physical contact took place." He also pointed out that the Countess was not present at any of the test experiments; therefore she could not be an accomplice. However, he admitted that "the girl would cheat if we let her. That is why various controlling devices, tactual and mechanical, were employed." There were many Continental psychical researchers who came to Eleonore's defence. Professors Hans Hahn, Richard Hoffmann, Hans Thirring and Karl Wolf, with Dr. Alfred Winterstein and Michael Dumba, issued a statement in Vienna which recorded that they had observed the Zugun girl for six months under the most exacting conditions and could not find the slightest trace of fraud. They also rejected firmly the charge that the Countess, who had been engaged in psychical research for many years, could have had any share in the alleged deception.

Count Carl von Klinckowstroem attacked Schrenck-Notzing and the pro-Eleonore scientists and the argument raged for several months. The Countess immediately appealed against the verdict of the Munich Criminal Court. In a long statement she analysed the charges and "so-called proofs" of Dr. Rosenbusch and published the full records of several séances held under strict control. But, as always in such cases, it was one person's word against the other's — with three or four taking the side of Dr. Rosenbusch and the others supporting the Countess. The genuineness or fraudulence of mediums certainly cannot be decided by a majority vote nor by the personal evaluation of sceptics and believers. And again, as always, there were recriminations, charges of bad faith, of financial and prestige considerations. The Countess's appeal was heard late in 1927—and again she lost. The appeal court refused to go into the rights and wrongs of Dr. Rosenbusch's statements—perhaps wisely the judges would not get involved in an occult dispute—but simply took the view that his was "justified criticism".

Under German law the case could not be taken to any higher cour
and the Countess had to be content with putting her arguments tc
her fellow psychical researchers, appealing to their judgment. If I sa)
that the majority accepted her side of the story, it still does not meai
that anything decisive and final had been achieved about the "Devi
Girl". Perhaps, as in so many other cases, hers was a "mixed" me
diumship; but no satisfactory proof has been ever offered that th«
Countess aided any deception by the girl in any way.

But not long after the argument had subsided, the whole problem
was settled—at least in a certain sense.

"A few months after she left my laboratory," Harry Price wrot«
about Eleonore, "the menses appeared and, almost overnight, th
girl became perfectly normal. No more stigmata, or falling coins
or flying stilettos were witnessed. She also 'grew up' mentally ver'
rapidly, and in addition there was a marked physical development. . ."

It has been the general experience of occultists that the delicat
physiological and psychological changes connected with puberty ar
always closely connected with the psychic "powers" of young mediums
With a girl it is the catamenial period that appears to be the dividin;
line between the appearance and disappearance of phenomena. Th
development of sexual functions either *stops* mediumship or revea]
the latent powers. This has been recorded again and again in psychica
research though no satisfactory explanation has been offered for i
and there are, of course, not enough mediums to provide a statistica
basis for a thorough study of the subject.

Anyhow, Eleonore, as the Countess announced, had lost her psychi
powers. But her foster-mother had foreseen that this would soone
or later happen. She apprenticed the girl to a Viennese ladies' hair
dresser. Here she did extremely well and gained a diploma. The la\$
Harry Price heard about her was a message on a neat business car
announcing that the "Poltergeist girl" had set herself up in busine\$
in Czernowitz, Rumania. She was doing well, happily and lucrativel
catering for the never-ceasing desire of women to look their be\$
whatever their natural assets might be—from the top of their head
to their fingertips. And *Dracu* seemed to have been banished for ev«
to whatever limbo he had emerged from.

*   *   *

CHAPTER EIGHT

Margery: Spooky Fingertips

Never Underestimate a Woman—the famous advertising slogan proclaims. And if any mere male would be rash enough to risk such an attitude, he would need only to be reminded of Mrs. Le Roy Goddard Crandon, the second wife of a Boston surgeon who, for almost twenty years, dominated psychical research in the United States, almost wrecked the American Society for Psychical Research and set scores of famous scientists, psychologists, magicians, journalists and others at loggerheads.

She did this by her personal charm—for she was a very personable lady—and by the amazing variety of the occult phenomena she produced (or didn't produce, according to the view you took of her mediumship). Most mediums specialize in one or other phenomenon. Certainly, they are usually divided into the two main categories of physical and mental mediums. But not Mrs. Crandon. She was a veritable da Vinci of occult, a *polyhistor*, a "compleat psychic". She would do automatic writing in several languages, apports, telekinesis, direct voice, clairvoyance, materialised "hands" and teleplasmic forms, cross-correspondence tests—you named it and she would deliver it. She was probably the most versatile lady in all psychical history.

At least twenty books could be filled with only the main writings about her. Acres of newsprint have been covered with charges and counter-charges. Her champions and her attackers balanced each other fairly evenly and in the dust raised by the conflict not only the truth but even the simple facts disappeared—often without trace. To tell Margery's story, a vast amount of condensation and over-simplification is necessary. A book which one of her stoutest champions, J. Malcolm Bird, (at one time editor of the "Scientific American" and later Research Officer of the American S.P.R.) wrote about her runs to over 500 pages. Between 1925 when this weighty volume was published and 1930 when Theodore Besterman devoted a chapter to

Margery in his "Some Modern Mediums", the literature dealing with the lady had grown at least tenfold. It can be divided sharply between pro and contra-Margery writings with only few "in-betweens". And in the following account I have felt it necessary to mark clearly the nature of the sources I have used.

★ ★ ★

In an early paper on the Margery case Dr. Crandon provided biographical sketches both about himself and his wife. According to these, Margery was born Mina Stinson in rural Ontario, near Toronto, in 1883. She was educated in Toronto, studying Latin and French for one year but no other languages. When she was about seventeen, she went to Boston where she became secretary to the Union Congregational Church.

Dr. L.R.G. Crandon was born in Boston; his maternal uncle was Rear-Admiral J.E. Pillsbury, U.S. Navy; his father's family came from Plymouth, Mass., a "direct descendant from twenty-three of the original Mayflower passengers." His great-grandfather was Collector of the Port of Plymouth for thirty years; his father President of the Boston Ethical Society. He graduated from Harvard in 1894, received his M.D. degree in 1898 and an A.M. in philosophy in 1909. We are not given details of his first marriage nor the exact date of his wedding to Miss Stinson. They had one child.

Margery was five years younger than her brother Walter, (who was killed by a railway-engine in 1911 when he was twenty-eight). There was a slight psychic inclination in the family; in his youth Walter had tables tilt and levitate in his presence in daylight (Dr. Crandon reported) and Margery's mother did automatic writing for many years.

It was Malcolm Bird who gave Mrs. Crandon the pseudonym of Margery while he baptised Dr. Crandon "F.H." (Friend Husband). The idea was to keep the medium's identity a secret—though this was soon discarded.

Dr. Crandon, a voracious reader, became interested in psychical research in 1923 when he read *On the Threshold of the Unseen* by Sir William Barrett and Crawford's book on the *Reality of Psychic Phenomena*. He began to study the available literature and "the subject came to occupy a major place in his extra-professional mental life."

As a result, but more as a joke, Mrs. Crandon and her friend Mrs. Katherine Brown, went to a medium who informed them that a "male spirit" was present who gave the name of Walter and claimed to be Margery's brother. A few days later Dr. Crandon visited the same clairvoyant and obtained from him "evidential messages from his brother-in-law." Margery had been told that she was herself "a potential medium of great power."

Inspired by this, a table was made and on one of the closing days of May, 1923, the Crandons, Dr. Edison W. Brown and his wife, Frederick Adler (superintendent of the building in which Crandon had his office) and Alexander W. Cross, a young Englishman whom Dr. Crandon had more or less adopted and who acted as his secretary, sat down for a séance in a room on the top floor in the Crandons' Lime Street, Boston, house. At this very first sitting the table moved and tilted; later one of the usual codes of raps was formulated and soon, as Besterman says, "the mediumship began its formal course."

Between May and November 1923 most of Margery's simpler phenomena were developed.

In December 1922 the *Scientific American* had offered $2,500 to any medium producing "a visible psychic manifestation" under its test conditions. The committee investigating the claims of those who were to submit to the tests consisted of Dr. William McDougall, the eminent psychologist, Dr. Hereward Carrington, the psychical investigator, Dr. D.F. Comstock, a retired professor of the Massachusetts Institute of Technology; Dr. W.F. Prince, then research officer of the American *Society For Psychical Research* and Henry Houdini (Erich Weiss), the famous magician. J. Malcolm Bird acted as secretary and as he put it "stage manager" to the group—though, according to W.F. Prince "not by action of the committee." He was chiefly responsible for procedure—"the strict function of committee members being to act as judges."

About two-fifths of J. Malcolm Bird's long book is devoted to the 133 sittings which Margery held from May 1923 to April 1924. The materials for this had been furnished by Dr. Crandon. At the first 63 sittings no record was made of the arrangement of the sitters or the degree of control and even in the subsequent seventy sittings this information was provided only "incidentally or otherwise". Certainly, nothing like Schrenck-Notzing's or Harry Price's scrupulous, methodical procedure was followed and Bird himself calls it "the informal stage of the mediumship." Yet Dr. Crandon and Bird (a most enthusiastic champion of Margery) claimed that an immense variety of psychic phenomena took place.

In December 1923 Dr. Crandon and Margery visited Paris and London. According to Dr. Crandon: "Margery enters a laboratory in Paris or London for the first time, and, under conditions laid down by the most experienced men in the world, the phenomena begin within a few minutes." Yet Theodore Besterman wrote soberly: "Nothing especially notable occurred during the five sittings then given" ("then" refers here to the European visit.). Certainly, even Bird's account is rather restrained about this period. Margery herself had some "psychic photographs" taken by the notorious Mrs. Ada Emma Deane whose crude "spirit pictures" produced on Armistice Days around the London Cenotaph were found to be impudent frauds—the photographs of very much alive footballers. Bird actually printed some of her crude fakes in his book, with two "spirits" hovering in a cottonwool cloud to the left above Margery's head; the caption declared: "The one nearer Margery is the one recognized as Walter."

In any case, by January 1924 the Crandons were back in Boston and private sittings of the circle continued until April. In that month Dr. Crandon decided to enter his wife as a contestant for the *Scientific American* prize which none of the previous competitors had managed to earn. The séances took place between April and August. What *really* happened during them, became a matter of the fiercest controversy.

Here is first Dr. Crandon's version, published in the symposium "The Case For and Against Psychical Belief", edited by Carl Murchison and published by Clark University, Worcester, Mass., in 1927:

"In 1924, came a period of observation and investigation by a committee selected by the Scientific American. This was largely a period of comedy. One member, the most experienced student of this subject in the world, declared the phenomena to be of first quality and supernormal. The Secretary of the committee (J. Malcolm Bird) reached the same conclusion. One member said at the end of every sitting, 'There are plenty of psychic phenomena here', but he wouldn't write it. Perhaps he was wisely discreet. The third member was deaf. At a sitting in the dark, therefore, with eyes and ears missing as it were, he might as well have been absent! A fourth member, whose knowledge of wriggling out of strait-jackets and handcuffs was as great as his ignorance of psychics, came with his mind made up before he started. The last member saw apparatus used, of his own making, under his own conditions, over forty times, but decided it could not be true because he would not believe it. These inexplicable occurrences did not fit into his already formed philosophy, and the intellectual hole he found himself in was a bit uncomfortable. The signed notes of the Scientific American Committee are entirely accurate and contain no implication of normal production of phenomena."

In other words, four out of the six members of the committee (if we include Mr. Bird) were either incapable or unwilling to accept the mediumship of Margery. This, her husband insisted, was their fault. An ancient and familiar argument; to discredit the critics, it has been always convenient to cast doubt upon their good faith or ability. But the Boston surgeon would hardly be anything but a vigorous and persistent advocate of Mrs. Crandon.

In the same symposium, Dr. Prince presented the investigators' case in some detail, providing chapter and verse for his statements (*all* psychical investigation reports bristle with footnotes; Malcolm Bird's book was largely—and justly—attacked because it lacked this apparatus.) These were his main points:

"That bane of scientific research—premature publicity—was precipitated in spite of protests from the committee. Never was an investigation more hampered, both at this and subsequent stages, by prohibitions and arbitrary rules.

An investigator ought to be able to see, at least in some kind of light. But the darkness was relieved by red light, more or less, only when 'Walter' gave the signal, reminding one of the magician who withdraws the curtain after a wonder is prepared behind it. Darkness might be required by a 'psychic law' but it is also convenient for hoaxing.

It ought to be possible to make reasonable use of those important instruments of investigation, the hands. But hands were held fast except momentarily under strict regulations. The 'ectoplasmic limb' may shove, lift and throw objects, slap sitters and pull their hair, and even overturn the table or rip away the wing of the cabinet, but the slightest touch laid upon it unbidden, it is explained, might fearfully shock the medium. This seems unreasonable and yet investigators obeyed the inscrutable law."

(It will be remembered that this was not the case with the Schneider brothers or D.D. Home. Within certain limits, the 'ectoplasm' could be touched and even handled.)

"Investigators ought to be permitted cautiously to test how far alleged laws are actually valid. An investigator on one occasion ventured to move his own and the psychic's hands slowly into the area between her and the bell-box, and no objection being made continued to do so. Since the bell rang nevertheless, the law against this founded on the theory of 'psychic rods' seemed disproved, yet, after-experimentation of the kind was forbidden. If in his (Prince's) one daylight sitting the two momentary muffled tinkles really came from the box and not from beneath the medium's skirts five inches distant, the important discovery was made that the box-bell could be rung under the most favourable conditions. . .He never could get another daylight sitting. Scientific investigators are supposed to plan the nature, particular time and duration of their tests. But here 'Walter' autocratically directed, consenting or refusing, unexpectedly switching phenomena or terminating a series of particular type before the hiatus in the proof was filled. . ."

Dr. Prince was expecting too much. All 'controls' whether imaginary or genuine, working with fraudulent or honest mediums, are notoriously capricious.

Dr. Prince went on to complain about a number of rules Dr. Crandon introduced which amounted to "an effective device to hamper investigators to be so bound and to embarrass them after an unfavourable verdict." Every member had to sign a blanket report composed of individual observations dictated during the sitting by different members but could not make the reservation that he was responsible only for his own observations; the members were "vigorously scolded for not repudiating the observations of Houdini." Nor were they allowed to amend these dictated notes later. Everything that was considered important had to appear in the contemporaneous record—which meant that anything that did *not* appear in it was supposed to be unimportant. This was an "absurd rule." Crandon also demanded that "any observed indication of fraud must be announced immediately." This rule, of course, would actually coach a fraudulent medium and prevent the development of the fraud to the point of proof. "Friend Husband" insisted that he should always be one of the controllers of the medium. This, Prince said, was "scientifically suspect" and even Bird admitted that "Dr. Crandon's testimony as to continuity of control is unreliable."

The *Scientific American* Committee report was adverse by a majority of four to one. "Rigid proof has not yet been furnished," said Dr. Comstock. "As long ago as November 1923," Professor McDougall declared, "I was inclined to regard all the phenomena I had observed as produced by normal means. . .Since that date. . .the inclination described above has grown steadily stronger in the main, in spite of some minor fluctuations, and has now become well-nigh irresistible." Dr. Prince was even less cautiously damning: "No sitting at which I was present was to me convincing. . .In fact, I could write a chapter of indications which, in the absence of contravening proof, seem to tell the story of normal and deceptive production." Houdini was quite blunt: "Everything which took place at the séances which I attended was a deliberate and conscious fraud." Even Dr. Carrington who voted for Margery, had his reservations: "Many of the observed manifestations might well have been produced fraudulently—and possibly were so produced." He added, however: "But I am convinced that genuine phenomena have occurred here"—plumping therefore for a "mixed mediumship."

Dr. Crandon naturally did not like this result; Margery did not get the $2,500 prize. And in addition there was the confused and unpleasant incident of the carpenter's rule. Houdini had devised a strong cabinet to immobilise the medium. Then came a séance at which "Walter" declared that the magician had placed a wooden two-foot rule in the cabinet so that he—Houdini—could accuse the medium of trickery. Houdini replied that it was Margery who took the rule into the cabinet so that *she* could accuse *him* of framing *her*. A little melodramatically, the great escape artist swore by the grave of his dead mother that he had no knowledge of the rule.

By December 1924 the controversy had exploded upon the front pages. "HUSBAND OF 'MARGERY' ASSAILS PSYCHIC TESTS; HOUDINI IN HOT RETORT. TRICKS PLAYED AT SEANCES, DR. CRANDON SAYS. $5000 CHALLENGE, WIZARD'S ANSWER: HE OFFERS TO DETECT, AND DUPLICATE EVERY EFFECT MEDIUM PRODUCES," the *Boston Herald* proclaimed on December 18. Four days later it was: "HOUDINI ANSWERS PROF. McDOUGALL WITH FRESH CHALLENGE OF ABILITY. WIZARD DENIES HE WAS PUT OFF MARGERY BOARD. ASKS COULD OPPONENT BE BOXED UP AND THROWN INTO RIVER AND ESCAPE? NETTLED BY CLAIM TO DEEPER KNOWLEDGE. SAYS HE STUDIED SPIRITU-ALISM 40 YEARS—REPEATS $5000 OFFER." And by December 30, the main frontpage headlines of the *Boston Traveller* (under the topical banner: "*Police to Keep Hub Dry on New Year's Eve*") read: "HOUDINI POSTS $10,000 TO 'SHOW UP' MARGERY. MAGICIAN CALLS ON MAYOR HERE. TERMS SPIRITUALISTIC MEDIUM AS 'DANGEROUS'—LIST OF JUDGES CHOSEN—DEMON-STRATES TRICKS."

The headlines more or less tell the story. It was just a glorious free-for-all, a farrago of personalities, of challenges and counter-challenges, in many ways startlingly childish. Whether Margery could get out of a straitjacket or not really had little to do with her mediumship. Whether Houdini had studied occultism for four or forty years did not make Margery less or more genuine. And the challenges—as in the case involving Rudi Schneider, Maskelyne and Harry Price—were equally worthless because each challenger set his own terms under which he would be prepared to redeem his pledge; and these terms were unacceptable to the challenged.

As always, the dispute was decided a long time afterwards and not in the way in which the participants expected it to be settled.

★   ★   ★

Dr. Crandon, apparently despairing of getting sufficient scientific acknowledgment of his wife's powers, decided to try and obtain it from a foreign source. He invited Dr. Dingwall, then Research Officer of the British S.P.R. His investigations covered the period January and February 1925.

Here again we find quite contradictory accounts of what happened. Dr. Prince wrote:

"The great feature of this series...was the production of 'Ecto-plasm', something like an ill-formed, cold hand feeling like 'blanc-mange' and lying on the table or in the medium's lap, sometimes a curious substance seen either issued from or poked into her ear.

The substance was never seen in the process of actual materialization. Unfortunately, Dingwall's hopes that the missing links of authentication would be supplied were disappointed, for in his report he says: 'The control of the medium appears to be rigid, and is faultless, if we accept Dr. F.H. (Crandon) as a *bona fide* investigator, which, under the circumstances, he is himself the first to admit is impossible.' The conditions, therefore, of the sittings are such that I cannot at present affirm my belief in the authenticity of the phenomena."

Dr. McDougall attended a number of these sittings and his doubts greatly increased. Some photographs of the "ectoplasmic hand" seemed to him to resemble lung-tissue, artificially shaped to resemble an ill-formed hand. In at least one photograph the annular bands of a trachea and a tubular opening were recognizable. It was only a year later that he could submit the prints to experts. Dr. W.B. Cannon, professor of physiology and Dr. H.W. Rand, associate professor of zoology, both of Harvard University, supported McDougall's suspicions, saying that the "ectoplasm" was undoubtedly composed of the lung tissue of some animal.

In the January, 1925 issue of M.U.M. (Magic-Unit-Might), organ of the Society of American Magicians, Houdini published a front-page appeal to Dr. Dingwall which he had sent off as a telegram to the British investigator:

"If I am rightly informed, you are lecturing this evening on Mrs. Crandon (better known as Margery), and the genuineness of her manifestations. I hereby offer five thousand dollars if you will appear before a committee of newspaper men, clergy or before the *Society of American Magicians, of which you are a member,* and convince either one or the other with proof positive that I did not detect her in fraud. If you are satisfied that Margery is genuine, I will pay another five thousand dollars if I do not detect her in every manifestation she presents three times in front of a committee in my presence. It is understood the money I forfeit is to be donated to charity, and I am willing to pay also all expenses of bringing the medium here to New York. Wire answer. HOUDINI."

A somewhat plaintive footnote added: "No answer up to time of going to Press." Indeed, Houdini's challenge was a little unfair. Dr.

Dingwall was obviously in two minds about the mediumship. During the many sittings in January and February 1925, the phenomena witnessed were the usual "Walter" voice, telekinetic movements of objects, handshaped materialisations which "appeared to exude from the various orifices of the medium's body" etc. It was not until June 1926 that the London S.P.R. published Dr. Dingwall's report. He stated that Margery's mediumship was "the most remarkable hitherto recorded" and of great importance. Whether genuine or a vast hoax, it was still the most important, Dr. Dingwall said, but during the whole long document he was unable to commit himself whether it was genuine or not.

"I did not succeed in achieving my primary purpose, of coming to a definite conclusion as to the genuineness or otherwise of the phenomena. During the course of the (twenty-nine) sittings the evidence seemed to me at one time for, and another time against, their supernormal nature, but never to incline decisively either way."

In January 1925 while the Dingwall-séances were still in progress, Sir Arthur Conan Doyle, an unflinching champion of practically all mediums, whatever their standing, entered the fray. The *Boston Herald's* front-page headlines presented his views: "MARGERY GENUINE, SAYS CONAN DOYLE; HE SCORNS HOUDINI. CRITICIZES THE EXPERT BODY IN SEVERE TERMS. ALL BUT BIRD AND CARRINGTON DERELICT IN SILENCE UNDER ATTACK. HE ANALYZES ALL EVIDENCE ADDUCED. SURPRISED AMERICAN GENTLEMAN SHOULD TOLERATE WIZARD'S CONDUCT." This broadside by the creator of Sherlock Holmes was evidently an answer to Houdini who, early in January, had staged a burlesque séance in Symphony Hall, Boston, "Harry Houdini", the Boston *Transcript* wrote of the occasion, "proved himself the greatest magician of them all last night. . .He accomplished his purpose: he sent home most of his audience convinced, at the close of a stormy forum, that the manifestations of spiritualistic mediums are fraud and knavery." Apparently the "wizard" exposed the tricks which, according to him, Margery had used in the recent test; he also attacked Conan Doyle and Sir Oliver Lodge as "Menaces of Mankind". It was an uproarious occasion and Houdini, one of the great extroverts of all ages, enjoyed himself hugely—and so did the thousands packing the large hall.

Dr. Dingwall came under fire both from the supporters and the critics of Margery. "Friend Husband" declared that the British investigator had been deeply impressed by the phenomena and had even written to Baron Schrenck-Notzing: "It is the most beautiful case of teleplasmic telekinesis with which I am acquainted. . .The 'control' is irreproachable." Yet, Dr. Crandon charged, Dingwall changed his attitude when he received a letter from Professor McDougall (written on January 18 1925) in which McDougall warned him that "it will be very unsatisfactory from every point of view, if your report and mine on the same series of sittings are in serious disagreement."

Confusion and contradiction; perhaps Theodore Besterman's summing up was the fairest: "Mr. Dingwall's investigation. . .led to conclusions generally regarded as adverse to the medium. . ."

★　　★　　★

In February and March, 1925, there were further private sittings in the Crandon circle. Dr. Crandon then organized a group of four Harvard instructors and a graduate student—the suggestion came from the indefatigable "Walter"—as a circle of study. The spokesman of the group was Mr. Hudson Hoagland. The University authorities gave them the use of a room at the Harvard psychological department and agreed that if the results constituted a substantial contribution to knowledge, he could submit them and their discussion as a Ph.D. thesis. A number of professors and physicians were invited to assist; Dr. Crandon stipulated that one or two should be admitted at a time. For the six sittings between May 19 and June 24, 1925, the investigations seemed to have been going well and the majority of the sitters were impressed by the phenomena. Several reports, against the investigators' wishes appeared in print. The last declared: "It is a joy to observe this study being made by honest men with open minds. . ." But on June 29th and 30th some of the investigators became convinced that they had observed trickery. This involved a luminous anklet which dropped on the floor (Hoadland distinctly saw the silhouette of a foot, its toes holding the luminous disc, and he traced the form of a leg to the knee); and on the second occasion Professor Shapley and Mr. Code saw the medium work both hands free from control and one of them detected her conveying objects from the region of her lap and afterwards returning them. "Internal search of the medium," Dr. Prince remarks plaintively, "has never been permitted."

In November 1925 Hoagland published a report in the *Atlantic Monthly*. Dr. Crandon tried to obtain an advance proof of it but failed; after its publication he protested that this was in violation of the agreement with the Harvard group. Hoagland's article alleged more than twenty items of evidence, direct and collateral, leading to a verdict of "normal production" of the "ectoplasmic limb" that was the "great phenomenon" of these séances. Once again the published report of the group was "adverse to the mediumship."

Dr. Crandon was incensed at this outcome—the second negative report on his wife's psychic talents. He published a pamphlet entitled: "Margery Harvard Veritas" in which a strong attempt was made to discredit the judgment of all sixteen persons composing the three accepted tribunals of the Margery mediumship—except Dr. Hereward Carrington. It was a heavily biased publication and in a long, painstaking analysis of it Dr. Prince showed how the séance records were censored and even doctored in Margery's favour. Hoagland's report was interesting because his theory was that Margery's trickery was "largely automatic, subconscious." But others argued that this could be applied "to every professional medium including those known to *purchase* their apparatus and to consult with each other as to methodology."

All members of the Harvard group signed a statement that "the group is in absolute agreement that the only conclusion possible to them is that trickery accounted for all the phenomena; that the only possible difference of opinion in the group is to what extent the trickery was unconscious." The signatories included Harlow Shapley, the director of Harvard Astronomical Observatory, S. B. Wolbach, professor of pathology, Edwig G. Boring, director of Harvard Psychological Laboratory, Hudson Hoagland, a Harvard assistant in psychology, S. Foster Damon, Robert Hillyer (the distinguished poet) and John Marshall, (these last three were Harvard instructors in English).

From June to August 1925 there were three series of investigations by the American Society for Psychical Research. The Society was split from top to bottom by the Margery dispute; many of its officials resigned and the "Margery-champions" remained in control. Margery's sympathisers became convinced of the genuineness of the phenomena and in their *Journal* kept up a "heroic defence" of the medium. Between September 1925 and January 1926 there were more private sittings in

Margery (Mrs. L.R.G. Crandon) in her glass control cabinet:
Photograph below shows Dr. Richardson handing a luminous disc through the "door" opening. During the seance it was claimed that "Walter's" hand would take the disc and levitate it everywhere within the cabinet. (insert above) Control for Margery's hands during the seance. The loop around wrist was made from 128 lb strength wire which was then secured to a tie–bolt outside the cabinet.

Flashlight photograph of Margery producing the alleged hand of her dead brother Walter Stinson "after the manner of a birth". The "hand" is about to make a thumb print in dental wax. Note the bowls of hot and cold water.

the Crandon circle. In January 1926 Dr. Crandon made yet one more attempt to obtain some official or scientific endorsement. A committee of the American S.P.R., consisting of two psychologists and one physicist sat on the case but after the fourth séance Dr. Crandon terminated the experiments.

"The professor of physics," Dr. Prince reported, "declares himself firmly convinced of fraud, says that the apparatus used serves only to give a deceptive appearance of scientific control, asks why instead of the cumbrous voice machine the use of a simple stethoscope to test the 'independent voice' is not allowed, affirms that on one occasion in the darkness he traced clear to Margery's mouth a small solid rod covered with something feeling like soft leather, etc."

The two other members of the committee did not report and the American S.P.R. was silent on the whole matter. Professor J.B. Rhine and his wife—pioneers of the E.S.P. experiments at Duke University and perhaps the most eminent explorers of extra-sensory perception in the United States—had a single séance with Margery about this time. They, too, were completely disillusioned.

Yet Margery went on, quite undismayed, stoutly supported by her husband and the comparatively few people who remained faithful.

In July 1926 she—or "Walter"—developed a new and striking "phenomenon"—spirit fingerprints.

Margery had produced "psychic" gloves or moulds as early as May 1924. Those were rather crude and no one was particularly impressed by them—though Dr. Crandon duly enumerated them among the seventeen different "manifestations of psychic energy" he claimed for his wife (similar experiments were made by Klusky, the Polish medium.)

More than two years after the "gloves", a determined effort was made to obtain prints of the extrusions or "fingers" which belonged to the crude materialized hands, seen and felt at the Margery séances (as to their origin, this was one of the main bones of contention between the two opposing camps.) The difficulty was that "Walter"—a cantankerous "entity" at his best, much given to unprintable profanity—objected strongly to getting printer's ink or lampback on his "teleplasmic terminal". At "his" suggestion they tried a bucket of hot wax and a sheet of plate glass. "Walter" dipped his terminal in the wax, then pressed it on the glass. There were some skin markings to be seen but they were not very good. Then the resourceful "Walter" proposed that the glass should be covered with soft wax and that he should press his fingers upon it. Again, the markings were not very good. Finally Margery's dentist came to the rescue. Dr. Kerwin, much interested in the phenomena, thought of "Kerr", a proprietary brand of dental wax which became plastic when warmed. This technique was successful—and for the first time in occult history a spirit obligingly and permanently recorded his three-dimensional thumb-prints (and *only* the thumb-prints) as requested.

The procedure was somewhat cumbersome. Into a bowl of hot water a slab of "Kerr" was placed, resting on the end of a napkin. This cloth trailed over the side of the bowl into another bowl containing cold water. "Walter's" terminal (in complete darkness) pulled the soft "Kerr" out of the hot water by tugging at the end of the cloth, pressed his thumb terminal on to the wax, continued the pulling of the cloth which resulted in the "Kerr" being deposited in the cold water where it quickly hardened. The napkin was used to save "Walter" from scalding his fingers in hot water—though one would think that a spirit would be immune to hot and cold. It also prevented his "hands" getting wet. (The sceptics said that it saved all this trouble for the medium and her possible confederates.) Photographs showing "Walter's" "hands" (which appear to be extruded from the medium's vagina) making the prints have been published. By the time the thumb-print technique had been perfected, "Walter" had also improved considerably the shape of the terminals. The new fingers were much better to look at than the previous crude "pseudopods" which, as Professor Mc-Dougall had pointed out, were exactly like "heaps of animal tissue carved into the resemblance of hands."

As the plastic "Kerr" technique was perfected, "Walter" began to deposit his thumb-prints (left and right) in great profusion. At the séances the sitters' finger-prints were often taken in order to demonstrate that they were quite unlike the prints left by "Walter". "Friend Husband" was at pains to point out that he had a deformed right index-nail which had never been seen in one of the wax glove casts.

In December 1929 the Crandons visited London, for the first time since 1923. They were interviewed on disembarkation by a representative of the *Daily Mail*. This was the period of Harry Price's experiments with Rudi Schneider. The doctor and his wife both "laughed at the complicated system of electrical control which has been introduced at (Price's) National Laboratory of Psychical Research." Margery said, somewhat ambiguously, that "the main aim was to make the phenomena control itself (*sic*!)" After this Price was not surprised that the Crandons did not sit with him. Dr. Crandon paid a brief visit to the National Laboratory and refused pointblank to give any sittings on the premises. Price—who had tried to get the Crandons for some tests—reminded him that he had promised three times to do so; but "Friend Husband" replied that the time was too short.

However, Price, being a persistent man, demanded in his official capacity as Foreign Research Officer and European representative of the American S.P.R. the right to attend one of the Margery séances and in the end Dr. Crandon consented. The sitting was held on December 7, 1929. Among those present were Professor F.C.S. Schiller, Dr. William Brown, Lady Florence Barrett, the gynaecologist, Sir E.N. Bennett, Lord Charles Hope and others.

The Crandons, as Harry Price put it, were "determined to impress" him—but he was not impressed. The medium sat in an ordinary wooden armchair. Her wrists and ankles were fastened with adhesive tape to the arms and legs of the chair and her neck was loosely secured to its back by a thick piece of rope. All this was done by her husband, though Harry Price and another sitter were invited to mark the various ties with a surgeon's blue pencil. Price was seated in the chair farthest away from the medium. When the lights were switched off, a flower basket was filled with "personal objects for identification." The basket was placed on a low table only a few inches from the medium's mouth. "A few moments later," Harry Price recorded, "I heard both the table and the chair move. The two sounds were quite different and these noises continued on and off all the evening. When first I heard them I came to the conclusion that the medium was tilting her chair forwards so that her hands *which were quite free*, could manipulate the articles in the basket. . ."

Margery described the various articles correctly, but according to Price this could have been done by a child of five if it had the chance of feeling them in the dark.

Next came some of the famous "spirit fingerprints".

" 'Walter' kindly made one specially for me," Price wrote. "These 'thumb-print' séances are always held in Stygian darkness and I must admit I was not impressed at what occurred at the séance I attended. Every alleged abnormal happening *could* have been produced normally by the medium, including "Walter's" thumb-print, if Margery had secreted a small thumb-print die on her person. As a matter of fact, after one of these London séances, a piece of wax was found, bearing an imprint of the thumb of Margery, who was supposed to be so controlled as to be incapable of reaching the wax."

Three years later the Margery mediumship—at least as far as the "spooky fingerprints" were concerned—was definitely and finally proved to be a bare-faced fraud.

★　★　★

Late in 1931 it occurred to Mr. E.E. Dudley, a former officer of the American Society for Psychical Research to ask every person who had ever sat with Margery to supply him with inked prints of his or her right and left thumbs. This was quite a chore for there had been scores of them—in J. Malcolm Bird's book, which covers only about eighteen months, the list of the participants run to fifteen pages though, of course, many were 'regulars'—but Dudley persisted and obtained most of them. Collating carefully this mass of material with the "Walter" prints, he was amazed to discover that the "spirit's" thumb-prints, left and right, were *identical in every respect* with those of Margery's friend and dentist, "Dr. Kerwin" *who was still living*. In this report, reprinted as Bulletin III of the National Laboratory of Psychical Research, London, 1932, Dudley said:

> "The identification of these patterns has been checked by five competent and unprejudiced experts, as well as by several laymen, who had not the slightest difficulty in satisfying themselves as to the identity. . .In the right thumb-print the reader should be able to find approximatively ninety identical minutiae, while nearly seventy can be counted in the left thumb-print. . .This means that there is not one chance in billions of billions that Kerwin's prints and the wax ("Walter's") prints did not belong to the same person. . ."

Many a murderer has been hanged because of fewer than *ten* correspondences between his own finger-prints and those found at the scene of the crime!

This was a bombshell indeed. Margery's dentist was completely exonerated in the whole affair. No one really solved the question as to how "Walter" palmed off the thumb-prints of a living dentist as the impressions of his own dead ones. Again volumes were written by both Margery's supporters and detractors. A finger-print expert, Professor Harold Cummins, stated: "There seems just ground for suspecting the use of artificial dies."

But can you forge finger-prints? The pro-Margery faction—which composed the sadly truncated but still active American S.P.R.—denied this. But Mr. Dudley's discovery prompted a number of people to experiment with the aim of ascertaining whether three-dimensional finger-prints, in the form of moulds or dies, could or could not be produced from two-dimensional inked prints on paper. Price argued that this could be done by depositing (electro-plating) a film of copper or silver on the graphite print, gradually building up the image until it became three-dimensional, capable of being made into a thumb-stall die or something similar. It was Professor Harold Cummins, of Tulane University (who took a great interest in the "Walter" prints) who succeeded in actually producing three-dimensional dies in hard wax and other substances from ordinary thumb-prints on paper. He also reversed and "mirrored" the prints which, when made into dies, impressed the original finger-prints on to any substance, like a rubber stamp. Thus he proved that finger-prints *could* be forged, copied and transferred (complete with sweat-gland markings) to any object which the original fingers never touched. Dr. Cummins published a detailed paper in *Police Science* (1934) on "Counterfeit Finger-Prints"

Though Dr. Crandon and his friends protested violently and brought forward the most esoteric arguments to account for the identity of "the Walter" and "Dr. Kerwin" fingerprints, Dudley's findings almost killed the Margery mediumship. In July 1936 there were still reports of "Walter" effecting a marvellous cure; in February 1935 "he" described some articles hidden in a plaster of Paris cake; in November of the same year there was a report of his taking part in cross-correspondence tests and as late as January 1938 "he" was achieving some incredible card-calling guesses. But Margery's reputation was tarnished and her fame, at least as far as the American public was concerned, had sadly declined.

"In spite of scientific investigations," Harry Price wrote, "committees of inquiry, and the work of individual researchers, not one of the vast and varied phenomena, alleged to be the work of 'Walter' has been proved genuine scientifically. If the phenomena are genuine,

Mrs. Crandon has been singularly unfortunate in not being able to demonstrate their genuineness before orthodoxy. If they *are* genuine, then 'survival' has been proved, and the 'independent' spirit voice demonstrated. If they are fraudulent, then the 'Walter' entity marks the greatest hoax in the annals of psychical research. . .I had instruments in my laboratory at Kensington which, in an hour, would have settled the validity or otherwise of some of the 'Walter' phenomena. It is to be regretted that Crandon would not permit me to test his wife's mediumship, which, whether genuine or fraudulent, is the most remarkable ever recorded. . ."

By 1933 very few people took the Margery mediumship seriously. Yet the feuds and arguments over it did psychical research a good deal of harm—especially in America. Much dissension arose among the members and staff of the American S.P.R. This led to the abolition of the post of Foreign Research Officer which Harry Price held. The Society lost many of its members and in 1935 Mr. Frederick Bligh Bond, the chief editor of the American S.P.R.'s publications, resigned. "This was another 'Margery' victim!" Harry Price remarked in his *Search of Truth*...

Mrs. Crandon died on November 1, 1941, carrying with her the secret of her real or assumed psychic powers. In the same year the American S.P.R. was re-organized on more strictly scientific lines. There is no doubt, however, that Margery's case did much to discredit psychical phenomena.

★   ★   ★

There are certain indications in the vast mass of the Margery literature that might offer a clue to the whole enigma—if not a complete solution. The character of "Walter" as it emerged during hundreds of séances, was a most original one. Boisterous, slangy, multi-lingual (he provided messages in Latin, Italian, Chinese, French, German, Swedish, Dutch, Greek, none of them of much importance) he was a very earthy spirit.

Here are a few extracts from the séance records to show "Walter's" informality of speech and behaviour:

"May 19, 1925; a séance held at Emerson Hall, Harvard:
Walter's voice at 9.20. Walter: 'The forces are low; you'll have to wait a few minutes.'" Code repeats this into dictaphone. "If

McDougall reads that! This is a nice, comfortable room: looks like the Charlestown jail. What's this, a free country? To hell with Harvard."

"May 27, 1925; the same locale.
9:50, Walter said: 'I'll break the bloody bellbox,' and rang it. 10:05: A poem by Walter:

> Shall we gather at Old Harvard,
> Shall we go to all the bother
>   For McDougall?
> Shall we gather at the river?
> Shall we eat a pound of liver
>   For McDougall?"

(Professor McDougall was, of course, "Walter's"—or, if you like, Margery's—pet hate since his adverse report on the mediumship).

"Another 'Walter' poem at the same séance:
Onward, psychic soldiers,
Marching as to war,
With the cross of Science
Going on before;
We are not united
All divided we;
Some prefer the English,
Some, Philosophy. . ."

"June 22, 1925, at the home of Hudson Hoagland:
10:05, Walter enquires whether F.H. is likely to leave before the end of the sitting, and says: 'If he does, put Code in his place. I'm used to him. He's a crook.'
10:31, Walter, moving paraffin dish, says: 'What is this blasted stuff, damned glue?" and then says: 'I'll wipe it on Shapley.'"

Walter was fond of playing practical jokes, hitting people on the head or battering their knees with the edge of a table. He used profanity freely and sometimes in quite unprintable form. He was fond of poetry —and produced some rather pitiful doggerel. His "dictated prayers" were of monumental flat-footedness. He would urge a sitter: "Blow, you son of a gun, blow!" When Dr. Wolcott, at one of the 1925 séances, addressed him in several languages (including Japanese), Walter "jokingly responded with unintelligible sounds."

Now Margery had a most genteel upbringing, conditioned by staunch New England traditions. Her first and only job was in a congregational church. She married a man many years her senior. She lived most of her life in Boston, still a bastion of New England puritanism.

It is perhaps no flight of fancy to assume that in her subconscious she must have revolted, at one time or other, against all the restrictions and limitations which her ordinary life entailed. She was a pretty and healthy young woman. As she grew older the conventions became more and more irksome. All that was in her subconscious (or a good deal of it) might go towards forming this image of a hard-swearing, boisterous young man—Walter was only twenty-eight when he died—and in a way she could have created a split ego. This would explain the theory of "unconscious fraud" which must have been aided by her husband. At what stage the "unconscious fraud" became skilful and deliberate trickery, one cannot say. But psychology might hold the key to the Margery riddle where natural science and occultism have equally failed to provide one.

★   ★   ★

Bibliography

Dr. Rudolf Schmidt: *Metachemik*. Vienna, 1921.

Dr. Rudolf Tischner: *Die Unwissenschaft der Wissenschaft*. Stuttgart, 1924.

Prof. Charles Richet: *La Metapsychie*. Paris 1914.

Prof. Max Dessoir: *Tiefenpsychologie*. Berlin 1916.

Dr. Karl Ludwig Schleich: *Bewusstsein und Unsterblichkeit* (Berlin & Stuttgart, 1920).

Sepher Jezirah, Sohar. (The Books of the Kabbala.).

Roger Bacon: *Opus Tertium*.

Heinrich Corselius Agrippa von Nettesheim: *Magia Naturalis; Philosophia occulta*.

Emanuel Swedenborg: *Heaven and Hell; The Divine Love and Wisdom*.

Georg Conrad Horst: *Demonomagia; The Magic Library; Deutaroscopy*.

Andreas Justinus Kerner: *Die Seherin von Prevorst* (1829).

Friedrich Zöllner: *Scientific Essays* (1878-79, Leipzig).

Mme Helena Blavatsky: *Isis Unveiled* (1877); *The Secret Doctrine* (1888); *The Key to Theosophy* (1889); *The Voice of Silence* (1889).

Buchard Wefer: *A Noble Woman and Her Antagonists* (1919).

Baron von Schrenck-Notzing: *Materialisation Phenomena* (Munich, 1925); *Physical Phenomena of Mediumship* (1927).

Dr. Alfred Lehmann: *Superstition and Witchcraft* Copenhagen, 1902

Bill Berthold: *Der Teufelsprophet* (Hanussen) 1951

Jane Burton: *Hey-day of a Wizard*.

Horace Wyndham: *Mr Sludge, the Medium*.

D.D. Home: *Incidents in my Life; Lights and Shadows of Spiritualism*.

Robert Browning: *Mr Sludge, the Medium*.

Harry Price: *Rudi Schneider*, 1930; *Fifty Years of Psychical Research*. 1939. *Leaves from a Psychist's Case-Book*.

Eugene and Marcel Osty: *Les Pouvoirs Inconnus de l'Esprit sur la Matière*, 1932.

Harry Price *Stella C.*, 1925.

camille Flammarion: *Mysterious Psychic Forces*.

Charles Richet: *Thirty Years of Psychical Research*.

Dr. J. Maxwell: *Metapsychical Phenomena*.

Bibliography

COLONEL DE ROCHAS: *The Exteriorisation of Motivity.*
HEREWARD CARRINGTON: *Eusapia Palladino and her Phenomena,* 1909.
COUNTESS ZOE WASSILKO-SERECKI: *Der Spuk von Talpa.*
HARRY PRICE: *Poltergeist over England.*
J. MALCOLM BIRD: *Margery.* 1925.
THEODORE BESTERMAN: *Some Modern Mediums.* 1930.
CARL MURCHISON (EDITOR): *The Case For and Against Psychical Belief,* 1927.
PROF. HAROLD CUMMINS: *Police Science,* 1934.
HARRY PRICE: *Search for Truth.*

Index